Building Financial Empowerment for Survivors of Domestic Violence

Violence against Women and Children

Series editor, Judy L. Postmus

Millions of women and children are affected by violence across the globe. Gender-based violence affects individuals, families, communities, and policies. Our new series includes books written by experts from a wide range of disciplines including social work, sociology, health, criminal justice, education, history, and women's studies. A unique feature of the series is the collaboration between academics and community practitioners. The primary author of each book in most cases is a scholar, but at least one chapter is written by a practitioner, who draws out the practical implications of the academic research. Topics will include physical and sexual violence; psychological, emotional, and economic abuse; stalking; trafficking; and childhood maltreatment, and will incorporate a gendered, feminist, or womanist analysis. Books in the series are addressed to an audience of academics and students, as well as to practitioners and policymakers.

Hilary Botein and Andrea Hetling, *Home Safe Home: Housing Solutions for Survivors of Intimate Partner Violence*

Judy L. Postmus and Amanda M. Stylianou, *Building Financial Empowerment for Survivors of Domestic Violence: A Path to Hope and Freedom*

PREVENTING CHILD MALTREATMENT IN THE U.S. MINISERIES:

Milton A. Fuentes, Rachel R. Singer, and Renee L. DeBoard-Lucas, *Multicultural Considerations*

Esther J. Calzada, Monica Faulkner, Catherine A. LaBrenz, and Milton A. Fuentes, *The Latinx Community Perspective*

Melissa Phillips, Shavonne Moore-Lobban, and Milton A. Fuentes, *The Black Community Perspective*

Royleen J. Ross, Julii M. Green, and Milton A. Fuentes, *American Indian and Alaska Native Perspectives*

Building Financial Empowerment for Survivors of Domestic Violence

A Path to Hope and Freedom

Judy L. Postmus and Amanda M. Stylianou

Rutgers University Press
New Brunswick, Camden, and Newark, New Jersey
London and Oxford

Rutgers University Press is a department of Rutgers, The State University of New Jersey, one of the leading public research universities in the nation. By publishing worldwide, it furthers the University's mission of dedication to excellence in teaching, scholarship, research, and clinical care.

978-1-9788-0490-6 (cloth)
978-1-9788-0489-0 (paper)
978-1-9788-0491-3 (epub)

Cataloging-in-publication data is available from the Library of Congress.
LCCN 2022012470

A British Cataloging-in-Publication record for this book is available from the British Library.

∞ The paper used in this publication meets the requirements of the American National Standard for Information Sciences—Permanence of Paper for Printed Library Materials, ANSI Z39.48–1992.

rutgersuniversitypress.org

Contents

Abbreviations

ABI	Abusive Behavior Inventory
ACP	Address Confidentiality Program
BRFSS	Behavioral Risk Factor Surveillance System
CCB	Checklist of Controlling Behaviors
CDC	Centers for Disease Control
CTS	Conflict Tactics Scale
COR	conservation of resource
DV	domestic violence
DV-FI	Domestic Violence–Related Financial Issues Scale
EAP	Employee Assistance Program
IDA	individual development account
IPV	intimate partner violence
KCADV	Kentucky Coalition Against Domestic Violence
LGBTQ+	lesbian, gay, bisexual, transsexual, queer
MOVERS	Measure of Victim Empowerment Related to Safety
NEWWS	National Evaluation of Welfare-to-Work Strategies
NISVS	National Intimate Partner and Sexual Violence Survey
NVAWS	National Violence Against Women Survey
PTSD	posttraumatic stress disorder
REAP	Redevelopment Opportunities for Women's Economic Action Program
SEA	Scale of Economic Abuse

SEA-12	Scale of Economic Abuse with 12 questions
SEA2	Revised Scale of Economic Abuse
TANF	Temporary Assistance for Needy Families
TPB	theory of planned behavior
VAWA	Violence Against Women Act

Building Financial Empowerment for Survivors of Domestic Violence

Introduction

For most people, "domestic violence" is a loaded term that conjures up pictures of women with black eyes and questions of why someone would stay in a physically violent relationship. For some, the term summons memories of celebrities whose abuse or role as an abuser was made public, with these memories deeply etched by disturbing pictures such as Rhianna's bruised and bloodied face after she was beaten by Chris Brown or the video of the professional football player Ray Rice punching out his fiancée, Janay. Some might have followed the Twitter feed for #WhyIStayed and learned that leaving an abusive relationship is not easy. Despite what we have learned about the varied types of domestic violence, most people still think of domestic violence as physical violence or, in a worst-case scenario, as homicide occurring within intimate partner relationships.

Can domestic violence be explained so simply? Unfortunately, no. Domestic violence is about power and control. To gain and maintain control over another person takes a combination of abusive tactics that range the gamut from physical to sexual to psychological to emotional to financial abuse, coupled with the abuser's intermittent apologies, promises to do better, and protestations of undying love that hint that such abuse will never happen again.

One of the most used tools in the domestic violence field is the Power and Control Wheel created in the 1980s by the Domestic Abuse Intervention Project (fig. I.1; Pence & Paymar, 1985). This wheel illustrates the variety of ways in which abusive partners establish and maintain power and control over their victims, including the broad range of nonphysical forms of abuse. Perpetrators use a range of abusive strategies and tactics to trap the woman in the relationship, including coercion and threats, intimidation, emotional abuse, financial abuse, isolation, minimizing and denying the abuse, blaming the victim, male privilege, and threatening children in the household.

Figure I.1. Power and Control Wheel (Pence & Paymar, 1985)

The Power and Control Wheel depicts each of these tactics and provides examples of the types of behaviors used to carry out these tactics.

For one of Postmus's research projects, she interviewed survivors of domestic violence and listened carefully as they described the multiple challenges they faced when trying to break free from an abusive partner and how their efforts were often thwarted by the varied tactics their abusers used to keep them trapped in the relationship. For example, Cathy[1] talked about how her boyfriend controlled her and the methods he used when she tried to leave the relationship. As part of the interview with Cathy, Postmus reviewed a list of possible tactics and then asked how often Cathy's abuser had used each tactic. In Cathy own words,

> He always had control of [the money]. Threatening to kill himself? Often. Threatening to hurt my stepchildren? He did that often. Threatening to hurt or kill me? He did that quite a bit. Promised he could change? Oh, sometimes. Threatened to expose family secrets? Oh yes, always. He knew one secret that nobody else did know, . . . which I'm sure he will expose eventually. Give lots of money and flowers? That was rare. He never did that. Claimed you were the only one? Oh, he did that one all the time. I still hear that. He told me if I left, the kids would go back to their mother. He had a real good one—one time, he threatened to pour Drano into the gas tank—when the gas hit it, it would explode. He told me I would never know when he was gonna do that. His favorite one was that he could always mess with my insulin and I would never know it. He could drain it out and put water in there, and you couldn't tell by the color of it. He threatened to do that quite a few times. He was drunk one night, and I threatened to call the cops and have him arrested. And he had a bottle of Jack Daniels. He told me, "I could pour this down your throat, and then the cops would believe you were drunk and they would have you arrested.
>
> I went to leave him one night, and he actually went and got a knife that his father used to kill, to slice the pig's throat, which is about this long, about eighteen inches long and about maybe, the blade's about six to eight inches wide. And he put it to his stomach, and he was gonna push it into his stomach. And, of course, I tried to take it away from him. He used to tell me that if I left him and the kids were in the house, he'd blow the house up. And his promises to change, he'd never hit me again, and everything would be nice again and all this as long as I stayed.

Cathy also described four previous times she had tried to leave and her rationale for returning each time. Her reasons for returning to her abuser varied from thinking the abuse was just an anger-management problem to fear that a child would be hurt to not having enough money to leave and not knowing where to go.

> The first time when he broke my arm and my fingers, I stayed away that time for a month. The second time, he was threatening to hit his son, and I stepped in between 'em. And he swung to hit him, and he hit me instead. And my nose was cracked, and this cheekbone was cracked. The third time, he locked me in the house for two days, and when he finally did decide that I could go . . . cuz it was my two days off from work, . . . when he decided that I could go back to work that night, I went to work. And I told my boss and my boss . . . I transferred to another store. And then I went back again. This is the last time.

When Postmus asked Cathy to describe some of her reasons for going back, she said, "The first time, I figured, okay, everybody makes a mistake—everybody loses their temper. I've lost my temper. The second time I went back because he threatened to hurt my stepson. The third time I went back, I'm not really sure why I went back. I don't know if it was the fact that . . . I think more or less the fact of it is that when I went back the third time, I didn't have nowhere else to go. So I went back."

Far from atypical, Cathy's description of her experiences is a common refrain heard from women around the world who are living in abusive relationships.[2] Other voices include comments from family, friends, coworkers, the media, and the public, with such voices asking, "Why does she stay?" or adding judgments such as, "If my partner ever did that to me, I would leave immediately." Unfortunately, leaving an abusive relationship is never easy. Many barriers exist that make it difficult—if not downright impossible—to leave an abusive relationship. These barriers exist at multiple levels including the organizational, community, family, and individual levels. For example, to leave a relationship, survivors need access to the various supports provided by organizations such as nonprofit groups, law enforcement and court systems, social service agencies, and health care entities. These organizations provide crucial services, including emergency shelter, restraining orders, counseling and support, and medical care. However, research has consistently found that when survivors turn to these organizations, they often report feeling "revictimized" because they have to repeat their story to multiple persons and relive their victimization multiple times. Some survivors who have sought help from such organizations have reported feeling judged and shamed by staff members who appeared to hold the survivor responsible for contributing to her abuse. Survivors who have sought help from these and other organizations have described staff responses such as disbelief in their narrative, lack of being taken seriously, being judged as somehow to blame for the violence, and given reassurances that the relationship "can't be that bad." It is hard enough for anyone to seek help from formal entities, but being treated poorly, humiliated, or blamed is enough for a survivor to believe that it might be better to stay—or that she has no other option but to stay with the abuser.

Barriers also exist at the community level, with individuals behaving in ways similar to the patterns seen among organizations. Many communities are not prepared to help survivors because they lack crisis centers and long-term services such as emergency shelters or affordable housing. Additionally, some communities have coalesced around a common culture based in ethnicity, religion, or even sports and because of a cultural bias might not hold the perpetrator accountable for the abuse. Certainly, after Ray Rice was identified as a batterer, his fans, his team, and his own sports association (i.e., the National Football League) downplayed the seriousness of his actions. Rice was not fired by his team or banned by the National Football League until public outcry, including sponsors, demanded Rice be held accountable for abusing his fiancée. Community attitudes can also influence the actions of survivors from communities of color or from immigrant communities. These survivors might be reluctant to seek help or to report abuse due to fears of being deported as well as fear that their abuser will receive preferential treatment from the criminal justice system, especially if their abuser is a man in a position of power or influence. Survivors from religious communities have expressed frustration with religious leaders asking them what they did wrong or demanding that they stay with the abuser because divorce is not acceptable according the tenets of their religion.

At the family level, survivors who want to leave face numerous barriers, starting with the abuser, who will do anything and everything to maintain power and control to keep the survivor trapped in the relationship. Negative tactics might include threatening to hurt his victim, children in the household, or pets if she tries to leave. Sometimes an abuser will threaten to kill himself, to kill his victim, or to kill her children—the ultimate form of control. He might deny that the abuse exists, or if the abuse is undeniable, he might minimize his behavior or responsibility. Even when an abuser admits to abusing his partner, he often blames the survivor's behavior for making him lose control. Conversely, he might use positive tactics to trap his victims in the relationship, such as promising he will stop the abuse or go to counseling. He will buy flowers or gifts, expressing his undying love and support, and he will treat his victim like a queen—until the abuse begins again. All of these tactics are used to trap the partner in the relationship.

Other members of the immediate or extended family might erect additional barriers to make it more difficult for survivors to leave an abusive relationship. For example, close relatives might refuse to acknowledge the abuse, professing a belief that such matters should be kept private. The abuser might have purposefully isolated his partner from her extended family, straining or even destroying the family bonds. Family members might express frustration, similar to helping professionals, at the survivor struggling over her decision to leave or not. Family members might also blame her for the abuse and encourage her to just "please him" so that he does not resort to violence.

Barriers that make leaving difficult also exist within survivors themselves. Because of living with an unstable, abusive partner, a survivor might have emotional or behavioral health issues such as depression, anxiety, or post-traumatic stress disorder. She might not have the resources to leave or might not have access to resources. Her ability to leave might be hindered by the physical injuries she has suffered, including physical damage from blows to her head, impaired vision, hearing loss, or brain damage. A survivor might also face health barriers such as nonspecific symptoms that include debilitating headaches or stomachaches. She might believe her abuser's threats to hurt her, the children, the pets, or himself—believing his claims that if she tries to leave the relationship, then she will be responsible if harm comes to others. She might even believe her abuser's continual messages that she is worthless and that no one will ever want her again. Despite all the physical and emotional pain, she might still love her abuser and believe he will get help and things will change.

Theresa is an example of a survivor who struggled with leaving. When she showed up at the shelter where Postmus worked, she had been badly beaten by her boyfriend, Vince. After giving her time to shower and rest, Postmus listened to Theresa's story, which started with meeting this wonderful man who promised to make life so much better for her—certainly better than her life as a single parent on welfare who was struggling to stay afloat financially. Vince showered Theresa with attention, gifts, and promises of a better life. Eventually, he convinced Theresa to leave her town, her friends, and even her son behind to travel with him. As they traveled around the country, she could recite the places where "they had the most incredible sex" or where "they scored the best drugs." She could also name the places where Vince beat her for any reason possible. The last time he beat her, they were partying with friends who lived in a trailer park. Theresa needed to go to the bathroom, but she could not get Vince's attention to ask permission, so she just left in search of a bathroom. When she returned, Vince was so angry that he beat her—all because she chose to attend to her bodily needs without his permission.

After a few weeks in the shelter, Theresa's wounds had healed and she began to struggle with staying away from Vince. He had been arrested the night Theresa entered the shelter and was sitting in jail awaiting trial. Theresa started communicating with Vince via letters, which she also shared with Postmus. In one letter she received from Vince, he claimed that while he was in jail, he "had found God" and wanted "to forgive Theresa for putting him there." While Postmus was aghast at the sheer audacity of Vince's "forgiving" his victim, Theresa's reaction was quite different. Theresa had tears in her eyes as she said, "I am so happy that he forgives me. I didn't think he would." Theresa knew that Vince "had problems," but she also believed that she was the only one who could help him—the only person who truly understood him. Theresa sorely wanted to believe in Vince—even as he blamed her for the abuse and his arrest, even as he told her that he was the only one who cared for her and that no one else would ever want her, and even as he exerted total control over her and made all decisions for her, including when she could use the bathroom.

Clearly, Theresa left a lasting impression. Postmus continued working with her, trying to build her self-confidence in her ability to be self-sufficient. However, the bond of "love" between Theresa and Vince was so strong that Theresa purposefully got herself arrested so that she could be closer to Vince in jail. Unfortunately, we do not know what happened to Theresa or Vince. Theresa believed Vince's messages that no one would want her, believed that he loved her, and believed his promises to change and to make her life better than the one she left behind.

Domestic violence has an impact on the lives of women around the globe and, like a virus, knows no boundaries of class, race, creed, or age. It affects women from all walks of life but disproportionately affects women living in poverty. Domestic violence in all its forms affects women from all communities and ethnic groups. Solutions are not as simple as just leaving the relationship. So what can be done to increase the safety of survivors and their children?

Since the 1970s, private and public programs have been created to provide survivors with crucial supports such as a safe place to live and someone to talk to about the abuse. These programs often started as emergency shelters created and staffed by survivors or concerned women. Over time, many of these emergency shelters evolved into programs that now provide a wide range of services, including temporary and transitional housing; twenty-four-hour hotline support; legal and personal advocacy; individual, group, and family counseling for survivors and their children; and public education about domestic violence.

Beginning in the mid-1990s, domestic violence programs and advocates have given increasing attention to addressing the financial needs of survivors. This shift of attention is critically important because the lack of financial resources often traps women in abusive relationships. Despite society's advances toward equality, women are generally in worse financial shape than men, especially when experiencing trauma, abuse, poverty, or other hardships (Hopley, 2003; Malone et al., 2009; Tamborini et al., 2011). Women typically earn less money than men, save less money, have inconsistent employment (often because of child rearing), and face greater financial difficulty after divorce (Schmidt & Sevak, 2006; Tamborini et al., 2011). Often, financial struggles leave women feeling trapped in their marital relationships (Schramm & Harris, 2011). Additionally, women are at greater risk of experiencing domestic violence than men, with one in four women experiencing domestic violence in their lifetime (Smith et al., 2017).

Domestic violence can take many forms, with physical, sexual, and psychological abuse being the more commonly identified and understood forms. However, abusers also use financial abuse as a way of dominating their victim and limiting her options. Abusers make their victims dependent on them for survival by controlling all money and assets, exploiting credit, or sabotaging her work efforts (Adams et al., 2008; Fawole, 2008; Postmus, Plummer, et al., 2012). Given that survivors of domestic violence list economic concerns as the top barrier to leaving an abuser (Sanders & Schnabel, 2006; Turner & Shapiro, 1986; Zorza, 1991), survivors clearly constitute one of the many groups in need of financial empowerment programs, especially programs designed to educate survivors about economic abuse, to create financial safety plans, and to encourage self-sufficiency. Such programs can be used by survivors to gain or regain their financial footing during and after abuse. Indeed, in light of the economic changes over the past twenty years, survivors and all women not only need to become better educated and empowered consumers but also need to develop their knowledge and skills toward understanding and managing complex financial products and information, rising consumer debt, global recessions, and volatile housing markets (Hilgert et al., 2003; Hopley, 2003).

Only nascent empirical information exists on the full extent of financial abuse, its short- and long-term effects, and how best to structure financial empowerment approaches for survivors of domestic violence. Indeed, even advocates whose work is to assist survivors with financial matters need more information and to increase their understanding of personal financial management. Financial empowerment programs designed specifically for survivors are relatively new to the advocacy community and represent an immense opportunity for developing or tailoring programs to the specific needs of survivors from diverse backgrounds and of varied abilities. Although cutting-edge survivor-centered programs are available, much work remains to be done to integrate financial empowerment efforts into the core advocacy services provided by domestic violence programs.

The limited but growing body of research on the prevalence of financial abuse and its impact suggests it is critical for advocacy programs to incorporate financial empowerment as a core service. Moreover, results of early studies suggest programs that focus on financial literacy and financial empowerment are effective in helping survivors improve their financial knowledge, increase their confidence in managing their financial affairs, strengthen their financial management skills, and develop financial behaviors that will improve their financial safety and security (Postmus et al., 2015). Although general financial literacy programs targeted to women and low-income populations have been found to be effective, when used with survivors of domestic violence, such programs should incorporate information specific to the unique, complex safety concerns that survivors face. Additionally, best practices grounded in empowerment theory suggest that financial literacy programs should be offered in conjunction with comprehensive advocacy services that assist survivors to gain or regain their self-confidence in managing finances and support survivors in taking action steps to improve their economic situation.

Because many domestic violence advocates might have limited knowledge of personal finances and other financial matters (Silva-Martinez et al., 2016), financial education should be included as a core part of financial empowerment efforts with survivors *and* advocates. As advocates increase their own knowledge, confidence, and skill in helping survivors navigate complex financial and safety concerns, these advocates will be able to enhance the empowerment of the survivors they serve. In addition to advocates, other professionals need to attend to their own financial education and understanding of financial abuse and other tactics used by abusers to trap survivors in abusive relationships. Professionals working in an array of settings ranging from human service agencies to the criminal justice system are likely to encounter survivors in their everyday practice and, thus, should remain mindful of addressing the financial capabilities of survivors. Similarly, professionals in financial fields, although knowledgeable about financial literacy, are likely to need a better understanding of financial abuse and the tactics abusers use to control and trap survivors of domestic violence. Last, managers and supervisors working in corporate settings need to gain a thorough understanding of the various tactics used by an abuser to sabotage a survivor's work efforts and then ensure that their organizations have policies and protocols in place to help survivors be safe at work.

The work of financial empowerment is critical not only to ensure the long-term safety of survivors but also to assist survivors in gaining long-term economic stability. Curiously, little of the research on domestic violence has sought either to fully understand the impact of financial abuse or to determine which intervention strategies are most effective toward the financial empowerment of survivors. This book aims to address this critical knowledge gap by providing those who work with survivors of domestic violence with practical knowledge on how to empower the financial well-being and stability of survivors. Specifically, every practitioner, human service provider, criminal justice practitioner, financial manager, and corporate supervisor should be screening the women they encounter for economic abuse, and when such abuse is found, they should be working with the women toward developing financial safety plans and referring survivors to financial empowerment programs to assist survivors to become free from abuse.

Overview of the Book

Chapter 1 provides the needed background for a book on financial empowerment with survivors of domestic violence by defining economic abuse, unfolding the story of economic abuse as a so-called invisible form of abuse, exploring theories to explain why such abuse occurs, and discussing dynamics that commonly occur in financially abusive relationships. To help unpack the definition of economic abuse, this chapter presents an intersectionality framework that emphasizes the points at which domestic violence intersects with poverty, race/ethnicity, and immigration status. Using examples shared by survivors of domestic violence, we discuss three forms of financial abuse: economic control, employment sabotage, and economic exploitation. The chapter concludes with practical tools and questions that advocates in the domestic violence field can use in assessing survivors' experiences of financial abuse.

Chapter 2 discusses the impact of financial abuse on survivors involved with human services, including welfare or child welfare agencies, or survivors who work in corporate settings. This chapter also focuses on the ways in which financial abuse affects the survivor's economic independence, economic self-sufficiency, and work efforts. In addition, the chapter examines the ramifications of financial abuse on survivors' behavioral health and psychological well-being, the effects on family formation and parenting practices, and the impact of domestic violence on children in the household. Further, the chapter covers the potential differential effects of financial abuse among women of color or immigrant women, as well as the challenges faced by women living at the intersection of race, immigration status, and poverty.

Chapter 3 discusses key theories, including capability theory, financial capability theory, and financial empowerment to provide practitioners a contextual and theoretical foundation for their efforts to financially empower survivors. Financial empowerment is conceptualized as both an outcome and a process in which survivors start with building a foundation of personal human capabilities and end with achieving financial empowerment. The chapter also includes application sections with program examples that demonstrate ways domestic violence organizations can integrate and increase financial empowerment in every stage of their intervention strategies.

In chapter 4, we propose a two-pronged intervention approach that focuses on (a) increasing the financial knowledge and skills of survivors and (b) creating and implementing interventions focused on increasing survivors' access to financial resources. The micro-level interventions include financial safety planning, financial literacy programs, asset-based savings programs, microloans, and employment assistance programs. The macro-level interventions include working with the criminal justice system to create a better understanding of economic abuse and to recognize such abuse as a form of domestic violence. In addition, macro-level interventions focus on providing employment protections to victims of domestic violence and increasing marginalized communities' access to mainstream financial institutions and products such as banking and savings accounts.

In chapter 5, Jolynn Woehrer, an advocate in the field of domestic violence, incorporates lessons learned from the field in providing financial empowerment to survivors of domestic violence. This chapter discusses, from the perspective of the field, practice implications and future directions. The chapter presents several concrete examples to illustrate the variety of roles organizations and advocates can play in increasing the financial empowerment of survivors.

Chapter 6 discusses the urgent need for advocates, practitioners, and domestic violence organizations to commit to making financial empowerment a primary component of their mission. For many domestic violence organizations, this commitment will mean integrating financial empowerment as a core element in their vision of service provision. In turn, making financial empowerment a priority will also require organizations to commit resources to training staff; implementing financial literacy programming for staff and survivors; and advocating for funding and policy changes to support collaborative efforts to improve survivors' financial knowledge, skills, and access to assets. This chapter provides an array of examples of the ways advocates and domestic violence organizations can use specific strategies to financially empower survivors.

The chapter also challenges staff from human service agencies (e.g., welfare, child welfare, criminal justice agencies) to screen their clients for domestic violence, including financial abuse, and to consider ways of integrating financial empowerment strategies in their work. Further, the chapter also challenges supervisors and managers working in the corporate sector to consider how they can provide a safe work environment for survivors and all employees and ways they can incorporate financial empowerment strategies into their workplace policies and protocols.

Last, this chapter challenges people working in the field of personal financial management to consider expanding their role to screen for economic abuse, to identify survivors, and to give survivors the tools to become financially empowered. In addition, advocates and domestic violence organizations are called to work closely with people working in all levels of the financial industry to create a better understanding of economic abuse across the industry and to develop ongoing collaborations with financial professionals with the expertise to provide financial education to survivors and to assist survivors with financial empowerment services.

Chapter 7 presents a three-staged approach to next steps and discusses directions for research, policy advocacy, and building community awareness and support. Additionally, this chapter not only includes suggestions for teaching financial empowerment strategies to advocates and practitioners but also covers how to advocate with policy makers and to educate the public about economic abuse and financial empowerment. Further, the chapter addresses implications of financial empowerment, focusing on academic audiences of researchers, scholars, and students in professional education programs, with the aim of encouraging these audiences to give greater attention to economic abuse and to incorporate economic abuse measures and financial empowerment strategies in their research, teaching, and practice. Implications are also discussed for policy advocates and policy makers with the aim of prompting changes to public policy and to support increased funding for organizations providing financial empowerment programs. Finally, implications are included for survivors regarding ways to use the information presented to help rebuild their lives. Specific attention is given to expanding financial empowerment efforts with survivors throughout the world.

The narrative in this book is practical and evidenced based; the book also provides illustrations to describe survivors' experiences with financial empowerment programs and the ways in which survivors found these programs useful in surviving their experiences of domestic violence, including economic abuse. Throughout the book, suggestions are included that outline ways in which the information can be used with survivors in various settings or used with policy makers to inform policy development. Additionally, the perspectives of advocates working with survivors are used to demonstrate the ways domestic violence organizations have successfully implemented financial empowerment programs and the advocates' suggestions for strengthening such programs.

Key Terms and Definitions

The field of domestic violence uses a substantial amount of specialized language to describe the complex phenomena that occur in abusive relationships; however, many of these terms lack a standardized definition. Therefore, we want to ensure we provide clear definitions of the terms used throughout the book. "Domestic violence" and similar terms such as "intimate partner violence" (IPV), dating abuse, and interpersonal violence are often used interchangeably by society, people working with "victims"/"survivors" (also called "parties harmed"), and people working with "perpetrators"/"abusers" (also called "batterers" or "harming parties"). For clarification, we use "domestic violence" or "IPV" as equivalent terms used to describe "physical violence, sexual violence, stalking, or psychological harm by a current or former partner or spouse" (CDC, 2012). In the context of IPV, the word "intimate" means that the perpetrator is known to the victim, but it does not require that the parties have or had a sexual relationship. Notably, the premise of this book expands the Center for Disease Control's description of IPV to include *economic or financial abuse.*

As noted, although violence occurs across all types of relationships—with male, female, cis- and transgender victims and perpetrators and among heterosexual and LGBTQ+ relationships—women are disproportionately the victims of IPV, whereas men are disproportionately the perpetrators of such abuse. In no way are we suggesting that males can never be victims or females perpetrators; nor do we want to diminish their experiences of abuse and trauma. However, we are relying on the research and our understanding of the disproportionality of the gendered nature of IPV. Hence, we refer to victims/survivors as women and perpetrators as men. We also use the terms "perpetrators," "batterers," and "abusers" to describe the men using abusive strategies to control and manipulate victims in a relationship marked by domestic violence. Additionally, we use the term "victim" to describe a woman currently experiencing abuse, whereas we use the term "survivor" to describe a woman identified as a victim of domestic violence who has reached out for help. Finally, we use the term "partner" to describe the other person in a relationship, which can include a spouse, lover, boy-/girlfriend, or significant other regardless of marital status or sexual orientation.

The terms "financial" and "economic" are used interchangeably throughout this book. Historically, the domestic violence field has identified economic abuse as a tactic used by abusers. From there, researchers have created measures of economic abuse, which have helped establish use of the term "economic abuse" widely across the United States and the globe (Postmus et al., 2020). However, Sharp-Jeffs (2015a) has argued that the field should use more precise language and, therefore, has proposed the use of "financial abuse" because the term is micro-focused and specifically related to personal finances and money. In contrast, the term "economic" is more macro-focused and tends to be used more generally as related to broad societal challenges such as transportation, housing, employment, and education. When discussing empowerment issues, the term "economic empowerment" is more commonly used in discussions of global settings focused on changing the broader society (i.e., macro-focused). However, this book uses the term "financial empowerment" because it is micro-focused on providing strategies, education, and support to the individual. As such, we use "financial empowerment" when discussing empowerment of survivors of domestic violence but use "economic abuse" and "financial abuse" interchangeably when referring to this pernicious form of domestic violence.

CHAPTER 1

What Is Financial Abuse?

Intimate partner violence (IPV) is a preventable, major public health concern affecting millions of women in the in the United States and across the globe. As previously described in the introduction, we use the terms "domestic violence" and "IPV" interchangeably to describe "physical violence, sexual violence, stalking, or psychological harm by a current or former partner or spouse" (CDC, 2012) and expand this definition to include economic and financial abuse. The CDC has documented the pervasive and ever-growing incidence of IPV in the United States using data from its National Intimate Partner and Sexual Violence Survey (NISVS; Smith et al., 2018). Survey results showed that IPV occurs in all socioeconomic groups and across all racial, ethnic, and cultural boundaries. The NISVS yielded alarming evidence of the pervasive extent of IPV in the United States, including the following:

- One in four women experience severe physical violence perpetrated by an intimate partner in their lifetime.
- One in ten women are stalked by an intimate partner in their lifetime.
- Nearly half of women in the United States experience psychological aggression perpetrated by an intimate partner in their lifetime.
- More than half of women who survived IPV acts of rape, physical violence, and/or stalking by an intimate partner reported that their first experience of IPV occurred when they were younger than twenty-five years old.
- Almost half (47.5 percent) of American Indian/Alaska Native women, 45.1 percent of non-Hispanic Black women, 37.3 percent of non-Hispanic White women, 34.4 percent of Hispanic women, and 18.4 percent of

Asian/Pacific Islander women experience sexual violence, physical violence, and/or stalking by an intimate partner in their lifetime.

When people without personal knowledge of IPV hear about an incident of domestic violence in their community or perhaps an incident involving a celebrity, most imagine scenarios with physical violence, black eyes, and broken bones. However, the IPV field—that is, the practitioners, scholars, researchers, and advocates working in the field of domestic violence—have long acknowledged that IPV involves various forms of both physical violence and nonphysical violence. Perpetrators of IPV use a wide range of abusive tactics to control and dominate their victims, including physical, sexual, psychological, emotional, and financial abuse. A perpetrator might use one, two, or half a dozen forms of coercive abuse tactics to manipulate his partner. In addition to horrific, often devastating physical harm suffered by many women at the hands of an intimate partner, the IPV field has also emphasized the equally painful and enduring negative effects that nonphysical forms of violence inflict on survivors and their children. In 1995, Mary Susan Miller published *No Visible Wounds: Identifying Nonphysical Abuse of Women by Their Men*, in which she identified four types of nonphysical violence: emotional, psychological, social, and financial abuse. Miller (1995) described the four abuse types as follows:

- *Emotional abuse* includes remarks or behaviors intended to damage the survivor's sense of value and self-worth; this type of abuse includes complaints, insults, name-calling, and public humiliation and embarrassment.
- *Psychological abuse* involves behaviors a perpetrator uses to undermine the survivor's judgment and thought processes; this form of abuse involves manipulating the survivor by making her feel as if she is losing her mind.
- *Social abuse* centers on isolating the survivor from her family and friends; abusers isolate their victims by persuasion, by force, by geographic isolation (i.e., moving the victim to a location where she has no social connections), or by threatening to harm the victim or the people close to the victim.
- *Financial abuse* focuses on creating financial dependency on the perpetrator; this type of abuse involves limiting the victim's access to cash, credit cards, and other monetary resources; refusing to let the victim maintain paid employment; and denying the victim any voice in how household money is spent.

Survivors often describe nonphysical IPV as the form of abuse that has the most invasive, longest lasting, and most devastating impact on victims.

Moreover, women who have survived nonphysical abuse have shared that these forms of abuse and threats of escalated abuse created a deep-seated fear of their perpetrator. Survivors often comment on the well-known nursery rhyme, "Sticks and stones may hurt my bones, but words will never hurt me," noting that words can inflict considerable harm. Indeed, survivors often speak about how broken bones can heal but the impact of psychological and financial abuse has long-lasting negative consequences that continued to erode their confidence, self-esteem, mood, health, functioning, and quality of life even after they found safety from abuse. Given this cascading, persistent negative impact of nonphysical IPV, the field has begun to give more attention to nonphysical forms of abuse and the impact of these abuse tactics on survivors and their children.

The Power and Control Wheel, found in the introduction (fig. I.1), highlights economic abuse as a primary abusive control tactic used by abusers, including actions such as preventing the woman from gaining or maintaining employment, forcing the woman to ask or beg for money, placing the woman on an allowance, stealing the woman's money, and preventing the woman from having access to shared finances. These financially abusive behaviors are not single, isolated behaviors but rather a pattern of behaviors aimed at gaining power and control over the victim. As such, financial abuse often overlaps with other abusive behaviors. An abusive partner might make financial threats toward his victim and/or her children, use emotional abuse to attack the woman's confidence in managing finances, minimize or deny his financially abusive behaviors, and exploit male economic privilege to gain control over shared financial resources. In addition, perpetrators often use a combination of physical and/or sexual violence with financial abuse, which perpetrators often deploy to punish victims for not giving their abuser access to her income or use to gain complete control over the woman's financial resources.

Why Does IPV Occur?

No single reason exists to explain why IPV, including financial abuse, occurs in relationships. Several theories help explicate the causes of domestic violence, ranging from the micro perspective (e.g., IPV is caused by a flaw within some individuals) to the macro perspective (e.g., IPV is caused by cultural or societal problems). However, several frameworks and theories have emerged as highly useful in tracing factors contributing to IPV. Practitioners, researchers, and policy makers rely on these frameworks in their efforts to increase the public's understanding of IPV, especially the causes of financial abuse. These frameworks and theories include the feminist framework, the intersectionality framework, coercive control theory, and dependency theory.

Feminist Framework

"Feminism is the struggle to end sexist oppression."

—bell hooks (1984)

The feminist framework has risen in prominence since the 1970s to become one of the predominant theoretical models in the IPV field. The feminist framework holds that IPV is the result of male oppression within a patriarchal society. Within this patriarchal system, men are the primary oppressors, and women are the primary victims (Dobash & Dobash, 1979; Walker, 1979). Through the lens of the feminist framework, IPV is a consequence of the historical power differential between men and women, which has continuously kept women in the subordinate position. Male violence occurs primarily through the persistent use of intimidation and coercion to dominate and control women (Dobash & Dobash, 1979). In the context of IPV, the feminist framework emphasizes the disproportionate number of men who perpetrate violence and abuse against women. Although people of all gender expressions have the potential to use abusive tactics to control and dominate a partner, most domestic violence incidents involve male aggressors against female victims. Feminist scholars often cite evidence from national crime surveys to demonstrate that as compared with men, women experience significantly higher rates of IPV (Tjaden & Thoennes, 1998).

Two studies used nationally representative samples to examine men's and women's experiences of IPV (Black et al., 2011; Breiding et al., 2008), with both providing evidence of the disproportionate rate of IPV perpetrated by male abusers against female victims. Breiding and colleagues' (2008) study used data on IPV experiences collected via the Behavioral Risk Factor Surveillance System (BRFSS). The BRFSS survey is a national telephone survey of U.S. adults, designed to "collect state data about U.S. residents regarding their health-related risk behaviors, chronic health conditions, and use of preventive services" (CDC, 2020). Breiding and colleagues' analysis of the IPV data obtained from the BRFSS indicated that as compared with one in seven men who experienced IPV, the rate was almost double for women, with one in four women having experienced IPV in their lifetime. Further, study results showed that as compared with male IPV survivors, female IPV survivors reported significantly higher lifetime rates of threatened physical abuse, attempted physical abuse, completed physical abuse, and unwanted sex.

Similarly, the study conducted by Black and colleagues (2011) used data from a national survey of adults, the National Intimate Partner and Sexual Violence Survey (NISVS). The CDC developed the NISVS to collect prevalence estimates of IPV, sexual violence, dating violence, and stalking victimization among the U.S. population. Findings from Black and colleagues' study of data from the NISVS indicated that as compared with one in nine men who experienced these forms of sexual violence, the rates among women were more than double the rates for men, with one in four women having experienced contact sexual violence, physical violence, and/or stalking by an intimate partner in their lifetime. Notably, findings from both the BRFSS and the NISVS provide evidence supporting the feminist framework and higher rates of IPV among women in the United States; however, neither of these surveys included measures of financial abuse.

To date, the only population study to include financial abuse items is the Australian Personal Safety Survey (Kutin et al., 2017). This survey documented lifetime prevalence of financial abuse at 11.5 percent, with the prevalence among women (15.7 percent) more than double the prevalence among men (7.1 percent). Although additional research is needed to document rates of financial abuse in intimate partner relationships across the globe, this initial population study illustrates that women are more likely than men are to be victims of financial abuse. In patriarchal cultures, men are expected to provide financially for their families, a role that includes the task of controlling how money is spent. In relationships in which financial abuse is present, abusers typically demand they control the couple's finances and make all decisions regarding how money is spent in the household. Because the male breadwinner role is ingrained in patriarchal cultures, abuse often occurs without women realizing they are experiencing financial abuse. Indeed, when we first started asking survivors about the different types of financial abuse they experienced, many survivors mentioned they had never realized their partner was controlling them using financial abuse tactics since gender, family, and cultural norms dictated that men controlled the money.

Intersectionality Framework

"There is no such thing as a single-issue struggle because we do not live single-issue lives."

—Audre Lorde (1982)

Similar to the use of the feminist framework to examine the role of gender in IPV, the intersectionality framework examines various identities of perpetrators and survivors (e.g., race/ethnicity, socioeconomic class, sexual orientation, gender identity, age, religion or spirituality, ability) and the ways these identities are shaped by systems of power and oppression. A guiding principle of intersectionality is the focus on "*simultaneous, multiple and interlocking oppressions of individuals*" (Mann & Grimes, 2001, p. 8, emphasis added). Thus, in this framework, IPV is caused by an abuser who uses intersecting opportunities to oppress a partner. For example, an abuser might gain power and control by using a combination of violence and threats to oppress his victim. In such a scenario, an abuser might use physical violence against his victim while also threatening to publicly humiliate his victim. In this way, victims with oppressed identities, or multiple intersecting oppressed identities, are more likely to experience IPV, whereas their partner is more likely to use oppression as an abusive tactic.

Intersectionality scholars have emphasized the need for the antiviolence movement not only to challenge patriarchy but also to challenge all forms of systemic oppression. Although intersectionality acknowledges the impact of gender inequality on IPV, gender inequality is neither the sole focus nor the privileged focus of the intersectionality framework. Rather, intersectionality focuses on the impact of all forms of power and oppression (Sokoloff & Dupont, 2005).

A significant amount of research using the intersectionality framework helps explain that even though IPV occurs across racial/ethnic and socioeconomic backgrounds, the most severe and lethal forms of IPV occur disproportionately among low-income women of color (Capaldi et al., 2012; Ellison et al., 2007; Ramisetty-Mikler et al., 2007). Further, Smith et al.'s (2018) analysis of NISVS data produced the following statistics regarding lifetime prevalence rates of physical violence, sexual violence, and stalking across racial/ethnic groups in the United States:

- 47.5 percent of American Indian/Alaska Native women
- 45.1 percent of non-Hispanic Black women
- 37.3 percent of non-Hispanic White women
- 34.4 percent of Hispanic women
- 18.3 percent of Asian/Pacific Islander women

In addition to race/ethnicity as a risk factor for increased prevalence of IPV, women in lower socioeconomic classes are also at increased risk of experiencing IPV. Studies have consistently found many homeless women were once victims of IPV (Browne & Bassuk, 1997). Results from the National

Crime Victimization Survey demonstrated that as compared with women with annual incomes of $10,000 or more, women with annual incomes of less than $10,000 had a four-fold likelihood of experiencing IPV (Bachman & Saltzman, 1995). Similarly, a 2002 study found that annual household income was a strong predictor of IPV among Euro-American, African American, and Hispanic families (Cunradi et al., 2002). Indeed, the intersection of IPV with socioeconomic status leaves survivors vulnerable to financial abuse at both the lower and upper levels of the socioeconomic continuum. Cultural norms such as gender norms play an important part in determining which partner holds the role of controlling and managing money in the household; however, men consistently hold that role regardless of their socioeconomic status. Therefore, to better understand what causes and contributes to IPV, we need to use a lens that incorporates an understanding of gender, race/ethnicity, and socioeconomic status as well as a range of other identities.

To exemplify the role of intersectionality and IPV, we present Ana's story. Ana, a Latina mother with a one-year-old child, was twenty-two years old when she left her child's father. During her relationship with her child's father, Ana experienced a range of abusive behaviors. He frequently threw her around, punched her, forced her to have sex, and threatened her with a weapon. Although he required Ana to work, he would often do things to keep her from getting to her job on time, would threaten to make her leave her job, and consistently prevented her from having access to the money she earned. Ana wanted to leave the relationship, but she had nowhere to live. When Ana moved into an emergency domestic violence shelter, Stylianou asked her what prompted her to enter the shelter.

> I didn't have anywhere to go. I kept telling [the child's father] that he really didn't give a shit. He had no place to go. I felt that he needed to go because I wasn't happy with me, having to wake up depressed all the time, and trust issues, insecurities that he gave me. I wasn't at ease. Even me sleeping. I was very uncomfortable there. As much as I try, it wasn't right, you know? The relationship wasn't healthy. . . . He cheated on me. I found out he had a wife and kids. Other girls were pregnant, had abortions. He was doing his own things. . . . I know the whole time it was just a matter of time before I left him. . . . I wasn't satisfied with the relationship, but he wasn't moving. I was like, I really have to go to a shelter? That's crazy. Maybe I'll just stick it out here, and if he has to stay here, then fine.
>
> But then, I thought, I can't come home to this from a long day of work having to take care of the kid and then clean up after him. It's like I can't deal with that. I'm gonna be even more unhappy. And killing myself for no reason. . . . And I lived in a basement, so everything was so gloomy. I thought

> I was going crazy. I started psychiatric help, and after I did that, he made it even worse for me because he made it sound like I was crazy. If someone can't support you and say positive things to uplift you, then you are never going to get better with them. I had stress when I was one-month pregnant. [He would say,] "I don't want to get a job because I don't want to deal with a boss." You aren't bringing nothing home. You are telling me that the baby is going to have everything, the basement was going to get fixed. I was giving him my money to fix the basement because it was a wreck. It's not like he was focused. He wasn't focused at all, and he put a lot of stress on me. And I came to a breaking point.

Ana's story illustrates the various forms of abuse victims of IPV experience. Victims often endure not only physical abuse but also psychological, social, and financial abuse. The effects of multiple types of abuse often leave victims of IPV feeling overwhelmed and exhausted, with few, if any, resources to escape the relationship. Ana's story is an example of a survivor facing "both dangerous intimate relationships and dangerous social positions" (Richie, 2000, p. 1136). Ana experienced two major threats: the threat of IPV and the threat of homelessness. Moreover, those threats occurred within the context of being a Latina woman who not only had to manage the challenges and expectations of her culture but also had to contend with the stigma and oppression from others outside her culture. These compounding risks create complex challenges and barriers for IPV survivors, forcing them to make impossible decisions in navigating their situation and finding safety for their children and themselves.

Coercive Control Theory

Coercive control theory defines coercive control as "a strategic course of self-interested behavior designed to secure and expand gender-based privilege by establishing a regime of domination in personal life" (Stark, 2013, p. 21).

Stark (2007) developed the theory of coercive control to expand the conception of domestic violence from a limited focus on physical abuse to a model that includes the broad range of coercive and overt behaviors perpetrators engage in to control, dominate, and manipulate their victims. The coercive control framework emphasizes that these abusive behaviors are ongoing, intentional behaviors that create cumulative harms for survivors and their children. The theory of coercive control holds that the combination of coercion and control is the most common and the most devastating form of abuse. Empirical evidence has confirmed the theory, providing support for both the prevalence and devastating impact of coercive control tactics (Stark, 2013). The concept of coercive control incorporates three core principles: (a) the victim/survivor experiences ongoing oppression (i.e., rather than episodic oppression); (b) coercive control produces multifaceted, cumulative harms for the victim/survivor, and (c) the perpetrator engaging in coercive control is using rational, instrumental behavior (Stark, 2013).

To understand coercive control, Stark (2013) recommends focusing on the four primary tactics used by perpetrators: violence, intimidation, isolation, and control. Perpetrators use violence and intimidation tactics to coerce the partner. Violence includes acts of physical violence that allow the abuser to physically dominate their victim, whereas intimidation is used to instill the victim with fear and shame and, thereby, gain her compliance and loyalty. Perpetrators often intimidate their partners through threats, degrading her verbally or physically and ensuring the victim knows that she is under constant surveillance by her abuser.

Coercive control tactics of isolation and control are used by perpetrators to exert authority and control over their partner. A perpetrator isolates his partner from her family, friends, and other support networks to dominate the partner, to gain control of her resources, to prevent the partner from getting outside help, and to make the partner emotionally and physically dependent on her abuser. Coercive control tactics also include a perpetrator controlling his partner's access to necessities for daily living (Stark, 2013).

Financial Dependency Theory

Financial dependency refers to "the degree to which one person relies on another for financial support and is used to describe situations in which one member of a dyad has exclusive or near-exclusive control over financial resources" (Bornstein, 2006, p. 597).

The financial dependency theory seeks to explain the ways in which financial abuse creates an environment in which the perpetrator gains complete control of his victim and how the dependency that results from financial abuse increases the difficulty survivors face in leaving abusive relationships. Historically, researchers have focused on financial dependency in terms of income disparity between two partners. More recently, the concept of financial dependency has been expanded to include factors that affect one partner's financial reliance on the other partner. Examples of these additional factors influencing a victim's financial dependence on her abuser include the need to care for young children, lack of alternative housing or housing availability, or a lack of access to financial resources and benefits. Related to this theory, the dependence model of commitment in intimate relationships proposes that individuals will remain in dissatisfying relationships if they have a high level of dependence on the significant other (Drigotas & Rusbult, 1992). In other words, if one partner has a great extent of financial dependence on the other partner, then the dependent partner will be less likely to terminate the relationship.

Numerous research studies have found that women's financial dependency plays a significant role in risk for abuse. Gelles (1976) was among the first researchers to report evidence supporting a link between financial dependency and risk for IPV. Although limited to a relatively small sample of forty-one women, Gelles found that a woman's occupational status predicted her decision to leave or remain in an abusive relationship, with women in low-paying occupations less likely to terminate their abusive relationships. Similarly, Woffordt and colleagues (1994) examined data from a national sample of couples and found evidence supporting the financial dependence theory. Specifically, Woffordt and colleagues found that as compared to women living in the middle class, women living in low socioeconomic households were significantly less likely to leave their abusive relationships.

Expanding the research on the link between financial dependency and risk for abuse, Rusbult and Martz (1995) examined financial dependency using multiple measures, including employment, income level, independent income, total money available, and amount of money on hand. Their study results showed that all measures of financial dependency were associated with a decreased likelihood of financially dependent women leaving an abusive relationship.

In addition to risks associated with financial dependency, women face additional structural risks around gaining and maintaining financial dependence. Ptacek (1999) coined the term "social entrapment" to provide a framework for understanding the phenomenon created by the combination of an abuser's control tactics with the social and institutional failures to adequately support survivors of IPV, which leaves survivors with few options for living safely. When the systems designed to support individuals and families are built on patriarchal, racist, and classist frameworks, then these systems effectively trap survivors in abusive situations (Moe, 2007). Therefore, survivors within a financially abusive relationship not only need to find ways to protect themselves and their children but also need to find ways to build their financial independence within a system that fails to provide key supports such as affordable housing, livable wages, affordable child care, and equal educational and job opportunities.

Why is financial dependency critical to our understanding of IPV and financial abuse? Because the primary reason women do not leave abusive relationships is their financial dependence on the abusive partner. Moreover, the effects of this dependency on women's decisions to leave, stay, or return to abusive relationships is compounded by the failure of systems to adequately support survivors in gaining financial independence (Kim & Gray, 2008; Sanders, 2015).

In summary, financial dependence theory highlights the factors that make financial abuse the primary barrier women face in attempting to leave abusive relationships. Coercive control theory frames financial abuse as a form of coercive control that includes a range of controlling and manipulative behaviors designed to gain power and control over the victim's financial resources. The intersectionality framework brings the attention to the multiple levels of oppression survivors experience as well as the multiple tactics abusers use to oppress their partners, including individual and societal-level oppressive tactics used to trap women in the relationship. In addition, the feminist framework underscores that women disproportionately experience abuse, in large part because society continues to perpetrate the oppression of women through the patriarchal norms. With these frameworks, advocates can collaborate with survivors in understanding the history of the abusive relationship, identifying the array of tactics the perpetrator used to gain power and control, recognizing societal oppressions, and exploring the meaning and impact of each tactic from the survivor's perspective. When the abusive relationship is viewed through the combined lens of these frameworks, the work with a survivor shifts away from intervention with a sole focus on physical safety to broaden the intervention to encompass a range of safety-planning steps focused on increasing the survivor's emotional and psychological safety, social safety, and financial safety. Interventions can also be directed to societal institutions that engage with survivors to help these institutions recognize and respond appropriately to the needs of survivors. Therefore, to create a path to hope and freedom for survivors, we must understand the dynamics of financial abuse behaviors and the array of coercive tactics used by perpetrators of financial abuse.

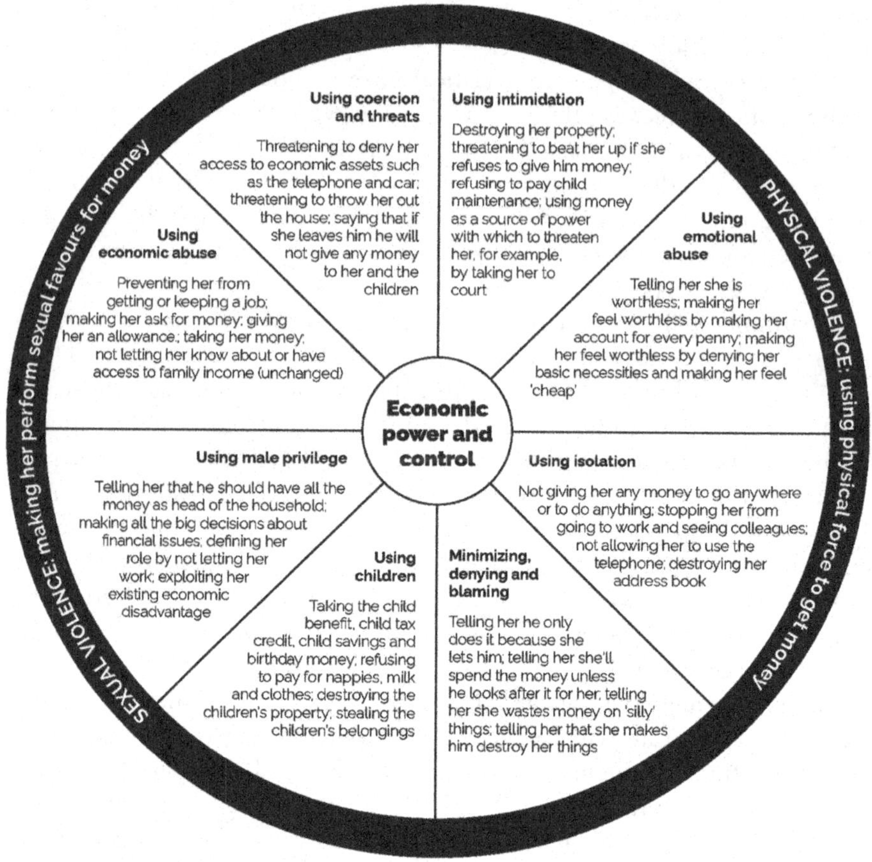

Figure 1.1. Economic Abuse Wheel (Sharp, 2008)

Financial Abuse: An Invisible Form of Abuse

Financial abuse includes behaviors that control a survivor's "ability to acquire, use and maintain resources thus threatening her economic security and potential for self-sufficiency" (Adams et al., 2008, p. 564).

Financial abuse is a form of abuse in which the perpetrator engages in behaviors aimed toward gaining control over the survivor's financial resources and creating financial dependency (Fawole, 2008). Often considered an invisible form of abuse (Postmus et al., 2020), financial abuse has long been considered a part of coercive control. Although some scholars differentiate between the terms "economic" and "financial" (Sharp-Jeffs, 2015a), the domestic violence literature uses the terms "economic abuse" and "financial abuse" interchangeably, and therefore, we use "economic abuse" and "financial abuse" as equivalent, interchangeable terms.

Nicola Sharp-Jeffs adapted the original Power and Control Wheel and created the Economic Abuse Wheel (fig. 1.1). In this wheel, she shows how she took the same categories in the original wheel but discussed them in terms of economic abuse. From our own work, we have found that financial abuse occurs in three forms: economic control, employment sabotage, and economic exploitation (Postmus et al., 2020; Postmus et al., 2016; Stylianou et al., 2013).

As illustrated in figure 1.2, behaviors identified as financial abuse include covert and overt behaviors. *Covert financial behaviors* are hidden behaviors such as an abuser hiding financial resources from his partner or not allowing the partner to have access to financial information. Because such behaviors tend to be secretive, recognizing that financial abuse is occurring is difficult for individuals outside the relationship. Indeed, many women in abusive relationships do not recognize these controlling behaviors as financial abuse or do not realize the full extent of such abuse. The impact of financial abuse on survivors is compounded by issues within the legal system. Generally, the behaviors constituting financial abuse are not criminal behaviors; therefore, the criminal justice system offers no options for protecting the survivor. However, these covert forms of financial abuse can completely undermine and destroy the survivor's ability to leave the relationship. The perpetrator creates a coercive situation in which the survivor is financially dependent on her abuser, who hides financial resources, makes financial

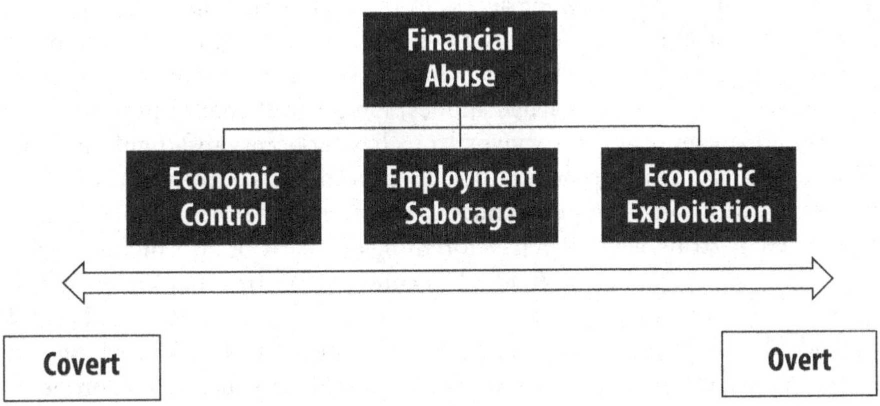

Figure 1.2. Financial abuse continuum

decisions without the survivor's knowledge, and prevents the survivor from accessing her own or jointly owned financial resources. Drawing from coercive control theory (Stark, 2013), the rationale for a perpetrator's use of coercive financial abuse tactics can be explained as the abuser seeking to control and isolate his partner, to create financial dependency, to dominate the survivor's financial resources, and to prevent the survivor from leaving the relationship.

A survivor at Stylianou's program told her,

> My husband sees where the money is going. If I need something, he has control over everything. He keeps track of what I'm spending and how much. I have to give him the details on every little thing I'm spending on. I don't have the freedom to spend lavishly. I have to think twice because I have to tell him where and when I'm spending so I don't have that much financial freedom. Even to buy clothes for myself. I have to keep requesting him for months. He can get things for me. It's very depressing when I have to wait for small things for long even though he can get things for me. He questions me a lot. Why did I spend? What did I spend? I don't spend a lot. I don't feel comfortable asking him for money.

Economic control **occurs when the perpetrator prevents the survivor from having access to or knowledge of the finances and from having financial decision-making power (Brewster, 2003; Postmus et al., 2016).**

Survivors of economic control report that their partners controlled and limited their access to financial resources (Sanders, 2015; Wettersten et al., 2004) and denied the survivor access to necessities such as food, clothing, or medications (VonDeLinde, 2002). A perpetrator might exert economic control by using tactics such as tracking the survivor's use of money, withholding or hiding jointly earned money, lying about shared properties or assets, and preventing the survivor from having access to a bank account (Brewster, 2003; VonDeLinde, 2002). By preventing a survivor from using banking institutions, the perpetrator forces the woman to be "unbanked." Unbanked persons generally pay for things in cash or use prepaid debit cards. Among unbanked individuals, economic control focuses on maintaining control over the family's cash income and expenses. Among banked individuals, economic control expands to include control over checking and savings accounts, retirement accounts, and other assets such as real property or investment accounts.

Survivors often emphasize the extent of control perpetrators derive from using economic control tactics. One survivor described how her abuser used money not only to exert control over her but also to have power over all family decision-making:

> We argue about the future of our son. I want us to put money away for college. He doesn't think ahead. I want to plan so he [son] has a better future. You do have to pay for college. He says, "He can get a job and pay for it himself." Or if he [son] needs braces or a medical thing or something unexpected—he [partner] makes the money, so he wants to do what he wants to do, like smoke cigarettes, things that he can sacrifice and give up, but he won't. I'm the one staying home, and I can make twice as much as he can. I'm sacrificing. I'm giving up my career, and he has the power when he has the money. And there is no medical, so I need to go out and get Medicaid. If you can't take care of it, you are behind on electric $700. I tried to leave him. He was not letting me do that. I would ask if he could watch the baby—he was threatened by me. (survivor interviewed by Stylianou)

Among most, if not all, couples, finances are the most frequent point of disagreement and intense emotion. However, among relationships with domestic violence, finances become a weapon for control. One survivor described to Stylianou the way her partner continued to use financial control even after she had left the relationship: "My husband doesn't want to pay me support because he's mad and he doesn't want to pay, so that's a sore point. It's all about power and control with him. The money is a way of control for him. That's why I have my own job right now, and I'm trying to support myself. I'm being financial responsible, but my husband isn't. I'm doing what I need to do, but he's still living way above his means and we're going to lose everything. . . . According to him, it's all my fault."

Numerous survivors have reported that perpetrators control the finances by "controlling the purse strings," that is, by providing or withholding money for necessary expenses. In turn, perpetrators use household finances to enforce their power and control in the relationship. For example, a perpetrator might refuse to give the survivor money to pay for food or medications that she or the children need or might agree to pay for necessities as a way of coercing the survivor to engage in unwanted behaviors and remain in the relationship: "When my daughter was home and my husband doesn't give me enough money for food—there isn't enough food for us nutritionally. She had to go to a nutritionist because she has arthritis. She had to gain weight; that was a problem. I told him she has to have protein and fruit every day and vegetables. He wasn't giving me enough money to buy food for her. We had to end up eating whatever we had. I went to a food pantry. I didn't have food" (survivor interviewed by Stylianou).

Survivors who are part of immigrant communities often face additional layers of economic control because perpetrators might hide financial assets in international accounts, with family members living in other countries, or with informal banking/lending groups within the immigrant community. These added avenues of economic control can create insurmountable barriers for survivors when trying to access financial resources.

> We are going through a divorce, and he is hiding all the assets, when I disclosed everything. It's a burden on me to discover his assets, which are not only in U.S. but outside U.S. Just to hire a forensic accountant is $2,500, and he can only get all the transactions. But if he [partner] bought land in India, he[accountant] cannot discover the land. He can only discover if money leaves his [partner] account because it's in India. The burden is on me, and he is hiding [assets]. The court mandated that he has to show his accounts, but he closed his accounts. I just showed everything I had without closing any accounts. But him, he went through all the money and closed a bunch of accounts and then disclosed only the statements are left over. So that is cheating. Even credit cards he closed, and he is only showing the credit cards which are open right now. It's very tough to get [information on] what exactly he makes. It's very tough. (survivor interviewed by Stylianou)

The second type of financial abuse is employment sabotage. This form of abuse occurs further down the continuum from covert behaviors and uses both covert and overt tactics of abuse.

***Employment sabotage* encompasses behaviors that prevent the survivor from obtaining or maintaining employment (Postmus et al., 2016).**

Numerous studies have documented the ways in which perpetrators interfere with their partners' employment or educational endeavors, including forbidding or discouraging the partner from attending work or school, as well as actively creating barriers and obstacles to hinder the survivor's job or school performance (Alexander, 2011; Brewster, 2003; Moe & Bell, 2004; Sanders, 2015; Swanberg & Macke, 2006; Tolman & Raphael, 2000; VonDeLinde, 2002). Perpetrators using employment sabotage engage in an array of behaviors to prevent or limit the survivor's ability to secure or maintain employment. Employment sabotage includes behaviors intended to prevent or hinder the victim's ability to get a job, such as ensuring that the woman is not at her best for a job interview by instigating arguments and keeping her up all night before the interview. If the partner has a job, the perpetrator might sabotage the victim's work performance and ability to maintain her employment as a way of keeping his financial control and making the woman financially dependent on him. These sabotaging behaviors include turning off alarm clocks, destroying the victim's work clothing, inflicting visual facial injuries, disabling the car, threatening to kidnap the children from child care, or failing to show up as promised to provide child care or transportation (Tolman & Raphael, 2000).

Studies have also established on-the-job harassment as a distinct form of employment sabotage. Examples of this harassment include repeated incidents of the perpetrator entering the victim's workplace, telephoning the victim repeatedly while she is working, or making repeated telephone calls to the victim's coworkers and supervisors (Riger et al., 2000; Swanberg & Logan, 2005; Swanberg & Macke, 2006; Wettersten et al., 2004). Researchers have also documented how perpetrators maintain control over their victims by interfering with the partner's ability to attend educational opportunities and by blocking efforts that the partner makes to access other forms of income, such as child support, public assistance, or disability payments (Anderson et al., 2003; Brewster, 2003; Moe & Bell, 2004): "I'm looking for education options where I can make myself educated and get a job and become financially independent. I would like to do nursing. I spoke with him about it yesterday. He refuses to let me work."

The third form of financial abuse, economic exploitation, is on the overt side of the continuum.

Economic exploitation **occurs when a perpetrator intentionally engages in behaviors aimed to destroy the survivor's financial resources or credit (Postmus et al., 2016).**

Over the past several decades, changes in financial systems have made getting and using credit commonplace. However, as consumer lending has increased, perpetrators of IPV have increasingly used debt as a means of gaining power and control over their victims (Littwin, 2012). This form of financial abuse can be carried out through intentional, planned behaviors such as the following:

- A perpetrator steals his partner's cash, checks, or ATM cards.
- A perpetrator uses the victim's line of credit without her permission.
- A perpetrator opens credit accounts in the victim's name without her knowledge.
- A perpetrator refuses to pay the mortgage, rent, or utility payments.
- A perpetrator runs up bills under the victim's name or under the names of his or her children.
- A perpetrator gambles jointly earned money. (Anderson et al., 2003)

In addition, a perpetrator might steal or damage his victim's possessions to maintain financial control and exploit the victim's dependence (Brewster, 2003). Many survivors describe a relationship in which the perpetrator spent lavishly on himself while highly restricting the amount the survivor could spend. The comments of one survivor summarized the experiences of many: "My husband blames me. It's my fault for not putting away enough money. I buy my nieces gifts. I do buy the cheapest I can find, [at] the dollar store. It gets me in trouble with my husband. It causes him to drink. It's a vicious cycle. He gambles on football in the casinos—the alcohol too, a $42 bottle of whiskey. I'm so tired of the police, of him" (survivor interviewed by Stylianou).

Overt financial abuse behaviors (e.g., forging checks to steal money from the victim or opening credit accounts in her name) are highly visible forms of financial abuse. Individuals outside the relationship often identify overt financial abuse as "inappropriate" behaviors. However, even with additional safety resources (e.g., consumer credit protections and laws) available to address overt financial abuse, these forms of financial abuse can have long-term, distressing impacts on the survivor and can have a crippling effect on survivors' ability to gain financial independence. For a survivor, reclaiming her stolen financial resources or repairing her credit history can take years. By engaging in overt financially abusive behaviors, the perpetrator creates an environment of financial intimidation and control: "Well, my situation pretty much is that my husband took me off our checking accounts over a year ago, and when he did his taxes, he didn't include me. He won't give me anything. It affects my ability to take care of the kids because it's all on me" (survivor interviewed by Stylianou).

Measuring Financial Abuse

Historically, financial abuse has not been a well-measured form of IPV. For example, the National Violence Against Women Survey (NVAWS; Tjaden & Thoennes, 1998), a nationally representative survey of U.S. households, included only one question to measure respondents' experiences of financial abuse. This question asked if the respondent's "current partner presents him/her from knowing about or having access to family income, even when (she/he) asks." The results based on this one question indicated that financial abuse was a rare phenomenon, occurring less frequently than physical abuse (Outlaw, 2009).

In contrast, the 2012 Australian Personal Safety Survey (Australian Bureau of Statistics, 2013) used a comprehensive measure to examine the prevalence of financial abuse among couples. The measure included five items inquiring about a current or former partner's behavior related to finances:

- Stopped or tried to stop you knowing about or having access to household money
- Stopped or tried to stop you from working or earning money or studying
- Deprived you of basic needs
- Damaged, destroyed, or stole any of your property
- Stopped or tried to stop you from using the telephone, internet, or family car

Survey findings revealed that 15.7 percent of Australian women experienced financial abuse from an intimate partner during their lifetime.

To date, prevalence of financial abuse in the United States has not been examined using nationally representative surveys. Some existing research suggests that financial abuse is a common element in abusive relationships. For example, Adams and colleagues (2008) found that of 103 survivors seeking domestic violence services 99 percent of the women reported experiencing financial abuse in their relationship. Similarly, Postmus and colleagues (2012) surveyed 120 women receiving domestic violence services and found that 92 percent reported experiencing financial abuse. These findings were consistent with those of Stylianou and colleagues (2013), who surveyed 457 survivors of IPV and found that 76 percent of the women reported that their abuser had exhibited at least one behavior representative of each form of abuse (i.e., physical, psychological, and financial abuse). However, among the 16 percent of the sample that did not report physical abuse, all reported experiencing both psychological and financial abuse, suggesting that financial abuse is more common than physical abuse.

To evaluate the state of knowledge regarding domestic violence and economic abuse, Postmus and colleagues (2020) conducted a systematic review of forty-six peer-reviewed research articles from six continents. Although the authors found some consistency in researchers' use of validated measures designed to assess economic abuse, the authors concluded that the field must continue to pursue global collaboration with the aim of standardizing the measures used in research to assess economic abuse. Among the forty-six articles that Postmus and colleagues reviewed, five articles used a validated tool designed as a specific measure for the construct of economic abuse; these tools included the Scale of Economic Abuse and the Scale of Economic Abuse–12. However, most reviewed research studies used general IPV measurement tools that included items designed to capture the construct of economic abuse. Examples of these measurement tools include the Checklist of Controlling Behaviors, the Domestic Violence–Related Financial Issues Scale, and the psychological abuse subscale of the Abusive Behavior Inventory. To clarify the existing options for assessing economic abuse, we review each of these measures.

Domestic Violence–Related Financial Issues Scale

The Domestic Violence–Related Financial Issues Scale (DV-FI; Weaver et al., 2009) was the first scale to incorporate a subscale measuring financial abuse experiences. The DV-FI was tested with a sample of 113 women seeking emergency shelter services for IPV. The DV-FI was developed to be a comprehensive assessment of the unique financial issues faced by IPV survivors. The DV-FI includes one five-item subscale measuring financial abuse; these five items focus on credit card debt and credit rating:

1 Credit card debt has played a role in my previous experiences of partner violence.
2 My partner prevented me from having access to money.
3 My partner negatively affected my credit rating.
4 My partner negatively affected my credit card debt.
5 My partner prevented me from obtaining necessary skills or education to obtain adequate employment.

Checklist of Controlling Behaviors

The Checklist of Controlling Behaviors (CCB; Lehmann et al., 2012) is an eighty-four-item domestic violence assessment tool used to access multiple levels of violence and coercive control in intimate partner relationships. The CCB was validated in research with a sample of 517 residents of domestic violence shelters. The checklist measures economic control using a seven-item subscale of financial abuse. The seven items in the subscale include the following statements about the partner's pattern of behaviors related to finances:

1 Did not allow me equal access to the family money.
2 Told me or acted as if it was "his money, his house, his car, etc."
3 Threatened to withhold money from me.
4 Made me ask for money for the basic necessities.
5 Used my fear of not having access to money to control my behavior.
6 Made me account for the money I spent.
7 Tried to keep me dependent on him for money.

Abusive Behavior Inventory, Psychological Abuse Subscale-12

The Abusive Behavior Inventory (ABI; Shepard & Campbell, 1992) is a widely used validated instrument designed to measure IPV. The ABI consists of two subscales: the physical abuse subscale and the psychological abuse subscale. Our discussion is focused on the twenty-item psychological abuse subscale. The ABI was developed as an alternative to the Conflict Tactics Scale (CTS; Straus, 1979) used to measure conflict and violence in familial relationships. Shepard and Campbell developed the thirty questions composing the ABI in consultation with domestic violence advocates and survivors. The ABI is a self-report measure grounded in the view of violence as part of coercive control (Stark, 2007) and based on the Power and Control Wheel (Pence & Paymar, 1985). The ABI psychological subscale includes two items specific to economic abuse measured on a scale of 1 ("never") to 5 ("very frequently"): one measures economic control (i.e., "Prevented you from having money for your own use"), and the other measures employment sabotage (i.e., "Stopped you or tried to stop you from going to work").

Scale of Economic Abuse

Adams and colleagues (2008) were the first researchers to develop a full scale specifically to measure financial abuse experiences: the Scale of Economic Abuse (SEA). Development of the SEA drew from several sources, including anecdotal evidence, empirical research, and interviews with advocates and IPV survivors. During the development process, several patterns in perpetrators' behaviors emerged as key elements in financially abusive relationships: (a) the abuser prevents the survivor from acquiring resources, (b) the abuser prevents the survivor from using resources, and (c) the abuser exploits the survivor's resources. The SEA self-report instrument was tested with 103 IPV survivors who were receiving services from domestic violence organizations. The final version of the SEA is a self-report instrument of twenty-eight items that compose two subscales measuring (a) economic exploitation and (b) economic control. The twenty-eight items—presented below as subscales—are intended to probe the extent and impact of the economic abuse that survivors experienced. Survivors answer each of the items on a scale from 1 ("never") to 5 ("very often").

SEA economic control subscale

1 Steal the car keys or take the car so you couldn't go look for a job or go to a job interview.
2 Do things to keep you from going to your job.
3 Beat you up if you said you needed to go to work.
4 Threaten you to make you leave work.
5 Demand that you quit your job.
6 Do things to keep you from having money of your own.
7 Take your paycheck, financial aid check, tax refund check, disability payment, or other support payments from you.
8 Decide how you could spend money rather than letting you spend it how you saw fit.
9 Demand to know how money was spent.
10 Demand that you give him receipts and/or change when you spent money.
11 Keep you from having the money you needed to buy food, clothes, or other necessities.
12 Hide money so that you could not find it.
13 Keep you from having access to your bank accounts.
14 Keep financial information from you.
15 Make important financial decisions without talking with you about it first.
16 Make you ask him for money.
17 Threaten you or beat you up for paying the bills or buying things that were needed.

SEA economic exploitation subscale

18 Take money from your purse, wallet, or bank account without your permission and/or knowledge.
19 Force you to give him money or let him use your checkbook, ATM card, or credit card.
20 Steal your property.
21 Pay bills late or not pay bills that were in your name or in both of your names.
22 Build up debt under your name by doing things like use your credit card or run up the phone bill.
23 Refuse to get a job so you had to support your family alone.

24 Gamble with your money or your shared money.
25 Have you ask your family or friends for money but not let you pay them back.
26 Convince you to lend him money but not pay it back.
27 Pawn your property or your shared property.
28 Spend the money you needed for rent or other bills.

The Revised Scale of Economic Abuse

After publishing the Scale of Economic Abuse, Adams and colleagues advanced the measure of economic abuse by developing a Revised Scale of Economic Abuse (SEA2; Adams et al., 2019). The Revised Scale utilized a two-dimensional measure focused on abusers' use of economic restriction and economic exploitation to exert control over the economic domain of their partners' lives. The SEA2 includes fourteen items that compose two subscales: economic restriction and economic exploitation.

SEA2 economic restriction subscale

1 Decide how you could spend money rather than letting you spend it how you saw fit.
2 Make you ask him or her for money.
3 Keep financial information from you.
4 Keep you from having the money you needed to buy food, clothing, or other necessities.
5 Hide money so that you could not find it.
6 Demand that you give him/her receipts or change when you spent money.
7 Keep you from having a job or going to work.

SEA2 economic exploitation subscale

1 Spend his/her money however he/she wanted while your money went to pay for necessities.
2 Make you use your money to buy him/her things or pay his/her bills when you didn't want to.
3 Steal your property.
4 Put bills in your name, leaving you to pay them.
5 Force or pressure you to give him/her your savings or other assets.
6 Make you take out a loan of buy something on credit when you didn't want to.
7 Take out a loan or buy something on credit in your name without your permission.

Scale of Economic Abuse–12

Several years after the SEA was published, Postmus and colleagues (2016) developed a revised and shortened version of SEA. The revised version—the Scale of Economic Abuse–12 (SEA-12)—uses twelve questions to measure the impact of economic abuse on survivors, and the shorter version improved the scale's utility for use with IPV survivors in research or practice settings. Postmus and colleagues (2016) began the revision process in 2008 by first testing the original SEA with a sample of 120 female IPV survivors receiving services from domestic violence organizations and then reducing the scale items through an exploratory factor analysis. The scale was reduced to twelve items that compose three subscales: economic control, employment sabotage, and economic exploitation. The twelve items are presented below, arranged by subscale.

SEA-12 economic control subscale

1. Make you ask him for money.
2. Demand to know how money was spent.
3. Demand that you give him receipts and/or change when you spend money.
4. Keep financial information from you.
5. Make important financial decisions without talking to you first.

SEA-12 employment sabotage subscale

1. Threaten you to make you leave work.
2. Demand that you quit your job.
3. Beat you up if you said you needed to go to work.
4. Do things to keep you from going to your job.

SEA-12 economic exploitation subscale

1. Spend the money you need for rent or other bills.
2. Pay bills late or not pay bills that were in your name or both of your names.
3. Build up debt under your name by doing things like use your credit card or run up the phone bill.

To date, the SEA, the SEA2, and the SEA-12 are the measures of survivors' economic abuse experiences that have been validated through rigorous evaluation studies. The SEA-12 was developed and tested with survivors living in the United States; additionally, the use of the scale has expanded to Hong Kong, Taiwan, Australia, Israel, and New Zealand, where researchers are currently testing the cultural utility of the SEA-12.

Identifying Financial Abuse, or, What Does a Healthy Financial Relationship Look Like?

Before addressing how to identify financial abuse in relationships, it is important that we define and understand how to identify financially healthy relationships. In a financially healthy relationship, both partners have equal access to and decision-making power over household finances. These partners engage in open and respectful dialogue around their shared finances. What does a financially healthy relationship look like in today's world? Of course, the specific characteristics vary from relationship to relationship. In some relationships, the household financial decisions are made in conversation with both partners, and both partners share financial responsibilities such as monitoring accounts and financial security, paying bills, and planning for long-term financial needs. In other relationships, the partners split the financial responsibilities, with one partner managing some of the financial duties and the other partner managing the rest of the financial duties. For example, one partner might manage and make decisions regarding routine and day-to-day financial decisions, while the other partner manages and makes decisions regarding the couple's long-term financial planning. However, both partners have access to their shared financial resources, including all information about their resources, and they share decision-making power. In this scenario, if the partner managing the day-to-day finances expresses concern regarding recent decisions made about long-term financial plans, then the two partners would have an open conversation about those concerns and work together to make financial decisions on which they agree. Although these partners split the financial responsibilities for their household, both partners still have decision-making power over all their household financial decisions.

A third type of relationship takes a traditional approach to managing finances in which one partner (often the man) manages the finances, pays bills, monitors long-term savings and retirement accounts, and keeps track of spending. Through mutual discussion, these "household tasks" are assigned to the person who has better skills (and confidence) in managing financial matters. In a financially healthy relationship with this structure, if the partner who is not involved in managing the finances expresses concern about their financial situation, then the other partner would engage in a respectful conversation to explain decisions and discuss concerns. Similarly, if the partner not involved in managing the finances wants access to financial documents or shared assets, then the other partner would provide the documents and access to the financial resources. Even though one partner has taken on managing all the financial responsibilities, these partners still share mutual, equal decision-making power. Both partners have full access to household resources and information; that is, neither partner keeps money, resources, or the status of their finances hidden or secret from the other person. Decisions are jointly made about large expenditures made with household money (e.g., cars, housing, major appliances, pets, vacations). Both partners agree on the financial responsibilities and talk over household finances as needed. Therefore, in financially healthy relationships, the financial access and decision-making power is shared. Financially healthy relationships either share all financial access and responsibilities or maintain separate financial access and responsibilities in a mutually agreed upon decision.

***Group Activity*: Identifying behaviors that occur in a financially healthy relationship versus a financially abusive relationship is a highly effective group activity that can be used with teen dating-abuse prevention groups or IPV support groups. This activity helps to increase awareness and facilitate conversation around financial abuse, especially the "red-flag" behaviors that are often indicators of the potential for a relationship to become abusive. Such red flags may include calling or visiting you repeatedly at work, complaining about your job, restricting your spending, requiring detailed accounts of spending, restricting your access to money, or expecting you to cover all expenses.**

When assessing a survivor for financial abuse, we ask questions to understand how financial decisions are made in the relationship and whether the partners share financial power. The open-ended questions in figure 1.3 can be used to start a conversation with a survivor aimed toward assessing her financial abuse experiences.

Similar to the dynamics of psychological abuse, financial abuse in a relationship often begins slowly, escalating over time as the perpetrator gains increasing control over his partner. Early in the relationship, the perpetrator might make offers or suggestions around managing household finances that, on the surface, appear thoughtful and caring. Perhaps the perpetrator offers to manage the finances as a way of supporting his partner and easing her load of responsibilities, saying, "You don't have to worry about the finances. I'll take care of us." These sentiments align with the typical gender norm in which men are responsible for making and managing the money in a household. Such sentiments are probably the established norm for men and women whose parents' style of money management mirrored these stereotypical roles.

Who in your relationship . . .

- **Has access to money and other financial resources?**
- **Has access to financial information?**
- **Knows where the money is kept?**
- **Knows how the money is spent?**

How do you and your partner . . .

- **Manage the household finances?**
- **Make household financial decisions?**
- **Manage the day-to-day spending?**
- **Make decisions around employment?**
- **Plan for your financial future?**
- **Share financial information with each other?**
- **Share financial decision-making with each other?**
- **How satisfied are you and your partner with the way finances are managed in your relationship?**
- **What is shared and not shared in your relationship related to finances?**
- **How are financial concerns expressed in your relationship?**
- **How do you and your partner manage financial stress?**

Figure 1.3. Assessing for financial abuse

Over time, the perpetrator begins to funnel household resources into new accounts, opened in his name only, without informing his victim that he has moved funds or decreased her access to money. Survivors often report that their abusers gained financial control by using tactics such as deception and blame (Jury et al., 2017). In this scenario, an abuser might blame the woman for overspending and claim that he needs to control the money until she can demonstrate she can be trusted to wisely manage the household finances. At other times, an abuser might demand that his victim needs to work and support him financially as a way of demonstrating that she cares about him. Similarly, the abuser might accuse and blame his victim for not earning enough to provide adequate financial resources for the family, even if the abuser is the one creating the debt and spending the money.

When initially assessing for financial abuse with survivors, it is important to remember that the survivor may or may not be aware that financial abuse was or is occurring in her relationship. She may be completely unaware of any financial abuse, especially if the perpetrator engaged in covert financial abuse behaviors. Survivors are more likely to begin talking about other forms of abuse, including experiences of physical abuse or psychological abuse, rather than financial abuse experiences. However, research has demonstrated that substantial overlap exists between and among the different forms of abuse. As such, if a survivor has experienced physical, psychological, or sexual forms of IPV, it is highly likely that she has also experienced financial abuse. Given the high likelihood of financial abuse, it is critical for advocates to assess all survivors of IPV for financial abuse experiences, even when a survivor is not immediately reporting financial abuse.

Does financial abuse differ from other forms of abuse? If so, how does financial abuse differ from psychological abuse? To answer these questions, we must first consider two critical dynamics of financial abuse that will help expand our understanding of the differences between financial abuse and other forms of IPV. The first dynamic is the *spatial component* of abusive behaviors (Stylianou et al., 2013). The closer the perpetrator's physical proximity to the survivor, the greater the number of abusive tactics the perpetrator can use. For example, a perpetrator must be in close proximity if he intends to engage in physically or sexually violent behaviors. However, physical proximity does not limit a perpetrator's ability to engage in psychological abuse. A perpetrator can engage in psychologically abusive behaviors from any location across the globe where he can find a means of communicating with the survivor or with the survivor's friends and family members.

Similarly, financially abusive behaviors are not limited by spatial proximity, communication, or contact with the survivor. With just a few pieces of the survivor's personal identifying information, a perpetrator can carry out most forms of financial abuse from countless locations. The increasing use of smartphone technology and online banking options have made it easier for perpetrators of IPV to engage in financially abusive behaviors. Even when an environmental barrier prevents a perpetrator from carrying out physical, sexual, or psychological abuse (e.g., a survivor entered an emergency shelter), the perpetrator can engage in financial abuse. Given the "long reach" of financial abuse, survivors face a high risk of ongoing financial abuse—even after they have left an abusive relationship—and are likely to experience identity theft, substantial difficulty in trying to disentangle joint finances, and a long battle in trying to repair their credit history.

In a recent study, Jennifer Glinski (2022) was able to identify economic abuse that perpetrators use *after* the couple is separated and no longer living with each other. She too took the original Power and Control Wheel and overlaid her findings using some of the same categories. She found new tactics abusers employ, such as manipulating institutions or abusing court processes, as a way to financially control their partner after they have separated.

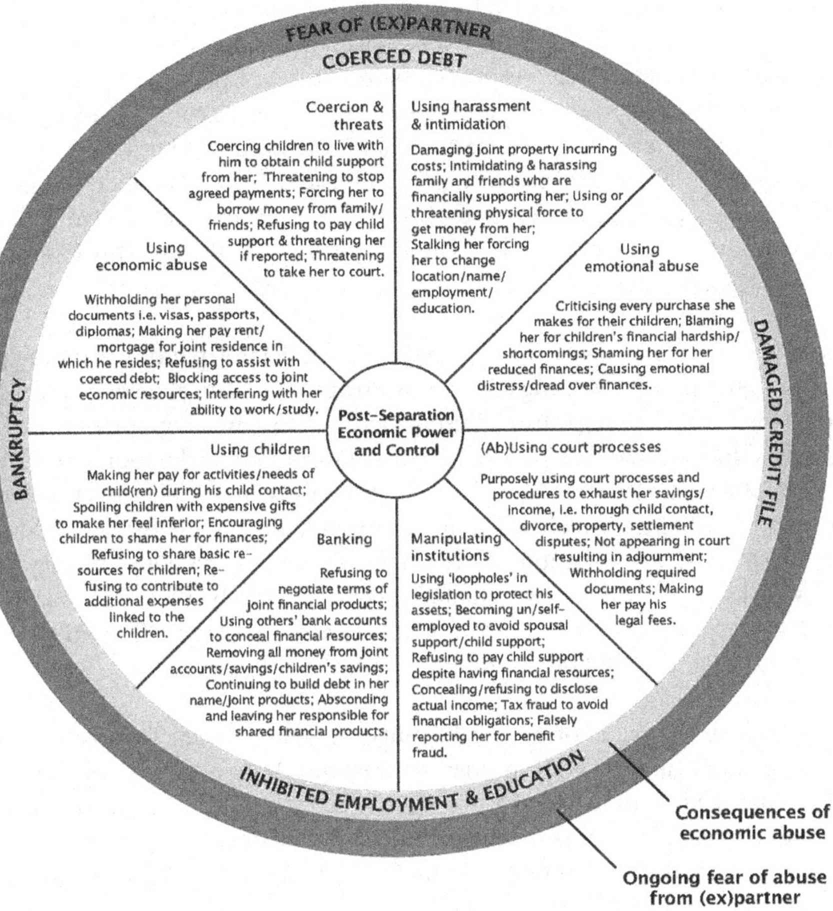

Figure 1.4. Post-Separation Economic Power and Control Wheel (Glinski, 2022)

The second dynamic differentiating financial abuse from other forms of IPV is a specific set of abusive behaviors intended to disrupt the survivor's financial security and, thereby, to make her financially dependent on the perpetrator (Adams et al., 2008; Miller, 1995). This dynamic differs from other forms of abuse in key ways. Specifically, financial abuse differs from other forms of abuse at the level of intention, that is, the perpetrator's intentions in choosing specific tactics. Whereas the perpetrator's intention in financial abuse is to control the survivor's ability to acquire, use, and maintain financial resources (Adams et al., 2008), in situations of emotional abuse, the intent of the abuse is to undermine the survivor's sense of self-worth and self-value (Miller, 1995). Similarly, financial abuse differs from both psychological abuse and social abuse. In situations of psychological abuse, the intent is to degrade the survivor's sense of logic and reasoning; in situations of social abuse, the perpetrator's intent is to isolate the survivor from her support network of friends and family (Miller, 1995). Financial abuse can have long-term and devastating effects on survivors because the perpetrator's focus on controlling or destroying the survivor's financial resources can create a cascade of negative effects that diminish the survivor's ability to establish a safe, independent life away from the abuser. This cascade of effects includes the following:

- Reinforces and maintains the survivor's financial dependency on the perpetrator, thus preventing the survivor from leaving an abusive relationship
- Prevents the survivor from gaining access to financial opportunities, hinders the survivor's ability to gain benefit from financial opportunities, and sabotages the survivor's efforts to maintain her financial opportunities
- Undermines the survivor's ability to provide financially for her children
- Destroys the foundation of the survivor's financial life and history (e.g., wrecks her credit score), which, in turn, negatively affects the survivor's future financial opportunities (Littwin, 2012; Postmus, Plummer, et al., 2012; Swanberg & Logan, 2005)

Through this cascade of negative events, financial abuse creates short- and long-term negative effects on survivors beyond those of psychological, physical, and sexual abuse. Given the unique nature of financial abuse and its impact on survivors' financial capabilities, it is critical that the field of survivor services adopts an intentional focus on better understanding the nature and consequences of financial abuse.

When assessing for financial abuse, remember that financial abuse often looks different at the level of individuals, couples, families, and cultures. Whereas physical abuse—and its host of negative effects—tends to look similar across cultures, financial abuse occurs in a range of forms that can look quite different in different cultures or socioeconomic groups. For example, among survivors with financial means, financial abuse might involve destroying the survivor's credit score and, thereby, limiting her ability to build financial independence. In contrast, among unbanked survivors navigating the cash economy, financial abuse might take the form of stealing the survivor's cash or possessions. Among immigrant families, financial abuse might involve hiding financial resources in the country of origin, especially if women have limited legal or civil rights in their country of origin. In addition, if a survivor's family is living in another country and receiving some financial support from the survivor, the abuser might threaten to stop all support payments to his victim's family as a way of gaining and reinforcing his power and control in the relationship.

Many survivors have reported that financial abuse often escalated into physical, psychological, or sexual abusive acts (Sanders, 2015); thus, it is critically important for those who are working with survivors to remain mindful of the risk for escalation. One study found that although only 16 percent of the sample of IPV survivors reported experiencing two forms of abuse (i.e., psychological abuse, financial abuse), nearly 76 percent of the IPV survivors reported experiencing three forms of IPV abuse: physical, psychological, and financial (Stylianou et al., 2013). Often abusers engage in a range of abusive tactics, including physical, psychological, and financial abuse tactics, and use these tactics and strategies interchangeably and in concert to gain power and control over the survivor.

Strategies to Improve Financial Safety

It is critically important to assess all survivors for experiences of financial abuse and to discuss financial safety strategies with survivors. Financial safety strategies leverage survivors' strengths and resourcefulness (Sanders, 2015).

To develop a financial safety plan, ask questions aimed at understanding the survivor's experience with managing money, including the methods used to manage money and the safety strategies or resources she has used to remain safe. The open-ended questions in figure 1.5 can be used to start a conversation with a survivor around developing financial safety strategies.

We know that IPV survivors' financial dependency on their partner is the number one reason they remain trapped in a relationship with abusive

---

- **How have you managed to survive financially?**
- **What have you done in the past to help your financial survival?**
- **What have you done in the past when your partner engaged in financially abusive behaviors?**
- **Who has supported your efforts to increase your financial safety?**
- **How have you managed to meet your needs (and your children's needs) in the past?**
- **What has worked in the past to increase your financial safety? What has not worked in the past to increase your financial safety?**
- **What resources have you used to increase your financial safety?**

Figure 1.5. Assessing for financial safety strategies

partners. All those who work with survivors must recognize the critical importance of assessing for financial abuse and the urgent need to help survivors create a financial safety plan—whether the survivor has left the relationship or remains in the relationship. Enhancing survivors' ability to identify and address their financial risks can lead to increased safety, security, and quality of life for survivors and their children.

Historically, the field of IPV has focused on the physical and emotional forms of abuse; however, a critical need exists for people in the field to build paths to hope and freedom for survivors experiencing financial abuse. Although the "typical" physical and emotional forms of abuse overlap across a range of coercive tactics, financial abuse is a unique set of abusive behaviors that perpetrators use to increase their control over survivors by making the survivor financially dependent. For survivors attempting to leave their abuser, their financial dependence on the perpetrator creates an array of barriers and obstacles. Therefore, the cycle of financial abuse is a recurring pattern of behavior in which a perpetrator engages in financially abusive tactics, with each recurrence increasing the extent of a survivor's financial dependence. In turn, as the survivor's financial dependence builds, the perpetrator is fueled to exert greater power and control over the survivor's financial assets and resources. Despite this pernicious cycle of abuse, financial abuse is often an invisible form of IPV. Nevertheless, financial abuse is a pervasive form of IPV and the leading reason women become trapped in an abusive relationship.

CHAPTER 2

Impact of Financial Abuse

"[I'm just] trying to get everything caught up to where I can stick to my financial plans and goals on a regular basis. Trying to get everything paid, caught up, and far enough out of the hole to where I can have a fresh start. I have set up so $100 a month out of my paycheck goes into savings and $100 into checking and $100 into another savings account. It goes away regularly, but the hole is so deep it's really been difficult to try and get out of it."

—a survivor who participated in an evaluation of a financial empowerment curriculum

Intimate partner violence has numerous and well-documented effects on survivors and their children that can emerge as short- or long-term impacts, including an extensive array of financial, social, and health consequences. Abusers often intentionally obstruct survivors' ability to manage their own finances, engage in work or educational activities, or use their wages to establish economic independence (Stylianou, 2018b; Stylianou et al., 2013). IPV is often associated with housing instability, employment volatility, and financial devastation (Adams et al., 2012) and is one of the leading causes of homelessness among women in the United States (Levin et al., 2004). Further, IPV is associated with increased risk for several serious mental health conditions, including depression, anxiety, posttraumatic stress disorder, substance use disorders, and self-harm. Additionally, IPV puts survivors at increased risk for multiple physical health conditions such as chronic pain and gastrointestinal symptoms (Davies et al., 1998). Because IPV often includes forced sexual activity, survivors have elevated risk for gynecological symptoms, including pregnancy complications and sexually transmitted infections.

IPV is among the leading causes of homelessness for women in the United States (Levin et al., 2004).

Children's exposure to IPV is an equally serious and growing public health concern. Estimates suggest that in each year, more than seven million U.S. children are exposed to IPV, either by witnessing violence or living in households in which IPV occurs (McDonald et al., 2006). IPV is so prevalent in U.S. households that it is estimated that 29 percent of U.S. children live in families in which IPV has occurred in the past year (McDonald et al., 2006). Researchers have documented the numerous negative effects that seeing, hearing, or attempting to intervene in IPV can have on children's developmental, mental health, physical health, and adult functioning (Holt et al., 2008; Hungerford et al., 2012). Children's exposure to IPV has been linked to short- and long-term negative outcomes such as deficiencies in cognition, poor academic achievement, impaired socioeconomic development, and criminal behavior as adults (Graham-Bermann & Perkins, 2010; Roberts et al., 2010). Children exposed to IPV also experience disproportionately high levels of child abuse and maltreatment (Hamby et al., 2010).

The IPV field has long emphasized the ways in which IPV impacts survivors and their children, and for decades, advocates and survivors have stressed that nonphysical forms of abuse are the most devastating forms of abuse, with negative effects reaching far beyond the impact of physical violence (Outlaw, 2009). Although physical, emotional, sexual, and financial forms of abuse overlap across a range of coercive tactics, financial abuse is unique because it aims to create financial dependence on the perpetrator. In turn, a survivor's financial dependence on her abuser creates a range of barriers for any survivor attempting to leave her abusive relationship. Therefore, the cycle of financial abuse is one in which perpetrators engage in financially abusive relationships that increase the survivor's financial dependence; as financial dependence builds, perpetrators are fueled to gain greater power and control over the survivor's financial assets and resources. As such, although financial abuse is often considered an invisible form of abuse, it is pervasive and the leading reason women remain in abusive relationships. Given the unique nature of financial abuse and the impact it has on the financial capabilities of IPV survivors, it is critically important that the field intentionally focuses on developing a better understanding of the nature and consequences of financial abuse. In this chapter, we delve deeper into understanding the multifaceted impact of financial abuse on survivors and their children across a range of financial, health, and well-being outcomes.

Conservation of Resources Theory

The conservation of resources (COR) theory is a theoretical framework that describes the connection between IPV—specifically financial abuse—and the range of negative short- and long-term consequences experienced by survivors and their children. The COR theory holds that the psychological distress that follows traumatic or highly stressful life events is strongly influenced by "resource loss"; that is, trauma often leads to individuals losing economic, social, and interpersonal resources central to their well-being (Hobfoll, 2001). For IPV survivors, this resource loss can include short- and long-term consequences such as having to relocate and leave family and friends; experiencing physical injuries; enduring health and mental health ailments; or experiencing a diminished sense of self, empowerment, or quality of life. The COR theory proposes that if this trauma-induced resource loss is followed by resource gain, psychological distress will be reduced and well-being will be increased. For example, if an IPV survivor experiencing financial abuse leaves her partner, gains employment, and establishes financial safety and independence, then the resource gains experienced after leaving the relationship have the potential to counteract the resource loss and reduce the negative impact of the trauma. However, Hobfoll (2001) has noted spiraling patterns of resource loss and gains, explaining that resource loss often results in additional resource loss, whereas resource gain often initiates further gains. For example, Stylianou and Pich (2019) conducted research on 347 IPV survivors residing in domestic violence emergency shelters. The study compared survivors with different levels of resources and examined the survivors' success in finding stable housing after leaving the domestic violence shelter program. These researchers found that the survivors with few resources were less successful in obtaining stable housing. In addition, the study results showed that the strongest association between discharge from the shelter and homelessness was found among survivors with less than a high school degree, those with no work history, and those with no income. Such spirals of resource loss mean that even after leaving an abusive relationship, survivors not only are facing a substantial number of barriers at the individual, community, and systems levels but are simultaneously facing numerous resource losses.

Intersectional Understanding of the Impact of Financial Abuse

Using an intersectional framework helps us understand the ways in which experiences of financial abuse can spiral into a broad range of negative outcomes. One premise of an intersectional framework (Crenshaw, 1991) holds that individuals have a variety of identities (e.g., race/ethnicity, socioeconomic status, sexual orientation, gender identity, age, religion/spirituality, ability), all of which are shaped by systems of power and oppression. Therefore, individuals might experience "simultaneous, multiple and interlocking oppressions" (Mann & Grimes, 2001, p. 8). Following the intersectional framework, Davies and colleagues (1998) defined two categories of risks that IPV survivors face. The first set of risks—*batterer-generated risks*—includes risks around physical, sexual, emotional, social, and financial safety, which are created directly by the abusive partner in an attempt to establish and maintain power and control. The second set is composed of *life-generated risks* and includes risks created by the interconnections between the effects of domestic violence with racism, sexism, classism, poverty, and structural inequality.

As discussed in chapter 1, although domestic violence occurs across racial, ethnic, and socioeconomic backgrounds, low-income women of color suffer disproportionate rates of IPV (Capaldi et al., 2012) and the structural inequity that compounds the effects of the two categories of risks (i.e., batterer-generated and life-generated risks). Although women's financial security can be limited by many factors such as structural inequalities, workplace inequities, child-rearing responsibilities, and oppressive social institutions (Bowie & Dopwell, 2013), a survivor's experience of financial abuse serves to heighten the financial vulnerability of many survivors and their children.

Research has found that women, especially women of color, are more likely to live in poverty, to experience IPV, and to experience more severe and prolonged IPV because they have restricted access to financial resources (Alcalde, 2006). Further, empirical evidence has documented historically higher rates of unemployment and job loss among people of color (specifically individuals who identify as Black or Latinx), and these disparities cannot be explained by single factors such as educational attainment alone (Cajner et al., 2017). When seeking employment, an African American woman experiencing IPV is likely to be confronted with both financial control from her partner and racism in the workplace. A Latina seeking to leave her abusive husband can be affected by both employment sabotage from her husband and the discrimination in the housing market. These are just a few examples of the ways in which interlocking systems of oppression interact to shape the experiences of IPV survivors. As Bograd (1999) has emphasized, "the trauma of domestic violence is amplified by further victimization outside of the intimate relationship, as the psychological consequences of battering may be compounded by the 'micro-aggressions' of racism, heterosexism, and classism" (p. 281). Even as survivors escape abusive relationships, intersectional risks can create a cascade of negative impacts, threatening survivors' safety, financial security, and well-being.

Conceptual Model of the Impact of Financial Abuse on Survivors and Their Families

Financial abuse includes behaviors that control a survivor's "ability to acquire, use, and maintain resources thus threatening her economic security and potential for self-sufficiency" (Adams et al., 2008). When the abuser has gained complete control over the survivor's financial resources (Fawole, 2008), the financial abuse, as discussed in chapter 1, includes three dimensions or forms of financial abuse: economic control, employment sabotage, and economic exploitation (Postmus et al., 2016; Stylianou et al., 2013).

Financial abuse not only affects survivors' intrapersonal consequences, such as financial knowledge, financial self-efficacy, and financial strain, but also influences their interpersonal consequences, such as access to financial

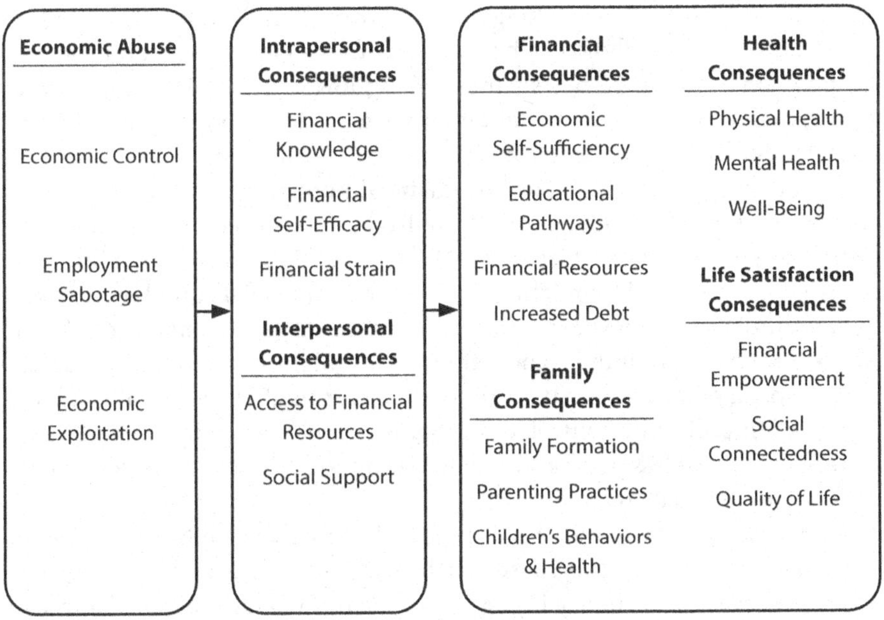

Figure 2.1. Conceptual model of the impact of financial abuse

resources and social support. In turn, the intrapersonal and interpersonal consequences lead to longer-term outcomes, including the following:

- Financial consequences (e.g., economic self-sufficiency, employment stability, income stability, financial resources and credit, and financial safety)
- Health consequences (e.g., physical health, mental health, and well-being)
- Family consequences (e.g., family formation, parenting practices, and child behavior and health)
- Life satisfaction consequences (e.g., financial empowerment, social connectedness, and quality of life)

Diving into current research can help us understand what we know and do not know about the consequences of financial abuse.

Intrapersonal Consequences

Financial knowledge or *financial literacy* encompasses the information and skills needed to "discern financial choices, discuss money and financial issues without (or despite) discomfort, plan for the future, and respond competently to life events that affect everyday financial decisions" (Vitt et al., 2000, p. xii). Therefore, financial knowledge is an important area of concern because an individual's level of financial knowledge is associated with their financial well-being over the long term (Gudmunson & Danes, 2011; Gutter & Copur, 2011). Households with low levels of financial knowledge are at risk for poor financial outcomes such as having low or no savings and investments, high credit card debt, and high mortgage debt (Braunstein & Welch, 2002). One study of 120 female survivors of IPV found significant relationships between the women's level of financial knowledge and their sense of economic empowerment, economic self-efficacy, and economic self-sufficiency (Postmus, Plummer, et al., 2013). These findings suggest that financial knowledge is a critical foundation for long-term financial confidence, stability, and independence (Postmus, Plummer, et al., 2013). Survivors of IPV who are members of immigrant communities might not have knowledge of U.S. financial practices, and thus, these survivors might be especially vulnerable to both economic control and economic exploitation by their partners as well as defenseless against the devastating longer-term financial consequences of financial abuse.

Economic self-efficacy is an individual's perceived ability to perform financial tasks. In turn, this sense of self-belief or self-assuredness (i.e., self-efficacy) serves as a primary influence on the individual's ability to improve their financial decision-making and behaviors. Women experiencing economic abuse typically have low levels of economic self-efficacy because their abusive partners give them ongoing negative messages about their ability to manage finances and restrict the women from having control over their own finances. Financial self-efficacy is critically important because research has found that economic self-efficacy is a pivotal predictor of financial success, even surpassing financial knowledge (Lapp, 2010). One Australian study compared levels of financial self-efficacy in a sample of women and found that the women with higher levels of financial self-efficacy were more likely to hold investments and savings and less likely to hold debt-related products (Farrell et al., 2016). When women experience economic abuse, the abuse erodes their sense of economic self-efficacy, negatively affects their financial behaviors, and increases their financial dependence on the abusive partner.

Financial strain encompasses a range of concepts, including individual control and mastery, interpersonal relationships, family tension, and resource constraint (Shippee et al., 2012). The notion of financial strain has been described as giving "psychological meaning to the experience of economic difficulties" (Gutman et al., 2005, p. 428). One study of 457 IPV survivors underscored the importance of this concept by showing that financial strain is associated with economic self-efficacy, economic self-sufficiency, and difficulty with income; given these critical associations, the researchers argued that financial strain is a significant component that must be considered in evaluating an individual's financial situation (Hetling, Stylianou, & Postmus, 2015).

Interpersonal Consequences

When an abusive partner exerts economic control over a survivor, the women often report losing *access to critical financial resources*. Survivors have reported that their abusers controlled and limited their access to financial resources, tracked their use of money, withheld or hid jointly earned money, prevented the survivors from accessing bank accounts, and lied about shared properties or assets (Brewster, 2003; Sanders, 2015). In many cases of economic abuse, the abusive partner controls the survivor's access to financial resources by restricting access, closely monitoring her access to cash or other resources, or completely controlling her access to financial resources of any type (Sanders, 2015). This lack of access often leaves survivors feeling "diminished, dependent, frustrated, and often unsure how to proceed" (Voth Schrag, 2019, p. 318). Moreover, the lack of access to financial resources is a main reason why many survivors feel they have no choice but to remain in the abusive relationship (Lyon, 1998; Sharp-Jeffs, 2015a).

Social supports provide survivors with much-needed relief, but survivors' support networks are often disrupted by the abuse. For many women who experience IPV, their family and friends are the first people they reach out to when disclosing their abuse. In many instances, survivors reach out to their support networks with requests for practical forms of assistance such as a safe place to live, financial support, or immediate needs of children (e.g., diapers or clothing). Reaching out to social networks is often a survivor's only option for coping with the financial stress resulting from abuse; however, abusive partners often take explicit, intentional steps to isolate survivors from their social networks. Abusers isolate survivors by demanding that their partners break contact with family, friends, and community members (Stylianou et al., 2018). Survivors who experience repeated cycles of abuse but have been able to maintain a few social supports also risk exhausting those social supports (Goodman et al., 2003). Supportive individuals who recognize the pattern of abuse are likely to feel frustrated or burned out by the repetitive pattern of the abusive relationship. Survivors might feel embarrassed to disclose abuse experiences or might worry about burdening family and friends, particularly if the abuse is repetitive (Dunham & Senn, 2000; Rose & Campbell, 2000). With ties to social supports weakened or broken, survivors are left alone and typically become increasingly dependent on the abusive partner.

Financial Consequences

Financial abuse affects the survivor's ability to gain financial self-sufficiency and financial resources (Adams et al., 2015; Postmus, Plummer, et al., 2012; Voth Schrag, 2015). Voth Schrag (2015) found that experiencing financial abuse created unique batterer-generated risks for survivors, with specific negative impacts on the women's later economic outcomes. In fact, as compared with women who had not experienced financial abuse, women who were survivors of financial abuse were more likely to report experiencing ongoing material hardship.

As compared with mothers who are not financially abused, mothers experiencing financial abuse are 1.3 times more likely to suffer material hardship (Voth Schrag, 2015).

Financial abuse also affects survivors' *economic self-sufficiency*. Economic self-sufficiency is the ability to accomplish tasks related to personal finances. For example, an economically self-sufficient person can "pay their own way" in daily life without borrowing from family or friends. Research has documented that financial abuse, specifically economic control, is a significant predictor of decreased economic self-sufficiency (Postmus, Plummer, et al., 2012). A survivor's ability to be financially self-sufficient is continuously diminished as the abuser exerts increasing control over financial decisions and imposes greater limitations on the survivor's access to financial resources (Postmus, Plummer, et al., 2012). Similarly, Adams, Greeson, et al. (2019) found that the greater the extent of financial abuse women experienced during their relationship, the less money they had to meet their needs, the greater their economic hardship, and the greater their material dependence on the perpetrator. Further, as women's experiences of financial abuse increase over their lifetimes, the money they have available to meet their needs decreases over time. Researchers have even documented the relationship between past IPV experiences and economic self-sufficiency among divorced women, with their findings suggesting that the impact of abuse on economic self-sufficiency continues after the abusive relationship has ended (Warrener et al., 2013). As such, financial abuse is an effective, persistent tool used by abusive partners to limit women's access to financial resources; that is, as long as the financial abuse continues, women's financial health declines.

---

59 percent of women experiencing IPV report that their partner demands that they quit their job (Postmus, Plummer, et al., 2012).

28 percent of women experiencing IPV report that their partner prevents them from having the money they need to buy food, clothes, and other necessities (Adams et al., 2015).

Given that employment is a key pathway for women to leave an abusive relationship, abusers who use financial abuse tactics will often use employment sabotage to create *employment and income instability*. Survivors of employment sabotage report having difficulty concentrating at work and performing their jobs (Logan et al., 2007; Wathen et al., 2015).

Research has documented the detrimental impact of IPV in the short term and the persistent effects of past IPV experiences on employment stability over time (Adams et al., 2013; Crowne et al., 2011). A study conducted by Adams and colleagues (2013) clearly demonstrated that as compared with women who had not experienced IPV, women who had recently experienced

IPV worked fewer hours at any one job and had significantly less stable employment and, thus, fewer job benefits.

As compared with women without IPV experiences, women who experience IPV work 3.06 fewer months at any one job (Adams et al., 2013).

Women who experience physical violence have twice the odds of low or moderate employment stability (Crowne et al., 2011).

Employment sabotage can take many forms, with survivors experiencing numerous work disruptions caused by their abuser, including harassing phone calls or text messages, in-person harassment or threats, stalking while at work, using physical tactics to interfere with work attendance, refusing to provide transportation or child care, sabotaging the car or hiding car keys, stealing transportation money, or making threats against or harassing coworkers (Logan et al., 2007). As a result of this barrage of abusive behaviors, it is not surprising that survivors report having difficulty concentrating on their work, difficulty performing on the job, increased absenteeism, and reduced annual work hours (Garcia et al., 2017; LeBlanc et al., 2014).

---

40 percent of women experiencing domestic violence report that their partner steals the car keys or transportation money as a job interference tactic (Swanberg & Macke, 2006).

40–49 percent of women experiencing domestic violence report that their partner harasses them on the phone or in person at work (Swanberg & Macke, 2006).

Experiencing domestic violence reduces a woman's annual work hours by 137 hours (Tolman & Wang, 2005).

Given the numerous tactics that perpetrator use to sabotage survivors' employment, it is not surprising that IPV is associated with job loss, unemployment, and employment instability (Adams et al., 2013). One study with a sample of thirty-four women IPV survivors found that the women had difficulty maintaining employment because the perpetrators sabotaged their work. In addition to the tactics already described, perpetrators sabotaged survivors' ability to work by using physical and emotional abuse to force women to leave their jobs and by causing the women to suffer from sleep deprivation (Borchers et al., 2016). Research not only has demonstrated the negative impact of IPV on job productivity, work interference, and job satisfaction (Banyard et al., 2011) but has also shown that increases in the number of victimization experiences leads to greater decreases in job productivity and greater reduction in job satisfaction.

36–75 percent of IPV survivors experience employment sabotage.

5–27 percent of survivors lose their job due to employment sabotage (Swanberg et al., 2005).

In addition to employment sabotage, abusive partners can *undermine educational pathways* through various forms of school sabotage (Sanders, 2015; Voth Schrag & Edmond, 2017). Educational pathways are critical to survivors' financial well-being because attaining education and credentials provides the foundation for higher levels of job security and better opportunities for high-wage employment. Voth Schrag and Edmond (2017) have defined school sabotage as behaviors involving coercive controlling tactics that directly affect a survivor's efforts to obtain educational credentials. An abusive partner engaging in school sabotage might interfere with the woman's receipt of financial aid, use physical violence to prevent her from attending class, stalk the survivor on campus, disrupt her academic studies, or induce guilt related to academic efforts. Research has found that such tactics pose effective barriers to survivors' ability to complete their educational programs; therefore, school sabotage tactics are also associated with decreased safety and reduced economic independence for survivors of IPV (Sanders, 2015; Voth Schrag et al., 2019).

As a way of reinforcing control over survivors of IPV, perpetrators often intentionally engage in behaviors aimed to *destroy the survivor's financial resources and credit* and/or *increase her debt*, thereby increasing the survivor's dependence on the abuser. According to the Consumer Bankruptcy Project, in the year before filing for bankruptcy, 18 percent of married or cohabiting female participants had experienced IPV (Littwin, 2012). Littwin (2012) has identified three ways in which perpetrators engage in economic exploitation: fraud, force, and misinformation. In today's consumer credit system, a person with access to another's personal information (i.e., birthdate, Social Security number) can fraudulently obtain credit in the other person's name; this fraud is more easily perpetrated by intimate partners.

Abuse perpetrators might forge the survivor's signature to use preauthorized checks, open lines of credit, or engage in immigration-related fraud. Among LGBTQ+ relationships, a perpetrator might impersonate their partner to steal identifying documents (e.g., passport or driver's license) or gain access to accounts at financial institutions. Additionally, perpetrators might use force or threats to coerce debt, including forcing a survivor to sign financial documents or threatening violence or other consequences if she refuses to give the perpetrator financial information or access. Finally, perpetrators might purposefully mislead survivors into signing financial documents by lying about the content or misrepresenting the purpose of the document (Littwin, 2012).

The relationship between a woman experiencing economic abuse and incurring outstanding debt has been well documented by researchers. In fact, the more a woman has experienced economic abuse, the more types of debt she owes (Adams & Beeble, 2019). Similarly, Adams, Littwin, and Javorka (2019) found that coerced debt—incurred from both coercive and fraudulent transactions—was a common problem among survivors of IPV. Moreover, these researchers found that coerced debt was significantly related to the abusive partner's control over financial information, damage to the survivor's credit, and the survivor's financial dependence on the abusive partner. Nearly three-quarters of the women involved in this study reported that they had stayed in the abusive relationship longer than they had wanted because they were worried about how they would financially support themselves or their children.

IPV survivors whose partners hide financial information are 3.6 times more likely to have coerced debt.

IPV survivors who have coerced debt from their partners are 6 times more likely to have their credit damaged.

Women with coerced debt are 2.5 times more likely to report financial dependence on an abusive partner than women without coerced debt (Adams, Littwin, et al., 2019).

Not only does the research evidence clearly show the devastating impact of financial abuse on financial independence among survivors of IPV in the United States, but a growing body of research has started to document the impact of financial abuse on women across the globe. Research in South Africa found that women who received a new loan experienced increased levels of past-year economic abuse (Ranganathan et al., 2019). Similarly, research in India has documented the relationship of household financial stressors with women's increased risk of IPV (Raj et al., 2018). However, lower likelihood of experiencing IPV was found among women who had joint control of the husband's income and among women who owned bank accounts.

As compared with women in South Africa who did not request a loan, women who received a new loan were 6.3 times more likely to have experienced economic abuse in the past year.

Women in India who gained joint control of the husband's income experienced a 70 percent reduction in the likelihood of reporting IPV relative to women whose husband maintains sole control.

As compared with women in India with no bank account, women who opened a bank account experienced a 56 percent reduction in the likelihood of reporting IPV (Ranganathan et al., 2019).

The risk for economic abuse is even greater for women in arranged marriages. Among South Asian families, it is often customary for bank accounts to be held in the name of the male head of the household. Although in theory this money is available for the entire family's use, women who marry into the family might be considered outsiders without any claim to the family's money (Anitha, 2019). South Asian woman might also experience coercive debt through the coercive sale of her jewelry or other assets that were part of her dowry (Chowbey, 2017).

For immigrant survivors of IPV, the experiences of economic abuse not only create barriers to financial self-sufficiency but also restrict access to social safety nets, thus creating additional financial challenges. Such economic barriers, faced in the context of abuse and immigration, affect immigrant survivors' ability to build economic self-sufficiency and achieve freedom from abuse (Hoge, 2016). Research has documented many of the unique challenges immigrant survivors of IPV experience in leaving the abusive relationship because of having less income and a lack of financial resources (Molina & Abel, 2010). Abusive partners of an immigrant survivor might restrict the woman's ability to learn English, a tactic that not only socially isolates the survivor but also negatively affects her ability to find and maintain employment. Abusive partners might interfere with the survivor's ability to gain documented status in the country, thereby creating further opportunities for the abusive partner to manipulate the survivor and prevent her from gaining financial independence.

These forms of economic exploitation have major negative effects on the lives of survivors. Economic exploitation can negatively impact a survivor's credit, which in turn can create barriers to housing, employment, or other necessities, thereby limiting the survivor's economic self-sufficiency. Further, the financial effects of economic exploitation can persist long after the survivor has ended the relationship. For some survivors, these financial barriers not only create major roadblocks to leaving the relationship but also can be the major reason a survivor returns to an abusive relationship.

For most survivors, the road to financial independence is not a linear process but rather a winding road with numerous bumps and turns on the way. For many, gaining independence and safety requires significant personal, emotional, and financial costs for the survivors and their children. As survivors build their financial independence, it is important that they have access to critical supports, including both short-term resources (e.g., housing, cash, and employment opportunities) and long-term resources (e.g., financial education, supported employment, affordable housing, long-term financial planning). (See chapter 4 for a detailed discussion of these critical supports and interventions.)

Health and Mental Health Consequences

In addition to leaving financial consequences, financial abuse by an intimate partner can also create devastating mental health and health consequences. The existing research has well documented the ways in which experiences of IPV lead to trauma symptoms and other *symptoms of poor mental health.* Scholars have linked IPV experiences to poor mental health outcomes through the effects of IPV on survivors' social support; self-esteem; feelings of powerlessness, hopelessness, and loss of control; coping response; job instability; and economic hardship (Adams et al., 2013; Voth Schrag et al., 2018).

Among women who report experiences of economic abuse, 46 percent meet the clinical cutoff for depression, and 25 percent meet the clinical cutoff for PTSD (Voth Schrag et al., 2018).

The intersectionality framework provides a foundation for understanding the interrelationships between the various forms of trauma—individual, interpersonal, community, and systemic trauma—experienced by survivors of IPV and the way in which each form of trauma and oppression can lead to psychological distress. Therefore, although psychological distress is a risk factor for any individual experiencing IPV, the risks are exacerbated among individuals with multiple oppressed identities. Chronic stress models emphasize that both interpersonal trauma and systemic marginalization can enable complex trauma, which can lead to psychological distress (Matheson et al., 2019).

The intersection of IPV and poverty among women creates complex traumatic experiences that can lead to constrained coping and increased psychological distress. For women with additional oppressed identities (e.g., LGBTQ+ survivors, immigrants, or survivors of color), the complex traumatic experiences of IPV are compounded by experiences of systemic trauma. Research has found that among survivors of IPV, the women's experiences of financial abuse were related to increased symptoms of depressive disorders and PTSD, greater levels of psychological distress, and increased suicide attempts (Nancarrow et al., 2009; Postmus, Huang, & Stylianou, 2012; Voth Schrag, 2015; Voth Schrag et al., 2019). Postmus, Huang, & Stylianou (2012) found that when testing for the intensity of and change in abuse experiences over time—including physical, psychological, sexual, and financial abuse—only financial abuse predicted depression over time. Specifically, these researchers found that mothers who experienced financial abuse were 3.5 times more likely to exhibit depressive symptoms five years later. Moreover, among the mothers who experienced increased financial abuse over the five-year study period, those mothers were 2.2 times more likely to experience depressive symptoms.

Mothers who experience financial abuse are 1.9 times more likely to exhibit depressive symptoms than mothers who do not experience financial abuse (Postmus, Huang, & Stylianou, 2012).

Research has established that experiences of financial abuse are uniquely associated with depression—even when accounting for other forms of IPV victimization. One study found that among women receiving services from domestic violence organizations, financial abuse experiences were associated with depressive symptoms, even when accounting for physical, sexual, and psychological abuse (Stylianou, 2018a). Voth Schrag and colleagues' (2019) study among female community college students also found an association between economic abuse and depression. Notably, when all forms of IPV (emotional, physical, sexual, and economic) were included in the researchers' analytic model, economic abuse was the only form of IPV to maintain a significant relationship with depression.

Research across the globe has documented similar relationships between economic abuse experiences and depression. In Australia, Nancarrow and colleagues (2009) found that among women who had experienced multiple forms of abuse, including physical, psychological, sociopsychological, and financial abuse, financial abuse was associated with severe psychological symptoms and severe depression. Further, financial abuse was found to be the highest risk factor for reporting depressive symptoms. A study conducted in the Philippines found that among women who reported multiple forms of abuse (i.e., physical, psychological, and financial), experiences of psychological abuse and financial abuse were the strongest predictors of psychological distress and suicide attempts (Antai et al., 2014). A nationally representative study conducted in Germany found that women who reported economic abuse had increased psychosomatic symptoms and severe psychological problems (Stockl & Penhale, 2015). A study using a sample of young women in informal settlements in South Africa found a significant relationship between economic abuse and symptoms of depression (Gibbs et al., 2018). In addition, Gibbs and colleagues (2018) found that if women reported that their partner diverted money needed for the household to spend on himself (e.g., for alcohol or tobacco), then the women were more likely to report suicidal ideation. Notably, the study reported that emotional and economic abuse had significant negative impacts on the women's mental health, and those impacts extended beyond the effects of physical or sexual IPV alone.

One potential explanation of the significant relationship between financial abuse experiences and depressive symptoms is the way in which financial abuse is used by perpetrators as a tool to create financial dependency and trap the survivor in the relationship. Therefore, financial abuse has the potential to unleash a cascade of negative effects on the survivor, including preventing the survivor from leaving the relationship, preventing her from gaining or maintaining economic opportunities, impacting her ability to financially care for her children, and destroying her financial foundation. Given the nature of financial abuse and its impact on IPV survivors' financial capabilities over the long term, the added dimension of the financial hardship created by financial abuse might explain the unique relationship between financial abuse and depressive symptoms. Notably, although other forms of abuse such as physical, sexual, or psychological abuse can lead to long-term negative effects, none results in oppressive or destructive consequences equal to those of the extraordinary burden of financial hardship.

In addition to financial abuse leading to increased depressive symptoms among survivors of IPV, early research has documented a relationship between financial abuse and PTSD (Voth Schrag et al., 2018). Trauma theory explains that chronic stress—that is, stress created by ongoing interpersonal trauma, poverty, or systemic marginalization—can create an environment that elicits complex trauma reactions from individuals. Common trauma reactions include flashbacks, nightmares, severe anxiety, intense feelings of shame, decreased attention or focus, emotional lability, somatic symptoms, poor interpersonal relationships, impulsive or harmful behaviors, and suicidal thoughts or behaviors.

A study conducted by Voth Schrag and colleagues (2018) among female community college students found that experiences of financial abuse and economic hardship were related to symptoms of both depressive disorders and PTSD symptoms. Further, when compared with other form of IPV, specifically physical abuse and sexual abuse, financial abuse was the only form of abuse found to be significantly related to depressive symptoms and PTSD symptoms. Similarly, Sauber and O'Brien (2017) compared outcomes of women whose partners did or did not use financially abusive tactics and found that women who experienced financial abuse reported more symptoms of depression and PTSD; lost more interpersonal, financial, and work-related resources; and were less economically self-sufficient. Qualitative research with survivors has documented reports by women of their partner's efforts to intentionally sabotage their efforts toward financial independence, which in turn contributed to the women's psychological and financial distress (Sanders, 2015). As noted by Voth Schrag and colleagues (2018), financial abuse creates ongoing safety risks for survivors, even after the relationship has ended. Additionally, experiencing financial abuse and the risk of economic insecurity exposes survivors to greater risk for traumatic reactions.

A large body of research has documented the effects of IPV on survivors' physical health outcomes. IPV is associated with numerous poor physical health outcomes, including poor functional health, somatic disorders, chronic disorders and pain, gynecological problems, and increased risk of sexually transmitted infections (Dillon et al., 2013). Not only have IPV researchers documented the effects of financial abuse on survivors' mental health outcomes, but early research has also documented the effects of financial abuse on survivors' *physical health outcomes*. To examine the physical health consequences associated with financial abuse experiences, Tenkorang and Owusu (2019) collected data from 2,289 ever-married Ghanaian women. This research team found that financial abuse had a negative impact on the cardiovascular, psychosocial, and overall health of the women.

In addition to substantiating the relationship between financial abuse experiences and health and mental health symptoms, research has also confirmed a connection between financial abuse experiences and negative effects on women's *quality of life*. Quality of life is a dimension of psychological well-being that reflects an individual's assessment of how things are going in their life (Adams & Beeble, 2019). Among a sample of ninety-four women with recent experiences of physical violence, a change in a woman's experiences of financial abuse over a four-month period was found to be significantly related to the woman's reported change in quality of life (Adams & Beeble, 2019). This finding demonstrated that experiencing financial abuse decreased women's quality of life beyond the effects of physical and psychological abuse experiences. For many survivors, financial abuse and its cascading impact of negative financial consequences decreased overall quality of life. Adams and Beeble (2019) used specific items to measure individuals' satisfaction with their personal safety, opportunities for fun and enjoyment, independence and freedom, and accomplishments and found that a strong relationship existed between financial abuse and a survivor's perception of her quality of life. These findings not only establish the evidence base supporting the relationship between financial abuse and physical and psychological distress but also point to the need to provide survivors with comprehensive services that incorporate health, mental health, and financial empowerment components. Developing service frameworks that incorporate trauma-informed counseling with advocacy around economic justice is critical for the financial and emotional security of survivors.

Family Consequences

A growing body of research has begun to demonstrate the relationships that exist between financial abuse and family formations, parenting practices, children's behaviors, and youth outcomes. Belsky (1984) applied an ecological framework to understand parenting behaviors and identified three domains that determine parenting behaviors. The first domain includes characteristics of the parent, such as their psychological well-being. The second domain includes characteristics of the child, such as obedience and temperament. The third domain include the social context of the family and the stressors experienced by the family. Belsky specified three contextual sources of stress, including the marital relationship, social networks, and employment. Belsky proposed that in buffering the parent-child interactions from stress, a parent's psychological resources were more important than the contextual sources, but in turn, the contextual sources were more important than the child's characteristics in predicting parenting behavior.

Within this family microsystem, IPV permeates each domain. Numerous research studies have indicated that IPV decreases the survivor's psychological well-being (Afifi et al., 2009; Cavanaugh et al., 2011). However, witnessing IPV has also been associated with problems among young children, including difficulties with social competence, temperament, internalizing behaviors, and aggression (Burke et al., 2008; Evans et al., 2008). Among contextual stressors, IPV has negative effects on the marital relationship, the survivor's social network, her employment status, and her criminal justice involvement (Gottlieb & Mahabir, 2019; Staggs et al., 2007). Given these consequences, research has indicated that IPV is associated with a decrease in the quality of maternal parenting (Casanueva et al., 2008; Huang et al., 2010).

More recently, studies have examined the relationship between financial abuse and parenting. To examine the long-term impact of IPV on parenting, Postmus, Huang, and Stylianou (2012) conducted a study using data from the Fragile Families and Child Wellbeing Study (Brooks-Gunn et al., 2011), which is a nationally representative sample of births in hospitals located in cities with populations of more than two hundred thousand people. Findings indicated that mothers experiencing economic abuse following the birth of their child reported decreased engagement in parent-child activities and increased use of spanking. This study provided insights into how financial abuse impacts maternal engagement with the child and the use of spanking. Interestingly, the study findings showed that the mother's experience of physical violence was not significantly related to parenting behavior (Postmus, Huang, & Stylianou, 2012).

Mothers who experience financial abuse from a partner are 1.5 times more likely to spank their child (Postmus, Huang, & Stylianou, 2012).

Similarly, Huang, Postmus, and colleagues (2013) used the same Fragile Families data set to examine the occurrence of and changes in economic abuse over time and how economic abuse influenced mothers' union formation. The study findings demonstrated that economic abuse increased in prevalence over time, and both the occurrence of and the increase in economic abuse were significantly and negatively associated with the likelihood of stable union formations such as marriage and cohabitation.

Mothers who experience financial abuse have 68 percent lower odds of marrying than being uninvolved with the child's father at year five and 53 percent lower odds of cohabitating than being uninvolved at year five (Huang, Postmus, et al., 2013).

Gottlieb and Mahabir (2019) also examined the Fragile Families data and found that although mothers who experienced any form of IPV were at greater risk of involvement with the criminal justice system, only physical and economic abuse were independently associated with a greater risk of criminal justice involvement.

Mothers who experience economic abuse have 51 percent higher odds of criminal justice involvement than mothers who have not experienced economic abuse (Gottlieb & Mahabir, 2019).

Initial research has also demonstrated the impact of exposure to economic abuse on children. Huang and colleagues (2015) examined the effects of exposure to IPV in early childhood (as measured by the experiences of the children's mothers with physical violence and economic abuse) on children's delinquency at age nine, based on children's self-report of their behavior. The results indicated with respect to physical violence and financial abuse that only the presence of financial abuse was statistically significantly associated with child delinquency at age nine. These findings highlight the persistent, long-term effects of children's early exposure to financial abuse.

Similarly, Voth Schrag and colleagues (2017) examined the impact of witnessing financial abuse tactics among a sample of 105 female youth involved in the child welfare system. Nearly half of the sample reported witnessing moderate or high levels of economic abuse. Moreover, the study findings indicated that greater levels of exposure to economic abuse were significantly related to increased rates of depression, increased PTSD symptoms, and decreased rates of financial self-efficacy (defined as the individual's belief in their ability to succeed at a given financial task in the future; Voth Schrag et al., 2017).

Life Satisfaction Consequences

Financial empowerment is defined as both an outcome and a process that enables women to develop the knowledge, skills, and confidence needed not only to meet their financial goals but also to access external resources (both formal and informal) to build the financial well-being of their families. (See chapter 3 on financial empowerment.) Because abusive partners often limit or prevent survivors from having personal power, survivors frequently lose their ability to access the various resources needed to obtain their financial goals. This removal of power often leaves survivors with less financial knowledge, less confidence, and less ability to manage their finances. One study, conducted among 120 IPV survivors, found that increases in financial knowledge and economic self-sufficiency were significantly related to an increase in financial empowerment (Postmus, Plummer, et al., 2013). A key component of financial empowerment is providing survivors with the opportunity to gain or regain their financial independence. Additionally, researchers have found that empowerment can attenuate the severity of PTSD among IPV survivors (Goodman, Fauci, et al., 2016; Perez et al., 2012).

In addition to financial empowerment, *improving social connectedness* is an important factor in improving the quality of life for IPV survivors. Research has demonstrated that women with recent IPV experiences reported decreased social functioning (Bonomi et al., 2006). This finding is important because connection to others is critical to enhancing positive outcomes in times of stress and trauma (Schultz et al., 2016). IPV survivors have identified support from their social networks as contributing to their safety and well-being (Goodman, Banyard, et al., 2016). For example, survivors who are undocumented immigrants and who cannot access formal support systems for IPV survivors because of fear of deportation or language barriers will often reach out to their social network to access housing or financial resources (Sauber & O'Brien, 2017; Schultz et al., 2016). Survivors have shared numerous stories of the ways in which supportive individuals have provided not just emotional support but also practical assistance that was instrumental in their recovery. Research has documented the positive impact of social support on survivors' well-being (Suvak et al., 2013).

Last, the field has begun to prioritize quality of life as a critical outcome for IPV survivors. Research has shown that women who report IPV were more likely to report low rates of life satisfaction (Zlotnick et al., 2006), including poor physical functioning, heightened emotional problems, reduced vitality, impaired social functioning, and mental health aspects of quality of life (Laffaye et al., 2003). One study, with a sample of ninety-four women with recent IPV experiences, found that changes in their economic abuse experiences was significantly related to change in quality of life (Adams & Beeble, 2019). This finding demonstrated that financial abuse decreased survivors' quality of life beyond the effects of physical and psychological abuse experiences.

In sum, research has established that economic abuse is associated with a range of negative outcomes across interpersonal, intrapersonal, financial, health, family, and life satisfaction. The literature provide evidence of the short- and long-term negative effects of economic abuse on the lives of survivors of IPV and their children. Additionally, the existing evidence also documents that the impact of economic abuse extends far beyond the impact of other forms of IPV.

CHAPTER 3

What Is Financial Empowerment?

Kerri was twenty-eight years old when she left home with her two children to enter a domestic violence emergency shelter. Kerri described how her partner would constantly criticize her, verbally attack her (e.g., putting her down to her family and friends), and physically maltreat her (e.g., pushing, grabbing, shoving, forcing her to have sex). To trap Kerri in the relationship, her partner refused to let Kerri work, put her on a strict allowance, and closely monitored her use of money. Although she ended the relationship because of the abuse, her partner refused to leave the house and continued abusing Kerri. The abuse escalated until one day the abuser threatened to kill Kerri. She went to the police, reported the abuse, and obtained a protection order. Even though her abuser was arrested, he continued harassing and threatening Kerri. Her now-former partner demanded that she drop the charges; when she did not comply with his demands, he made threats to kill her and her children. Because Kerri felt that neither she nor her children could safely stay in their home, she and the children entered a domestic violence emergency shelter. During Kerri's first week at the shelter where Stylianou worked, Stylianou asked her what it was like transitioning to life in the shelter.

> When I arrived here, on one hand I feel well because I feel protected. I feel good. But still, since it's something that just recently happened, it still has some roots present in me. But yes, I'm trying to overcome it. . . . To be honest, it was a difficult change because it's something radical to have to leave one's home life in order to find shelter in the midst of experiencing domestic violence. The truth is that it's not easy—because of all that this man has done to me, I had to give up everything. I had to give up my home after so many

> years, the place where I was bringing up my children. And in order to run away from him, I had to leave everything behind and make a radical change. *It's not easy—new beginning, new life, you know?*

Stylianou asked Kerri what she wanted to focus on while residing in the shelter.

> I would like to do something. . . . If I can work, then I'd like to work in order to save some money. You know, I don't have any [job] right now because of the situation. And once I get out of here, I have no idea what I'm going to do about it. . . . I'd like to receive support to help me find an apartment, housing, something . . . so that it can be more comfortable for me and the kids. Yes, I'd really like to receive a lot of support to be ready when I leave here because *if I have to leave here and haven't found a solution, I wouldn't know what to do.*

For many survivors of domestic violence, Kerri's story is all too familiar. Most survivors share a common story of struggling to become physically, emotionally, and financially independent from an abusive partner. Moreover, survivors frequently point out that their struggle was magnified by lacking access to resources, ranging from a lack of employment opportunities to a lack of access to joint bank accounts to lacking even small amounts of cash. In addition to the lack of resources, survivors' struggle for independence is made more challenging when the women lack the knowledge and skills needed to be independent and self-sufficient. Many survivors lack the self-efficacy, knowledge, and skills needed to survive: what they truly lack is *financial empowerment.*

What is financial empowerment? At its core, financial empowerment is an intervention approach that focuses on improving the financial security of survivors of domestic violence. A financially empowered survivor has the knowledge, skills, self-confidence, and resources to support herself and her family. Achieving financial empowerment occurs when a woman feels capable of managing her current financial situation and financial tasks *and* feels capable of confidently planning her financial future. The logical question that follows is, How does a survivor build her sense of financial empowerment? The process of building toward financial empowerment is critical given the long-term negative effects of domestic violence on women's psychological health and self-perception, especially among women who experienced financial abuse. In this chapter, we conceptualize financial empowerment as both an outcome and a process, with the aim of peeling back myriad layers of the process to reveal the various levels of financial empowerment. The process of financial empowerment begins with a survivor building a foundation of human capability, financial knowledge and ability, and financial resources and assets. At the end of the process, the survivor has acquired the knowledge, skills, and confidence to manage her financial affairs and to achieve financial well-being and stability. To provide a background for the discussion of intervention strategies for financial empowerment, we briefly examine two key theories—capability approach and empowerment theory—and then develop a framework that combines these two theories to yield a definition of financial empowerment. To provide greater insight to these theories, we have included examples taken from the stories of survivors. The chapter concludes with a comprehensive definition of financial empowerment that practitioners can apply to their work with survivors of domestic violence.

Capability Approach

The capabilities approach holds that when an individual has both internal and external capabilities in the political, social, and economic environments, that combining these capabilities results in freedom and opportunities that improve the person's quality of life (Nussbaum, 2011).

Developed by the Indian economist and philosopher Amartya Sen (1981), the capabilities approach was created to provide a means for comparing quality of life in countries around the world on the basis of individuals' capability of achieving the kind of lives that the individuals valued (i.e., what they are able *to be* and *to do*). Hence, rather than comparing countries on outcome measures of wealth, production of goods, or available resources, applying the capabilities approach allows comparisons using measures that account for diversity, environmental quality, and the life options that *people are free to do or realize*. Drawing from Sen's work, Nussbaum (2000) applied the capabilities approach to women. Nussbaum's premise held that women around the globe lacked support for the basic functions of life, citing as evidence the many countries that do not consider women fully equal with men under law, do not give women the same rights to property as men, do not give women legal rights to sign contracts, or restrict women's mobility and religious freedoms. In many countries and cultures, women have few or no personal rights, and therefore, they have no choice in whether to marry or whom they marry, how many children they bear, or whether they can leave a bad marriage.

Gender equality is not only a fundamental human right but also requisite groundwork for a prosperous and peaceful humanity. Conversely, gender inequality has been strongly linked to poverty, which in turn, leads to deficits in the capabilities that all humans need to thrive. Nussbaum (2000) expanded on Sen's original list of central human capabilities to define the threshold level of basic personal capabilities that social and political institutions should promote for all but especially for women. Nussbaum's expanded list includes the following ten central human capabilities:

- *Life*: The ability to live and not die prematurely
- *Bodily health*: The ability to have good health, including reproductive health, adequate nourishment, and safe shelter
- *Bodily integrity*: The ability to move freely from place to place, having the boundaries of one's body as sovereign, and having opportunities for sexual satisfaction and choices in reproduction
- *Senses, imagination, and thought*: The capacity to use the senses and have the freedom to imagine, think, and reason in a human way as cultivated by adequate education
- *Emotions*: The ability to form and maintain attachments to things and people outside the self; the ability to love others and grieve their absence; the ability to experience longing, gratitude, and justified anger; and the ability to avoid emotions driven by fear, anxiety, trauma, abuse, or neglect.
- *Practical reason*: The capability of understanding complex ideas, the ability to engage in critical reflection of the self and life for making life plans, and the capacity to protect personal freedom of conscience
- *Affiliation*: The ability to live civilly with others, to engage in social interactions, to have self-respect, and to be treated as dignified human beings
- *Other species*: The capacity to live with concern and empathy for animals, plants, and nature
- *Play*: The capability of laughing, playing, and enjoying recreation
- *Control of personal environment*: The ability to participate in political choices that include free speech, holding property, and the capacity to seek employment on an equal basis with others

Nussbaum (2000) argued that if social and political institutions addressed the ten human capabilities of what people are able to do and to be as humans, then the resulting political and economic processes would be attentive to women's problems and the well-being of all. Hence, rather than tyrannical demands, Nussbaum's list of central human capabilities provides universal values that not only facilitate change but also create space for choices.

Women trapped in abusive relationships lose their central human capabilities. As an abuser gains and maintains control over his victim's life, he uses psychologically abusive tactics to target the woman's emotions, reason, and thoughts. Abusers tightly control their victims' day-to-day life and social interactions by limiting the women's relationships, recreation, and affiliations. Abusers control every aspect of their victims' environments, including the women's access to financial resources and employment opportunities. Abusers exert control through threats or carrying out behaviors that harm the victim's bodily integrity and bodily health and, in extreme situations, end the victim's life.

Domestic violence or intimate partner violence is often thought of narrowly as an act of physical violence; however, domestic violence encompasses an array of abusive strategies and tactics aimed at eliminating the victim's capability in every area of her life. Therefore, interventions for IPV survivors need to focus on rebuilding the woman's human capabilities as well as the capabilities of children exposed to domestic violence. Similarly, any criminal justice interventions (e.g., arresting the abuser, obtaining protection orders) need to focus on ensuring the survivor's physical safety and fostering her ability to *feel* safe. When survivors have been asked to identify what they most needed to heal from domestic violence, they named a broad range of supports, including physical and emotional safety, financial safety, rebuilding social support, engaging in community, regaining control over their life, freedom to be themselves, and having access to education and job opportunities.

In one study that Stylianou conducted with survivors of domestic violence, she interviewed women during their first two weeks of seeking domestic violence services and asked, "What type of help are you hoping or expecting to get?" The following responses are the survivors' voices:

> I would like to do something. I would like to study, have the opportunity to study. And if I can work, then I'd like to work in order to save some money. (Brenda, twenty-seven years old, Latina, mother of two)

> As the days pass by, I have been thinking. Before I could not even think. . . . I am here, and I want to move out, study, work, get my own place to live. (Maria, twenty-six years old, Latina, mother of two)

> Be the woman that I know I am. . . . I want to be a human being. I want to go to college, see my grandson go to college. I want to see him go down the aisle. I want to live to see that. (Charise, forty-seven years old, African American)

> Expecting to reinvent the wheel of life. . . . I feel that I am suffocating. Start over. . . . Reestablish myself. (Ayita, twenty-nine years old, Native American, mother of one)

> To keep on the positive path of getting a job and going to school. Keeping my child very interactive with outside, social life. Keep myself together. The way it is supposed to be. (Mia, twenty-three years old, African American, mother of one)

> To gain independence. To further my education. To get a job. To be able to again get my own apartment for my kids somewhere safe, [where] there is no worries or fear for the kids or me. (Jaquita, twenty-five years old, multiracial, mother of two)

> Take time for myself, to clear my mind and focus on things that are important to better myself and not end up in vulnerable situation like it happened to me before. Counseling for me and for my daughter. . . . Get a job. Save some money. Find an apartment. (Maria, twenty-eight years old, Latina, mother of one)

> Trying to figure out how I can just start my life, like get a fresh start. . . . I want to go back to college and finish . . . and go back to work. I like working. I like feeling independent, and I feel like I've been deprived of that for two years, so it's really hard. I'm hoping to get back there. And also a safe, stable place for me to call home where I don't have to worry about leaving the house and having somebody watching me. And, you know, being able to leave whenever I want to. *You know, I feel like it's all about freedom. That's what I want.* (Tamara, twenty-three years old, gay Latina)

Defining Empowerment

"Empowerment" has been defined as a theory, a process, an intervention, and an outcome (Gutiérrez et al., 1995). As a *theory*, empowerment is based on the assumption that "the capacity of people to improve their lives is determined by their ability to control their environment, namely, having power" (Hasenfeld, 1987, p. 478). Other features of empowerment theory include an emphasis on activities aimed at reducing feelings of powerlessness and a focus on the ability of a person to have greater control of and influence in their personal and professional lives (Busch & Valentine, 2000). The *process* of empowerment happens when "individuals or groups gain greater control over their lives, acquire rights, and reduce marginalization" (Johansson de Silva et al., 2013, p. 96).

Most approaches to building empowerment recognize the dynamic interplay between gaining internal skills and overcoming external barriers (Kim et al., 2007). As an *intervention*, empowerment encourages people facing challenging circumstances to take an active part in identifying, designing, and implementing solutions to change their circumstances (Johansson de Silva et al., 2013). The *outcome* includes the transformation of individuals or groups as they obtain personal, interpersonal, and political power. This power includes the ability to access resources, the capacity to achieve a stronger sense of self-worth and self-confidence, and the ability to decrease self-blame at the individual or intrapersonal level (Zimmerman, 1995).

The literature on psychological empowerment describes empowerment as having three primary components:

- *Intrapersonal*: Encompasses the elements of cognitive empowerment, such as knowledge, confidence, self-determination, and a person's belief in their abilities
- *Interactional*: Refers to the ways in which people relate to each other and their environment
- *Behavioral* (political or environmental): Includes self-determined behaviors toward taking action to achieve goals (Rappaport, 1981; Zimmerman, 1990)

The notion of empowerment lies at the core of the field of domestic violence. The Empowerment Process Model (Cattaneo & Chapman, 2010) defines the process of empowerment as an iterative process in which an individual lacking power sets a personally meaningful goal aimed at increasing power and accomplishing intermediary steps toward achieving that goal. The series of steps focuses on first enhancing self-efficacy, knowledge, skills; followed by accessing community resources and supports; and then observing and reflecting on the impact of those actions (Cattaneo & Chapman, 2010).

To help evaluate the effectiveness of domestic violence programs in assisting survivors to reach their goals and positive outcomes, Goodman and colleagues (2014) developed the Measure of Victim Empowerment Related to Safety (MOVERS) scale. The thirteen-item MOVERS questionnaire measures the outcome of empowerment interventions for survivors of domestic violence by focusing on three main components of empowerment: internal tools, trade-offs, and expectations of support. The *internal tools* component focuses on the survivor's goals, her self-efficacy, her knowledge, and the skills she needs to develop or strengthen to achieve her safety-related goals. The *trade-offs* component encompasses the survivor's sense that pursuing her safety-related goals will create new safety-related problems for her or her children. The third component, *expectations of support*, incorporates the survivor's sense that others (i.e., formal and informal supports) can and will assist her in increasing her safety. Together, these components mean that professionals working to empower survivors of domestic violence should focus on partnering with the survivor to accomplish a set of tasks, including the following:

- Envisioning a set of safety-related goals
- Strengthening the survivor's internal resources needed for her to achieve her goals
- Informing and connecting the survivor with potential external sources of support
- Facilitating the acquisition of resources needed to decrease the potential emergence of new safety-related risks

Deborah's Story

Deborah, a twenty-five-year-old African American female, and her two-year-old son had been living with her boyfriend (not the child's father) for one year. Over that time, the relationship had become abusive, with the abuse escalating from verbal abuse (e.g., calling her "stupid" and "lazy," telling her that she was lucky that he put up with her) to physical abuse (e.g., slapping, pushing, tripping). One brutal physical assault left a scar on Deborah's abdomen and made her frightened for her and her son's safety. While her abuser was at work, Deborah gathered a few clothes, left the apartment, and went to her mother's house in a nearby town. Once she was at her mother's, she called her abuser saying that the relationship was over and that he should not try to contact her. However, her abuser began calling Deborah multiple times each day, threatening to harm her if she did not return. Although Deborah filed a police report, the threats continued. One night the abuser showed up at the mother's house and began banging on the door. Both women and the little boy were terrified. Deborah's mother shouted through the closed door that she was going to call the police if he did not go away and leave them alone. He left. However, the next morning, Deborah looked out the window and saw her abuser sitting in his car at the end of the driveway. She called the police, but the abuser drove off before the police arrived. That day, Deborah and her son moved into a domestic violence emergency shelter.

Deborah and her son stayed at the shelter for three months. While living at the shelter, Deborah received supportive counseling focused on identifying safety-related goals important to her and providing Deborah with the support she need to achieve steps toward her goals. Three months after Deborah and her son left the shelter, Stylianou called Deborah to see how she was doing. Deborah reported that the abusive phone calls had stopped and that she was working a full-time job, making $25,000 a year. Stylianou asked Deborah what it was like moving from a domestic violence shelter to living on her own with her son.

> You know, when you come from a DV [domestic violence] situation, everything is literally stripped from us, financial and everything. . . . I left with a lot of stress because, as you know, what doesn't kill me makes me stronger. What doesn't knock me down makes me stand tall. . . . It wasn't easy. It was tough. It was a lot of difficult challenges, but I overcame them. And, um, yeah, I'm just thankful that I always have a plan and I have supportive family around me that I can always count on no matter what. . . . I still had inner strength that kept me going, especially from the Lord above. So I never gave up hope and faith, and that's what got me to where I am right now. . . . I have my voucher now, and I'm looking for apartments. I'm still currently working. So I'm thankful for that. And, um, with the voucher, [I'm] now able to move into my own apartment. So that's the missing piece to the puzzle of my life. It's my apartment. I have everything going, thank God. . . . I'm feeling very comfortable, like I said, I'm a little over my head because it's a lot of responsibilities. I have to look for apartments and still have to work, and I have to take off some days to do these interviews with real estate agents and management just to find an apartment. But it's all worth it, you know. It's a bigger picture for me and my son, and we will finally have our own, a place that we can call our home. And, you know, it's all a part of it. It's all a part of the growth: me living in a shelter to my own place. Like I said, that's the missing piece of the puzzle of my life. Like, I have everything going great. I'm in school. I have good health. I have a terrific son. I have a truck. I have a good job. I have some money. I just need an apartment, you understand? I would never—my mind will never be at ease or at peace until I have my own place. And I think that goes for every woman, any mom, you know? *To have your own place to call your own is something very serious, powerful. It's just something that is needed for every family.*

Defining Financial Empowerment

Financial empowerment is both an outcome and a process in which women are able to develop the knowledge, skills, and confidence needed to meet their financial goals as well as access the needed external resources (both formal and informal) to build the financial well-being of their families.

Although the MOVERS tool (Goodman et al., 2014) focuses on the overarching concept of survivors' empowerment, the scale's developers did not include financial empowerment as a specific concept or measurement component. To address this gap, others have attempted to quantify financial empowerment outcomes. Using quantitative indicators based on a microfinance intervention with domestic violence survivors in South Africa (Kim et al., 2007), researchers developed the following nine indicators of financial empowerment:

1 Improved self-confidence
2 Improved financial confidence
3 Ability to challenge gender norms
4 Autonomy in decision-making
5 Perceived contribution to the household
6 Good communication within the household
7 Healthy relationship with partner
8 Social group membership
9 Participation in collective action

Notably, these nine indicators can be organized into the three areas of psychological empowerment (table 3.1). For example, the first five indicators can be grouped in the individual or intrapersonal level (i.e., from self-confidence to perceived contribution to the household). The next three indicators (i.e., good communication, healthy partner relationship, and social participation)

Table 3.1. Indicators of Financial Empowerment Organized by the Three Levels of Psychological Empowerment

Intrapersonal or individual level	Interactional or interpersonal level	Behavioral/environmental or political level
Self-confidence Financial confidence Ability to challenge gender norms Freedom to make decisions Perceived contribution to the household	Good communication regarding finances Healthy relationship with partner Active member of social group(s)	Participates in collective action such as voting

fall under the interpersonal or interactional level of empowerment, and the final indicator (i.e., participation in collective action) is part of the behavioral/environmental or political level of empowerment.

Further, financial capability expands on the notion of financial empowerment and suggests that individuals not only need financial knowledge and skills but also need access to mainstream financial products and services. Hence, the notion of financial capability does not reside solely within the individual but also captures the relationship between an individual's internal ability and external environment (Huang, Nam, & Sherraden, 2013; Johnson & Sherraden, 2007). In addition, within the field of domestic violence, financial empowerment cannot be addressed without a consistent focus on the survivor's safety—and the safety of her family—throughout the empowerment process.

As seen in figure 3.1, the concept of financial empowerment is an interactive process encompassing five phases or stages. Given that empowerment is a process as well as an outcome, each component interacts with the other components and builds toward financial empowerment. However, each component can also be considered a unique outcome separate from the other components.

At the core of the financial empowerment process is a consistent focus on the survivor's safety. This core focus is carried out through partnering with the survivor to envision a set of safety-related goals focused on increasing her central human capabilities. Although this stage often focuses on the immediate physical safety needs of the survivor and her children, advocates and practitioners working with survivors in this phase should also emphasize supporting the woman's efforts to increase her human capabilities, including life, health, bodily integrity, emotions, and play (Nussbaum, 2000).

The second stage of financial empowerment focuses on increasing individual (or intrapersonal) financial empowerment. This stage focuses on providing tools and opportunities for the survivor to gain (a) financial knowledge, including adequate education and practical reasoning; (b) economic self-sufficiency, including financial skills and abilities; and (c) economic self-efficacy.

In the third stage of building toward financial empowerment, relational (or interpersonal) financial empowerment is addressed. In this stage, the survivor focuses on communicating with her household about financial matters, engages in relationships that allow for continued financial safety, teaches others in her life about financial empowerment, and joins with others in ways that encourage financial health and growth. Part of this process includes counteracting financial abuse and challenging financial gender norms.

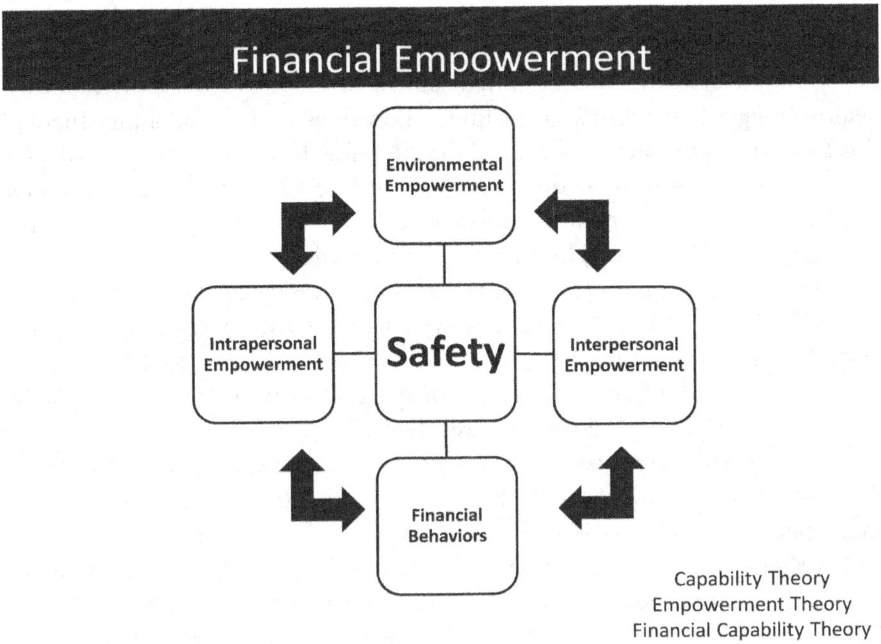

Figure 3.1. Five stages of financial empowerment

In the fourth stage of building financial empowerment, the survivor focuses on external (or environmental) financial empowerment by gaining access to resources. The survivor connects to external resources for financial support, engages in formal financial systems, and facilitates the acquisition of financial resources needed to decrease the potential emergence of new financial-related risks

In the final stage of financial empowerment, the individual engages in financial behaviors that increase her financial well-being and the financial well-being of her family. Hence, financial empowerment strategies with survivors might focus on a single component of the financial empowerment framework or on all components of the framework. In the following sections, we describe ways in which practitioners can address each stage or step of the financial empowerment framework with survivors.

Step 1: The Safety Core

As survivors begin the process of building financial empowerment, the primary focus is on any safety concerns the survivor has identified. Safety includes being protected from physical, sexual, emotional, psychological, legal, financial, political, or occupational injury or risk of injury. Personal safety might also include an individual having control over their bodily health, integrity, emotions, or feelings. Indeed, as part of capability theory, this foundation of safety is a critical first step for the empowerment process.

Since the inception of domestic violence services, the primary focus has been on safety as the foundational step of empowerment. By providing emergency shelter or "safe homes" for survivors fleeing abuse, advocates can minimally keep survivors physically safe. Indeed, most shelters are in confidential locations, often with security systems to provide a safe environment. For example, the shelter where Postmus worked had a ten-foot-high fence surrounding the property and had security cameras at the locked gate and at the locked front door to ensure the residents' safety.

Once survivors have been provided with physical safety, advocates from domestic violence programs can begin to address other ways to keep women safe. Specifically, advocates will need to work with survivors on developing comprehensive safety plans that address all aspects of their lives. A safety plan is a personalized, practical plan that helps the survivor identify potentially dangerous situations and then determine the best way to react when they encounter those situations. Typically, a safety plan addresses ways to remain safe while in the abusive relationship, while planning to leave, or after leaving the relationship.

Other domestic violence services focus on fostering survivors' emotional safety by providing individual counseling and support groups. Services to increase legal safety assist survivors in obtaining restraining orders or ensure that an advocate is available to accompany victims to court for criminal cases. Additional services often include a 24/7 hotline that maintains strict confidentiality, therapeutic programs for children exposed to domestic violence, and educational programs designed to increase community awareness and community responsiveness to domestic violence. Recently, some domestic violence organizations have started including economic justice programs in their array of services, with particular attention given to addressing financial abuse and developing financial safety plans for survivors. Chapter 5 provides detailed information on the steps in creating a financial safety plan.

One survey of 622 shelters in the United States for domestic violence survivors identified fifteen common safety-related objectives:

1 To secure battered women's safety
2 To promote a violence-free life
3 To achieve self-sufficiency and independence
4 To increase the safe surroundings for battered women and their children

5 To increase access to material resources
6 To increase legal protection
7 To reduce battered women's isolation
8 To change cultural beliefs and values that promote violence against women
9 To change institutional and community decisions that support individual men's use of abusive tactics against women
10 To end violence against women
11 To create a model organization of shared power and leadership
12 To build a political movement of women
13 To increase the collective power of women
14 To end racism
15 To end homophobia (Roche & Sadoski, 1996)

Early research on shelters and advocacy organizations indicated that such organizations were well equipped to improve survivors' emotional health and safety by enhancing women's internal resources and social support through counseling, support groups, advocacy, and shelter services (Berk et al., 1986; Cox & Stoltenberg, 1991; Mancoske et al., 1994; Sullivan & Bybee, 1999; Tutty et al., 1993). For example, support groups have been shown to be an effective approach in increasing women's self-esteem, their sense of belonging, and their locus of control (Tutty et al., 1993). Shelters and advocacy organizations are also equipped to enhance survivors' material and institutional resources through advocacy, referral, collaboration, and education (Hart, 1993; Sullivan et al., 1992, 1994; Weisz, 1999; Weisz et al., 1998). For example, as compared with survivors who did not participate in advocacy services, survivors who participated in community-based advocacy services reported a higher quality of life and greater social support (Bybee & Sullivan, 2005; Sullivan & Bybee, 1999; Sullivan et al., 1992). Additionally, survivors who participated in advocacy services had less difficulty than their counterparts obtaining community resources over time (Bybee & Sullivan, 2005; Sullivan & Bybee, 1999; Sullivan et al., 1992). In other words, advocacy organizations are well equipped not only to address survivors' stress but also to connect survivors with other systems and resources that can help them gain stronger emotional health and a greater sense of feeling safe.

Step 2: Individual (Intrapersonal) Empowerment

Recent attention to survivors' financial empowerment has centered on the individual or intrapersonal step. Components of financial empowerment within this level include (a) financial knowledge, (b) economic self-efficacy and self-confidence, and (c) economic self-sufficiency.

Financial Knowledge

Financial knowledge includes the necessary information to participate fully in the economy.

One of the basic human capabilities includes having adequate education and practical reasoning ability (Nussbaum, 2000). Applying this capability to financial empowerment enables survivors to acquire financial education to improve their knowledge regarding financial matters and to increase their financial management skills.

The early feminist Frances Wright believed that for women to advance, they must have educational equality. Indeed, Wright believed the only way to achieve any type of equality—whether equality of gender, race, or class—was through education (Gardner, 2013). Wright further emphasized that knowledge of the self and of the world empowered the individual to participate in their society. Hence, it is imperative for women not only to have their own thoughts, observations, and opinions from formal education but also to develop thoughts and opinions from watching, learning, and ingesting information around them (Gardner, 2013).

Given the complexity of gender issues, it is not surprising that research has produced mixed findings regarding the role that education plays in relation to domestic violence. Some research has demonstrated that women's secondary education is generally a protective factor that buffers against the risk of recent and lifetime experiences of violence (Weitzman, 2018). However, evidence from other research has demonstrated that educational attainment can increase a woman's risk for domestic violence; specifically, women who achieved higher education than their partners were found at increased risk of domestic violence (Vyas & Watts, 2009). In addition, research has established that education, especially postsecondary degrees, helps boost women's ability to obtain well-paying jobs and potentially helps to alleviate poverty (Butler & Deprez, 2002).

Financial education has garnered increased attention, especially during recent economic crises and periods of financial distress for individuals, families, organizations, and communities. In the recent economic context, financial education has focused on increasing consumer knowledge and improving financial management skills to specifically address consumer debt, to encourage savings, and to provide knowledge about the ever-growing amount and complexity of financial information (U.S. Government Accountability Office, 2004; Gudmunson & Danes, 2011; Hilgert et al., 2003;

Hopley, 2003). Research has produced compelling evidence of the association that exists between an individual's financial knowledge and their financial well-being, including survivors of domestic violence (Gudmunson & Danes, 2011; Gutter & Copur, 2011; Joo & Grable, 2004; Postmus, Hetling, & Hoge, 2013). However, recent research has suggested that improving financial knowledge alone is not sufficient to change individuals' financial behaviors (National Endowment for Financial Education, 2006).

Questions remain regarding how much education, including financial education, is needed to financially empower survivors of domestic violence. Although contradictory theories exist regarding whether enhanced education helps or hurts survivors, perhaps financial education could act as a protective factor from further abuse. Regardless, knowledge or financial education by itself is not enough for survivors to become financially empowered. To achieve financial empowerment at the individual (or intrapersonal) level, survivors need knowledge and financial skills and abilities, self-confidence in their financial capability, and access to resources and to the financial mainstream.

Economic Self-Efficacy and Self-Confidence

Economic self-efficacy is the individual's *perceived* ability and personal confidence to perform financial tasks.

Financial educators and behavioral economists have recognized that financial education alone is not enough to change individuals' financial behaviors or improve their financial capability (Rothwell et al., 2015; Sherraden, 2013). In fact, behavioral psychologists have long acknowledged the role that self-efficacy plays in changing an individual's behavior (Fishbein & Ajzen, 2010). Research has found that higher levels of financial self-efficacy translate into positive financial behaviors (Danes et al., 1999; Vitt et al., 2000). A study conducted by Farrell and colleagues (2016) examined women's personal finance behaviors and found that a woman's financial self-efficacy was one of the strongest predictors of the type and number of financial products she held. Specifically, the results showed that women with higher levels of economic self-efficacy (i.e., greater confidence in their financial management capabilities) were more likely to hold investment and savings products and less likely to hold debt-related products.

Self-efficacy is an individual's confidence in their ability to exert control over their own motivation, behaviors, and actions to be able to carry out specific tasks or behaviors (Bandura, 1997; Wood & Bandura, 1989). The focus of self-efficacy is not on the individual's ability to execute a specific behavior but rather emphasizes the individual having the self-confidence that they have the skills to cope whatever circumstance they face. Therefore, economic self-efficacy is an individual's belief that they have the capabilities or confidence to manage their finances.

In one of our recent studies, we revised the General Self-Efficacy Scale (Schwarzer & Jerusalem, 1995) to include economic language (Hoge et al., 2020). We named the revised ten-item scale the Scale of Economic Self-Efficacy. The following statements are examples of the Likert-type scale items:

"I can solve most financial problems if I invest the necessary effort."
"I can always manage to solve difficult financial problems if I try hard enough."
"If I am in financial trouble, I can usually think of something to do."
"I am confident that I could deal efficiently with unexpected financial events."

Other researchers examining the disproportionate rate of domestic violence among women living in poverty have documented an association between financial insecurity and low economic self-efficacy among survivors of domestic violence (Weaver et al., 2009). Because of survivors' domestic violence experiences, they often have great difficulty identifying and believing in the validity of their accomplishments. However, raising self-efficacy expectations for specific tasks can increase the likelihood that survivors will attempt new behaviors that further their educational and career goals (Chronister & McWhirter, 2003)

This body of research demonstrates that economic self-efficacy or self-confidence is needed to complement survivors' knowledge and self-sufficiency. As an example, Postmus often reflects on how her mother learned to manage a checkbook. For years, Postmus's parents had a traditional marriage in which her father managed the checkbook because he had better math skills. Although Postmus's parents made joint decisions about purchases or financial endeavors, her mother expressed no interest in taking over the chore of balancing the checkbook. As her parents aged, Postmus's father developed a chronic health condition that prevented him from managing the checkbook. Her oldest sister sat down with her mother and taught her about managing their finances. Her mother learned the necessary components (knowledge) for paying bills, entering deposits, and balancing the account every month. She had the skills needed (economic self-sufficiency) in that she could add and subtract (backed up with the help of a calculator) and could write checks. However, Postmus's mother struggled with this task. Why? She lacked the confidence in her knowledge and skills and believed that she would "mess things up." In time, and with support from her adult children, she developed greater self-confidence in her abilities to successfully manage that fiscal task for her household.

Economic Self-Sufficiency

Economic self-sufficiency is having the abilities or skills needed to manage finances and maintain financial independent living.

"Economic self-sufficiency" is a widely used term but is not defined clearly in the literature. In fact, definitions vary depending on the focus of who is to be economically self-sufficient. For example, economic self-sufficiency is routinely linked to populations receiving cash assistance or other forms of "welfare" and public assistance. In this context, self-sufficiency is reached when individuals no longer need such assistance. Other definitions have focused on work-related outcomes such as length of employment (Acs & Loprest, 2007) or increasing the rate of hourly wages to meet a minimum standard that enables self-sufficiency (known as the "living wage"). However, these definitions place the responsibility for reaching economic self-sufficiency on the individual but without accounting for environmental challenges (e.g., lack of available jobs, poor salary opportunities; Breitkreuz & Williamson, 2012).

Usually, economic self-sufficiency is linked to people living in poverty and is often measured as an alternative to traditional income-based poverty measures (i.e., the federal poverty line). Instead, economic self-sufficiency should be viewed as a person's having an adequate level of resources to avoid living in poverty (Gu et al., 2010). Categories used in measuring economic self-sufficiency include the funds needed for basic necessities such as food, housing, child care, transportation, and health care, with the funds needed for each category based on household characteristics such as the number and ages of children and the geographic location (Gu et al., 2010). However, this definition and associated measures of economic self-sufficiency focus on poverty and having the resources needed to avoid living in poverty. Others scholars have expanded the definition to include having enough resources to be independent from relying on either government programs or partners (Scott et al., 2007). Still other scholars have extended the definition of economic self-sufficiency to include enhanced levels of financial self-respect, increased choice and hope, and the ability of a parent to be a financial role model for their children (Morgen, 2001).

Defining economic self-sufficiency becomes even more challenging when focusing on survivors of domestic violence. As discussed in chapter 2, abusers often use a variety of financial abuse strategies to trap women in the relationship, including tactics such as employment sabotage, economic control, and economic exploitation (Postmus et al., 2016). Moreover, many survivors have reported that their economic dependence on an abusive partner was a primary reason they felt trapped in the relationship (Kim & Gray, 2008; Sanders & Schnabel, 2006). Thus, economic self-sufficiency appears to be intricately interwoven with domestic violence, given that low economic self-sufficiency creates a barrier to leaving an abusive relationship.

As welfare reform was emerging in the early 1990s, several researchers met with survivors to learn how the women defined economic self-sufficiency (Gowdy & Pearlmutter, 1994). From those discussions, the researchers identified four domains of economic self-sufficiency: (a) autonomy and self-determination, (b) financial security and responsibility, (c) family and individual well-being, and (d) basic assets for living in the community (Gowdy & Pearlmutter, 1993). Further examination of these domains led to the creation of three dimensions of economic self-sufficiency specific to survivors of domestic violence: (a) the ability to manage financial needs, (b) the ability to have discretionary funds, and (c) the ability to maintain independent living (Hetling et al., 2016).

The first dimension, the ability to manage financial needs, includes items such as the individual being able to meet their financial obligations, being able to stay on a budget, being able to make payments on debts, and being able to pay their own way without borrowing from family or friends. The second dimension of economic self-sufficiency specific to survivors of domestic violence includes items such as being able to buy extras for self and family, being able to put money in a savings account, or being able to afford to take trips. Last, the ability to maintain independent living includes items such as being able to be free from government programs and being able to afford a reliable car, decent housing, and decent child care (Hetling et al., 2016). In essence, economic self-sufficiency means that the individual has the abilities and skills needed to manage their finances and maintain independent living.

Step 3: Interpersonal (Interactional) Empowerment

Although steps 1 and 2 are critically important to ensure that survivors are safe and have opportunities to build their individual knowledge, confidence, and abilities, they alone are not sufficient to reach financial empowerment. Individuals do not act in a bubble but rather make behavioral decisions as they interact with the social environment. Financial socialization is a continual process that occurs as the individual interacts with their immediate family, family of origin, friends, community, organizations, culture, media, and society at large (Lusardi et al., 2010; Shim et al., 2013; Xiao et al., 2011). Through these interactions, the individual internalizes the values and norms of their social environment.

Financial socialization is "the process of acquiring and developing values, attitudes, standards, norms, knowledge, and behaviors that contribute to the financial viability and well-being of the individual" (Schuchardt et al., 2009, p. 86).

The interpersonal level is the third level in the financial empowerment process for survivors of domestic violence. This level includes two components: (a) counteracting financial abuse and (b) challenging financial gender norms.

Counteracting Financial Abuse

Given the extent of negative financial socialization that occurs between a perpetrator of financial abuse and a survivor trapped in the relationship, survivors often experience a serious diminishment of their sense of financial empowerment. For example, the perpetrator might restrict a survivor's access to financial resources (Brewster, 2003; VonDeLinde & Correia, 2005; Wettersten et al., 2004), which in turn limits her ability to gain experience in performing financial behaviors. The perpetrator might also undermine the survivor's financial capability by managing the finances without the survivor's input or consent on decisions (Anderson et al., 2003; Brewster, 2003). Additionally, the perpetrator might use psychological abuse tactics to verbally undermine the survivor's confidence in managing household finances. Finally, as mentioned in chapter 1, abusers who use sabotage to interfere with the survivor's work efforts often create situations that leave the survivor in a precarious position at her work.

To combat the negative impact of a financially abusive relationship on a survivor's financial socialization, advocates and other practitioners can be a positive influence by counteracting the negative experiences and negative messages survivors have received. Those who work with survivors can provide opportunities for survivors to build financial knowledge and gain experience with engaging in financial behaviors in a supportive environment (Christy-McMullin, 2003; Correia, 2000; Sanders & Schnabel, 2006). Advocates and practitioners can work closely with the survivor's place of employment, especially employers and direct work supervisors, to ensure that the workplace has appropriate policies and protocols in place not only to protect the safety of survivors and their coworkers but also to make sure workplace policies do not unfairly penalize survivors for problems caused by their abuser.

M. A. Zimmerman (2000) coined the term "empowering organizations" to describe organizations that cultivate activities to generate or facilitate empowerment among community members. Research has noted that processes that facilitate individuals' empowerment are important, especially for individuals who have experienced oppression or are members of communities with less access to resources, such as women or people of color (Becker et al., 2002; McDonald & Keys, 2008; Peterson & Hughey, 2002). An empowering organization aims to provide its members with opportunities to develop skills and a sense of control in a setting where individuals with shared experiences can exchange information and develop a sense of identity with each other (Zimmerman, 2000). Developing empowering relationships plays a critical role in the financial empowering process because these relationships not only facilitate the development of financial knowledge and skills but also provide the social and emotional support survivors need as they move through the financial empowerment process.

Challenging Financial Gender Norms

To be financially empowered at the individual level, the first step includes enhancing financial knowledge, strengthening skills (or economic self-sufficiency), and increasing confidence (or economic self-efficacy). The next step includes challenging misperceptions about money, especially as they relate to the roles or norms around gender and financial ability. Families are the primary socialization unit in which children develop attitudes, beliefs, norms, roles, and values regarding money and the management of finances (Gudmunson & Danes, 2011). Indeed, as Hallerod and colleagues (2007) have noted, "money ties people together, causes conflicts and injustices, allows independence, and creates dependence" (p. 143).

Such views on money are all learned and influenced by the cultural norms and attitudes regarding money as well as the norms and attitudes toward gender held in families and in society. For example, the dominant narrative in most Western cultures has been the expectation for men to be the breadwinner and to provide housing for women; this attitude has persisted over time, even when women make more money than men (Luken & Vaughan, 2005). Historically, men have also been tasked with managing the household finances; however, this expectation is most common in middle- to upper-class families (Joseph, 2013). Women in working-class families have historically managed the household finances, with their husband or partner turning over their paychecks to the woman and then expecting her to wisely budget and make purchases to fulfill all the needs of the household, regardless of whether the income is adequate to meet the demand (Zelizer, 1994).

The challenge, of course, is to understand the norms around money, who manages it, and, more importantly, who controls it—that is, who has the financial power in the family. Over the past forty years, researchers have tried to understand the transfer of resources between family members as well as the actions and decisions made within the family (Nyman & Dema, 2007). For example, early on, Blood and Wolfe (1960) noted that as compared with women who had no income, women who had their own income had greater influence over financial decisions, and this finding was confirmed in later research (Bernasek & Bajtelsmit, 2002). More recently, research has documented that when women controlled the household finances, more money was spent on meeting the women's and children's needs, with these expenditures enhancing the well-being of the children (Thomas, 1990). Other researchers have determined that the person who has more access to a range of alternatives outside the family (e.g., social support, position in the labor market) appears to hold the greatest power in the household regarding money-making decisions (England & Farkas, 1986).

However, the key is remembering that *managing* money coming into the household does not automatically include *control over* the money. The person managing the household funds has the task of making ends meet, buying food, and paying bills; in essence, the manager implements the decisions that are made. The person who controls the money is usually the one who also makes the decisions. Curiously, the managers (i.e., the women) in lower-income homes may or may not have control over the funds, whereas in higher-income families, the money managers are usually men who also have the power and control over the funds (Nyman & Dema, 2007).

How, then, do these historical gender financial roles apply to domestic violence survivors? In healthy relationships, the couple controls and makes joint decisions about money but might assign one person to be the manager of the funds and be responsible for paying bills and balancing the budget. In relationships where financial abuse is present, the abuser controls the money in the household, while the survivor might or might not be the manager of the funds; however, she has no voice in decisions regarding money. Therefore, a critical part of survivors achieving a step toward financial empowerment at this individual level will include challenging gender norms around money and gaining the right to participate in decision-making about money.

Step 4: Environmental Empowerment

From a feminist empowerment perspective, inequality and subordination in the lives of women must be addressed to promote social and economic justice. A feminist empowerment model provides a foundation for considering the multiple factors that affect all women in patriarchal societies, including economic inequality. Therefore, to increase financial empowerment among survivors, survivors need increased access to mainstream financial services and institutions.

Having the necessary knowledge, skills, and confidence, as well as counteracting the effects of financial abuse and challenging gender norms by participating in decisions, will definitely help survivors achieve financial empowerment at the individual level. However, to enhance their financial empowerment, survivors must also have access to resources, including a perceived contribution to the household. Access to resources does not necessarily mean a certain threshold of money that must be available. Indeed, one of our recent studies demonstrated that after completing a financial literacy curriculum, survivors reported less financial strain and less perceived difficulty living on their income; what makes this finding more impressive is that 44 percent of the women made less than $10,000 a year (Postmus, Hetling, & Hoge, 2013). Instead of a target dollar amount, to be financially empowered at the individual level requires the individual to have access and autonomy in decision-making related to resources, whether those resources are cash, connections to informal sources, or in-kind sources.

The World Value Survey has revealed that globally an alarmingly large number of men hold power in the household allocation of resources for vital services such as food, education, and health care (Fawole, 2008). Research has consistently shown that women hold lower levels of wealth, have lower earnings, and live longer than men (Fisher, 2010; Gottschalck, 2008). Historically, women have been dependent on men for financial security (Schmidt & Sevak, 2006); although this dependency might be changing, the economic well-being for women is still less than it should be (Fisher, 2010).

Curiously, research on household asset wealth and domestic violence has shown both clear and contradictory trends. Theorists have proposed that if policies were put in place to eliminate the gender gap in wages, the resulting wage equality would be more than likely to decrease the incidence of domestic violence (Farmer & Tiefenthaler, 2003). Higher household socioeconomic status (or greater household wealth) seems largely to protect women from experiencing violence over the past year or ever. Indeed, women living in the lowest income households have seven times the abuse rates of those in the highest income households, whereas women with the highest personal incomes experience the least amount of abuse (Farmer & Tiefenthaler, 1997; Greenfeld & Rand, 1998; Vyas & Watts, 2009). Additionally, when women have greater control over income and spending decisions in the household, those households have better outcomes, including better child outcomes (Bruce et al., 1995). Hence, women's greater contribution to household income can also lead to women having stronger bargaining power within their marital relationships (Slegh et al., 2013).

However, others have theorized that increases in women's wages could put women at greater risk of increased domestic violence (Vyas & Watts, 2009). Moreover, even if a survivor has a job or career, her partner might block her access to those wages, making her economically dependent on him and making it more difficult to leave (Postmus, Plummer, et al., 2012; Sanders & Schnabel, 2006; Turner & Shapiro, 1986; Zorza, 1991). Along with the high costs to society, domestic violence forces many women into poverty, and they become trapped by poverty. Domestic violence is a primary cause of homelessness among women; being homeless poses significant barriers to women's workforce participation. In addition, because of direct negative consequences from abuse (e.g., physical and mental health problems, abuser's sabotage of a survivor's work or education efforts), many survivors tend to be employed in low-wage work (Moe & Bell, 2004; Riger & Staggs, 2004; Swanberg et al., 2005; Tolman & Raphael, 2000). However, only recently have advocates, social workers, policy makers, and researchers given critical attention to the intertwined relationship between violence and poverty in women's lives (Pyles, 2005).

To address the needs of women living in poverty, asset-based programs have been created and tested to improve women's wages and to help lift individuals out of poverty. The term "assets" refers to financial capital, such as savings and investments, and property capital, such as home ownership and other real property. According to asset-based theory, having assets can stimulate and facilitate the development of human capital and, thereby, might indirectly contribute to the financial empowerment of impoverished people. For example, an asset-building program can assist individuals with lower income to save and accumulate financial assets for postsecondary education, which is one of the most promising ways to obtain a living-wage job (Zhan & Schreiner, 2005). One such asset-building program is the individual development account (IDA), which has received substantial attention from practitioners and researchers interested in the financial empowerment of individuals (Reutebuch, 2001; Shobe & Boyd, 2003; Zhan et al., 2004). (See chapter 4 for a more detailed discussion of asset-building programs and their effectiveness.)

Although evaluations of financial literacy and asset-building programs have provided limited evidence that these programs financially empower domestic violence survivors, these programs do not address the larger structural conditions and forces, such as wage and job discrimination, that work against women, especially women of color or immigrant women (Sanders et al., 2007; Shobe & Dienemann, 2007). Research studies have shown that what survivors needed most to move out of poverty and violence altogether was a living-wage job (Brandwein & Filiano, 2000; Lein et al., 2001). Here, a "living-wage job" refer to a job with wages and benefits that not only cover basic needs such as food, clothes, and housing but also cover costs of child care, transportation, and health care. According to the living-wage movement, a living wage amounts to enough money from a full-time job (i.e., forty hours per week) to cover costs of food, clothing, transportation, and health care, as well as housing costs of no more than 30 percent of income. The amount constituting a living wage varies from community to community, largely because of variations in housing costs. For example a living wage of $12.31 an hour is needed for a single person renting a one-bedroom apartment in Lawrence, Kansas, whereas the same person would need $24.38 an hour if living in central New Jersey (Universal Living Wage, 2018).

In summary, if advocates and practitioners focus on increasing women's access to earning money, providing more resources, and enhancing their decision-making power, women will experience economic growth and poverty reduction (Johansson de Silva et al., 2013). Indeed, much attention on financially empowering women, including domestic violence survivors, has focused on this individual or intrapersonal step of financial empowerment. Such attention has been given to improving women's financial knowledge, enhancing economic self-sufficiency, increasing economic self-efficacy and self-confidence, challenging gender norms, providing greater access to resources, and ensuring autonomy in decision-making. Nevertheless, these efforts represent only the first few steps in helping survivors of domestic violence to achieve financial empowerment. The final step is to address survivors' financial behaviors.

Step 5: Financial Behaviors

The final step in financial empowerment of domestic violence survivors centers on their developing and practicing financial behaviors to improve their lives. The theory of planned behavior (TPB; Ajzen, 1985) is perhaps the theoretical approach that is best suited for understanding the potential impact of financial interpersonal, intrapersonal, and environmental empowerment on survivors' financial behaviors. The TPB postulates that to change behavior, an individual has to address their behavioral intentions, which in turn are determined independently by their attitudes toward the behavior, subjective norms, and perceived behavioral control or confidence to perform the behavior. Perceived control (with intention) is also regarded as a codeterminant of the behavior.

Research has demonstrated strong support of the TPB in a wide variety of behavioral domains, including IPV perpetrator treatment (Kernsmith, 2005), IPV prevention (Casey & Ohler, 2012), and survivors' behavior related to staying in or leaving the relationship (Byrne & Arias, 2004; Edwards et al., 2015). In addition, research has demonstrated strong support for the TPB, as this theory has been found successful in influencing a variety of financial behaviors, including use of the Earned Income Tax Credit (Zimmerman et al., 2015), budgeting behavior (Harrington et al., 2016), savings behavior (Jamal et al., 2015), and the financial attitudes and behaviors of youth and college students (Serido et al., 2015; Van Campenhout, 2015).

As part of our evaluation of the *Moving Ahead* curriculum, we relied on the TPB (Ajzen & Fishbein, 1970; Fishbein & Ajzen, 2010) to provide a framework for the variables selected to examine when determining change in financial intentions and behavior. Specifically, we examined survivors' intention to engage in personal financial planning. For example, we asked a series of questions about their *planned* financial behavior in the short term:

"How likely are you in the next month to . . ."

- Review and evaluate your spending habits?
- Track down where money is spent?
- Estimate your monthly household income and expenses?
- Identify your own financial goals for the future?
- Follow your financial goals?
- Follow a weekly or monthly budget?

We also asked survivors about their intentions to use financial institutions in the next month, using a series of questions such as the following:

"How likely are you in the next month to . . ."

- Make payments toward your debt?
- Use a bank account?
- Pay more than the interest on your loans, credit, etc.?
- Contribute to a retirement savings account?

We then asked survivors about their recent financial behaviors using questions similar to those just presented. For example, to understand survivors' engagement in personal financial planning, we asked the following:

"How often in the last thirty days did you . . ."
- Review and evaluate your spending habits?
- Track down where money was spent?
- Estimate your monthly household income and expenses?
- Identify your own financial goals for the future?

We also asked survivors about their budgeting behaviors using questions such as the following:

"How often in the last thirty days did you . . ."
- Pay your bills on time?
- Follow your financial goals?
- Follow a weekly or monthly budget?

Finally, to examine survivors' financial behaviors related to the use of any extra funds, we asked questions such as the following:

"How often in the last thirty days did you . . ."
- Make payments toward your debt?
- Use a bank account?
- Pay more than the interest on your loans, credit, etc.?

All of these questions were created from the economic empowerment curriculum developed by The Allstate Foundation in cooperation with the National Network to End Domestic Violence (www.purplepurse.com). We compared outcomes of survivors who did or did not receive the *Moving Ahead* curriculum and found that survivors who received the curriculum were significantly more likely to improve their financial intentions *and* their financial behaviors at two key time points: at the implementation of the curriculum and one year after receiving the curriculum (Postmus et al., 2015).

Several survivors who participated in the *Moving Ahead* curriculum talked about the changes they had made in their financial behavior:

> I still manage my credit card and what they are charging me for, check the credit card very frequently.
>
> The biggest one [change] is just the savings. Making sure I put at least something in there every time I get paid. I started a 401K. I put in biweekly.

> Also, the class has led me to spend more but be responsible. I bought a place as a way of investing in mine and my daughter's security. Gave me a push to be financially responsible. Since everyone [in the group] is doing it, I should be able too.

> Just trying to stay on a strict budget and not going over and saving what I need to be saving.

> I use the budgeting information the most. I learned a lot regarding managing my money, how to make a budget, and also how to get rid of debt. All of this information is very useful to me, and I use it all the time.

> I try to save 10 percent of my income every month. As far as the little things, to try and sell stuff.

> There were many strategies they taught us: save money, not spend on things that are not necessary. Before I used to go out and buy things that weren't necessary, and now I make a list and only buy what I need.

In summary, to effectively help IPV survivors achieve financial empowerment, advocates and practitioners must start by partnering with survivors to help them *achieve safety* as the core of those efforts. The second step addresses *intrapersonal empowerment* by increasing the survivors' knowledge, enhancing their economic self-efficacy, and improving their economic self-sufficiency. In the third step, advocates and practitioners need to address survivors' *interpersonal empowerment* by counteracting the survivors' experiences of financial abuse and challenging financial gender norms. The fourth step moves on to addressing the survivors' *environmental empowerment* by helping them to access mainstream financial services, institutions, and resources. The final step in the financial empowerment process is enhancing survivors' *financial behaviors* by focusing on their intentions and actual budgeting, spending, and saving behaviors.

CHAPTER 4

Current Practices on Financially Empowering Survivors

"I was working at the Wal-Mart and at Burger King, and he [abusive partner] managed to call and tell them that I was in jail, when I wasn't even in jail. I was at home sick. He told them that I was in jail, so I lost both my jobs. Because he knew I was moving out, 'cause I had already two paychecks, and I was just waiting on the third one, because my first two were for rent and deposit and my third one was gonna be to get my water and utility turned on, because, you know, they require $50 deposit. And I was like, 'Okay, I'm almost in my third one.' And he knew I was this close to moving away from him and that I would need him no more. So he turned around, made me lose both of my jobs. He did the one for saying that I was in jail for Wal-Mart, and then he wouldn't let me leave the house to go to work to Burger King. He kept pushing me back on the bed, and he would not let me leave the house for nothing. I mean, I was almost there, but . . . I mean, I have my own place now, but it was better when I had both of my jobs, when I didn't have to depend on [welfare]. I liked having both of my jobs. I mean, I didn't see much of my kids, but they don't care. They seen the money too. They seen that they were finally getting stuff that they've been wanting for a while and I haven't been able to get them. So it's different."

In recent years, service providers have given increased attention to building survivors' financial empowerment. Generally, this attention has focused on creating and implementing financial empowerment interventions at the micro (i.e., individual) and macro (i.e., system and societal) levels that address survivors' short- and long-term needs. However, a major challenge for these service providers stems from the perceived conflict between providing short-term crisis services and meeting long-term financial needs. Hence, to fully implement financial empowerment programs, agencies that focus on short-term crisis intervention only will need to mitigate this perceived conflict by rethinking that focus and expanding their views on empowerment to include interventions that address the financial challenges survivors face (VonDeLinde & Correia, 2005).

In contrast, most of the financial empowerment interventions implemented in other countries tend to focus on policy and systemic (i.e., macro) reforms to improve women's financial self-sufficiency (Calvès, 2009). Examples of macro reforms include policy changes that support women in rural areas by giving priority to agricultural investments and changes in system perspectives to advance the view of women as stakeholders in national development rather than solely beneficiaries of development.

In this chapter, we present a two-pronged intervention approach focused on interventions offered at the micro and macro levels that increase survivors' financial knowledge and skills and/or increase their access to financial institutions and products. The micro-level interventions discussed include financial safety planning, financial literacy programs, asset-based savings programs, microloans, and employee assistance programs. The macro-level interventions discussed include increasing survivors' access to financial institutions (especially survivors living in marginalized communities), providing employment protections to survivors of domestic violence, and advocating for the criminal justice system to recognize financial abuse as a form of domestic violence. We review the available research for women with low income and the existing research on programs for survivors. In addition, we present arguments regarding which interventions should be used with survivors and which interventions need further testing to ensure the financial empowerment of survivors.

Micro-Level Financial Empowerment Interventions

Survivors of domestic violence have identified financial insecurity as one of the greatest barriers to independence. To address financial insecurity, most interventions implemented in the United States focus on the micro level of improving the financial self-sufficiency of survivors. For example, micro-level efforts include creating financial safety plans, increasing financial knowledge and self-efficacy, building assets, using employee assistance programs, and distributing microloans.

Financial Safety Plans

Part of the day-to-day practice in work with survivors includes safety planning (Logan & Walker, 2018a). Although a widely implemented and useful intervention, safety plans predominantly addresses physical safety, followed by emotional safety. Unfortunately, these plans rarely focus on financial stability and security (Logan & Walker, 2018a). However, financial safety planning is a critically important task that service providers should engage in with survivors as they take steps to separate themselves financially from an abusive partner. In addition to evaluating the impact of financial abuse on the survivor's life, financial safety planning might involve strategies such as the following:

1. Saving money in an individual bank account
2. Collecting information about individual and shared accounts, assets, and liabilities
3. Securing copies of important documents including bank statements and transaction receipts
4. Changing passwords and personal identification numbers (PINs) for accounts
5. Reviewing the survivor's credit history

Most important, service providers should ensure that safety plans are woman defined and individualized because survivors' financial situations can vary based on a survivor's culture, socioeconomic status, and geographical location (Bader et al., 2019).

A key way that a service provider can help a survivor to develop a comprehensive financial safety plan is by first educating the survivor about financial abuse and then engaging her in the first steps of financial safety planning: identifying and protecting resources (Hetling, Postmus, & Kaltz, 2015). For example, in Powers and colleagues' (2009) research on women with disabilities who suffered intimate partner violence or other forms of interpersonal violence, the researchers developed a scale of safety-promoting behaviors to educate women about financial abuse. The scale uses three questions that not only educate the woman but also assess her plans for protecting her money and resources from her abuser: "Do you have someone you trust who could help you handle your money?" "Do you keep your money in a safe place?" "Do you have your own bank account?"

Financial safety might also involve examining the ways in which an abusive partner controls the woman's access to resources, exploits existing assets, or sabotages the survivor's employment efforts. This step might involve reviewing the survivor's credit report and financial history to determine if an abusive partner has damaged her credit or exploited her financial standing by opening up credit accounts or businesses in her name. Additionally, reviewing a credit report can help the survivor determine if her abuser has hidden assets. If the survivor is married to her abuser, joint assets could be available to the survivor through legal proceedings (i.e., divorce). A review of a survivor's credit report might also help her determine if she and the abusive partner hold joint banking accounts and whether she might be able to move some of those assets into an individual account.

For service providers to effectively use financial and other forms of safety plans in their daily work with survivors, they should receive ongoing training, especially to stay abreast of policy changes and changes in financial products and regulations (Logan & Walker, 2018b). Not surprisingly, some survivors find it difficult to implement all aspects of their safety plan; hence, service providers need to seek formal feedback and evaluation of the plans they have developed with survivors to ensure that the providers are effective in their work with survivors (Logan & Walker, 2018b). Additionally, it is not only crucial that service providers fully understand the various ways abusers can manipulate the couple's finances but also critically important that providers have an in-depth understanding of current policies, laws, and banking regulations related to joint assets (Silva-Martinez et al., 2016). Indeed, service providers need their agency's support through standardized procedures, helpful documents, and agency policies regarding timing, staffing, training, and adherence to safety planning (Murray et al., 2015).

Financial Literacy / Financial Education Programs

A key component of financial empowerment is having sufficient financial knowledge to make thoughtful decisions around personal financial management. Indeed, as compared with individuals who have little financial knowledge, those who are financially literate make fewer financial mistakes and have better skills and behaviors (Lusardi & Mitchell, 2007). "Financial literacy" is a complex term without an accepted standardized definition. Most scholars and practitioners consider someone as financially literate if one has "the attitude, skills, and knowledge to manage one's finances in order to meet financial goals that assist in meeting life goals" (Buckland, 2014, p. 17). Others have defined the term using the theory of planned behavior—and more recently the reasoned-action approach (Fishbein & Ajzen, 2010)—which considers a person to be financially literate (and practicing positive financial behaviors) when they improve their attitudes, skills, knowledge, self-efficacy, and intentions to perform positive financial behaviors (Postmus et al., 2015).

Last, the U.S. President's Advisory Council on Financial Literacy (now called the President's Advisory Council on Financial Capability) defines financial literacy as the ability to use knowledge and skills to manage financial resources effectively for a lifetime of financial well-being (Collins & Holden, 2014). Hence, to be financially literate, a person must have not only a basic understanding of finances but also the capacity to apply that understanding to make financial decisions and use positive financial behaviors.

The economic crash of the Great Recession (2007–2008) prompted tremendous growth of financial education programs (also called financial literacy programs), covering topics such as credit counseling, home ownership, and retirement planning (Meier & Sprenger, 2013). Typically, many of these programs are targeted to specific groups such as women, high school or college students, low-income families, older adults, and persons from underrepresented and marginalized communities (Vitt et al., 2000). Few of these programs have included rigorous evaluation of effectiveness, with most using low-level consumer satisfaction surveys to test participants' knowledge retention. These evaluations have produced mixed results regarding program efficacy or positive changes in participants' financial behaviors (Collins & Holden, 2014; English, 2014; Meier & Sprenger, 2013). Additionally, most existing financial literacy programs have failed to address the challenges faced by racial, ethnic, or immigrant communities, an omission that has left these groups vulnerable to predatory practices in relation to car loans, mortgages, credit cards, check-cashing services, and payday loans (Postmus, 2010). Moreover, many financial literacy programs do not include information on economic abuse and financial safety planning, thus ultimately failing to address the challenges faced by victims and survivors of IPV.

To address these gaps in the existing financial education programming, several domestic violence organizations have developed economic justice and financial education programs that can be incorporated into the standard services offered to survivors. Similar to other financial education programs, these new programs cover a range of financial education topics such as saving money, budgeting, getting or repairing credit, cash-flow management, purchasing a home, predatory lending practices, financing major purchases, investing, and wise spending habits (Hopley, 2003). In addition, these comprehensive programs include information on financial abuse and financial safety planning to help survivors develop financial goals and improve their overall financial management skills. However, to date, only two of these comprehensive financial literacy curriculums have been evaluated: the Redevelopment Opportunities for Women's Economic Action Program's curriculum and The Allstate Foundation's *Moving Ahead through Financial Management* curriculum.

The Redevelopment Opportunities for Women's Economic Action Program (REAP) curriculum was the first domestic violence program to incorporate financial education with other services and then evaluate the impact of the financial component on survivors' outcomes. The REAP curriculum focused on the intersection of poverty, oppression, and violence while providing financial information to domestic violence survivors (Sanders et al., 2007). The program evaluation examined the curriculum using pre- and posttest surveys of a sample of sixty-seven survivors who were randomly assigned to the treatment group (i.e., received the curriculum) or to the control group (i.e., did not receive the curriculum; Weaver et al., 2009). As compared with survivors who did not receive the REAP curriculum, study results indicated that the survivors who participated in the REAP curriculum experienced significant increases in both their knowledge (financial literacy) and confidence in managing finances (financial self-efficacy), thus enhancing their confidence and sense of ability to effectively manage their financial matters (Sanders et al., 2007). The study findings also showed a significant correlation between a woman's financial literacy and the length of time she remained with her partner (i.e., abuser). Significant limitations of this study included the small sample size and the lack of a later data collection to follow up and assess whether the positive results persisted over time.

The second curriculum evaluated, *Moving Ahead through Financial Management*, was developed through a partnership between The Allstate Foundation and the National Network to End Domestic Violence. The goal of this program was to provide domestic violence service providers with the education and tools needed to facilitate financial literacy programs with abused women and, ultimately, to enhance survivors' financial empowerment. The curriculum covered five modules: (1) Understanding Financial Abuse, (2) Learning Financial Fundamentals, (3) Mastering Credit Basics, (4) Building Financial Foundations, and (5) Creating Budgeting Strategies.

Throughout the implementation of the *Moving Ahead* curriculum, it has undergone evaluation, using the theory of planned behavior as a guide to determine the program's impact on the financial and emotional well-being of survivors. The first pilot study was conducted in collaboration with fifteen IPV organizations located across ten states (Postmus & Plummer, 2010). Over the one-year study period, the researchers conducted three rounds of interviews after survivors had received the curriculum, yielding a sample of ninety-three interviews. Results indicated that survivors, the majority of whom lived below the poverty line, changed their financial behaviors by setting financial goals (88 percent), creating a budget (76 percent), paying off debt (71 percent), or starting a retirement account (22 percent). Additionally, the survivors reported significant improvements in financial literacy, financial self-efficacy, and financial self-sufficiency (Postmus & Plummer, 2010). Further data analyses revealed that both financial literacy and financial self-sufficiency were significant predictors of financial empowerment among survivors (Postmus, Plummer, et al., 2013).

Following the *Moving Ahead* pilot study, the research team conducted a randomized controlled study of the curriculum (Postmus, Hetling, & Hoge, 2013). Study participants were all survivors of IPV and were randomly assigned to either the experimental group, which received the curriculum, or the control group, which did not receive the *Moving Ahead* curriculum. The team recruited survivors from fourteen different IPV organizations located in seven states and Puerto Rico. The pre- and posttest interviews were conducted with a two-month interim and were completed by three hundred study participants, of which almost half identified as Latina. The results showed that survivors in the experimental group improved their financial knowledge by 40 percent (Hetling, Postmus, & Kaltz, 2015) and demonstrated an 18 percent improvement in financial behaviors such as saving money, budgeting, and using checking and savings accounts. The study results clearly indicated that the *Moving Ahead* curriculum is an effective financial literacy program that can improve survivors' financial knowledge and self-reported financial behaviors (Hetling, Postmus, & Kaltz, 2015).

The research team also collected data to assess whether the *Moving Ahead* program's effects were sustained over time (Postmus, Hetling, & Hoge, 2013). Data were collected through two interviews conducted at six-month intervals (i.e., interview three was conducted six months after the posttest interview, and interview four was conducted six months later). All four interviews were completed by 195 study participants; of these participants, 94 had been assigned to the experimental group (i.e., received the curriculum), and 101 had been in the control group. The results indicated that survivors who received the *Moving Ahead* curriculum had substantially better long-term outcomes than survivors in the control group on a number of financial measures, including significant improvements in financial knowledge, financial intentions, and financial behaviors. Additionally, analysis of the data collected in the short- and long-term follow-up interviews showed that survivors in the experimental group had decreased financial strain and significant improvement on other financial measures such as financial self-efficacy and financial self-sufficiency (Postmus, Hetling, & Hoge, 2013).

Building from the randomized controlled study (Postmus, Hetling, & Hoge, 2013), a longitudinal study was launched with a subsample of Latina participants to assess the impact of study participation and to gather the participants' comments regarding the impact of the curriculum on their lives.

In this longer-term study, the research team interviewed Latina participants more than two and a half years after they had participated in the original study and received the *Moving Ahead* curriculum (Hoge & Postmus, 2014). Here are some of their stories:

> In that course [*Moving Ahead*], I learned how to save, to not spend poorly. . . . In doing that, for example, now when my daughters come, I know that there is a method like how to use coupons well. Also, it helped me to have control, control of all my bills. I always do that. I control all my bills that I am spending on, how much I save. . . . I have that control now. That is what helped me most, in my ability to control my bills and to control to not spend poorly.

> [The *Moving Ahead* curriculum] helped me a lot, because there [in the group] was when I started to first see that I was abused economically also. Because I worked and I deprived myself of many things, to the point where I asked myself, "Why I should send this money there [home]?" So I saw that I could move forward. Cutting back on many things and doing other things, and then that was when I started to see that I could move forward. And a lot of help that they gave us; they gave us examples. Because they gave us a big binder that still is useful to me, because sometimes when I need to know something, I look it up because there are many things there, including how to buy a house. They taught us all those things.

> It [*Moving Ahead*] gave me more security, because I was so insecure. Yes. Not knowing how I was going to more forward alone . . . I had so many dreams, and then I didn't even know how to start. But, yes, it gave me a lot of security. And that was when I started to work, to manage my bills from there, my spending. Yes, it helped me a lot. . . . I started to think that I was strong, that I had to move forward, above all, that I had three daughters. I had to move forward. So it was from there that I changed my form of thinking and, above all, my form of thinking about . . . Those therapies helped me a lot to not go back to letting myself be abused emotionally, physically, or economically.

> Before, I didn't have the ability to manage money in my home, what came in and what I had to pay. There [at the group] they taught us what you have to pay and what you don't. I didn't know about any of that. Sometimes I took from one payment to cover another. I was making things worse and worse. So now I have organization. Now I have my goals. I write down how much comes in, how much I pay, and now I'm fine. I'm not late with my rent anymore. My electricity and gas are paid.

> Before [participating in *Moving Ahead*] we didn't have the ability to decide. . . . Like, we have such and such problems. We didn't really focus on the things that were more important, but instead we focused a lot on what was happening. So it helped a lot, the therapies and those courses. Yes, it helped us.

> It changed me! Before, I was very depressed, very much a person that didn't value herself, that thought that everything was over. And finding the therapy, the program, I feel more useful, more sufficient. I looked for work. So that helped me a lot. I feel much better than how I was before. . . . Yes, although there will always be challenges, but I feel I have more strength to be able to move forward because I have more understanding. Yes, . . . more secure, yes, to move forward and with more strength. I don't feel so weak because when someone experiences domestic violence, it makes you feel like you are not worth anything. So you stay with your self-esteem really low. So then you go on advancing and you go with . . . having knowledge about how to do things, so that helps you feel better.

Both the REAP and *Moving Ahead* programs demonstrated that financial curriculums were effective in increasing survivors' financial knowledge, financial self-efficacy, and financial self-sufficiency and improving their financial behaviors. Additionally, these programs demonstrated that financial empowerment interventions can make a difference in supporting survivors—even those with limited resources and limited financial knowledge or skills—to become financially independent from their abusive partners. Moreover, both curriculums were effective with survivors who were not in financially or emotionally stable environments. Both programs provided survivors with the information they needed to address financial well-being and safety. Evaluation results support that the use of financial interventions is effective when implemented with survivors of IPV. Given the anecdotal and empirical evidence, service providers should make financial literacy and empowerment interventions a priority among the services their agencies provide to survivors of domestic violence (Postmus et al., 2015).

Asset-Based Building and Savings Programs

Acquiring financial knowledge is one way that survivors can improve their confidence or self-efficacy as they attempt to manage their finances and practice positive financial behaviors. However, to reach their financial goals, survivors need to have access to assets or other resources. The ability to access money and other forms of assets has been shown to have a variety of positive associations linked to stronger self-efficacy and less financial strain; for example, access to assets is associated with positive outcomes such as opportunities to attain higher education or purchase a home (Christy-McMullin et al., 2009). Similarly, having access to assets has also been shown as positively associated with elevated levels of social support, community involvement, social status, and participation in civic opportunities (McBride et al., 2003). For example, a person might use their assets or savings to own a reliable vehicle, which in turn improves that person's opportunities to obtain well-paid employment, health care, child care, and social supports (Brabo et al., 2003). Last, assets provide a safety net that can cushion economic shocks (e.g., job loss, unexpected illness) as well as provide the means to help weather economic crises or help meet future consumption needs or wants (Sanders, 2014). Given the importance of assets, some domestic violence service providers have turned to asset-building strategies that have been shown to be effective when used with lower-income populations, applying those strategies to work with survivors. These strategies include programs such as individual development accounts (IDAs), many of which offer financial education and incentives such as matched savings to support participants in achieving their savings goals. Other asset-building strategies include programs that support participants' efforts to increase their job-readiness skills, find secure employment, or further their education.

Individual development accounts. The first IDA programs were developed as part of the welfare reforms that came about with the passage of Temporary Assistance for Needy Families (TANF) in 1996. The U.S. government created the Assets for Independence Program, which funded 611 state and local IDA programs (U.S. Department of Health and Human Services, 2010). These IDA programs were targeted to low-income individuals, many of whom were receiving public assistance. Notably, the IDA programs exempted participants from the asset limits imposed in most public assistance programs; without such exemptions, participants' savings would have reduced their monthly assistance amount or made them ineligible for assistance. Although IDA programs vary considerably in design, length, and target audience, nearly all provide participants with incentives to encourage them to save money and reach their savings goals. Incentives such as matched funds have been provided by government, corporate, foundation, or private donor sources. IDA participants receive the matched funds when they use their savings for qualified purchases such as buying a computer, making a down payment on a home, paying costs of higher education, or starting a small business. The IDAs set up by states imposed saving ceilings that ranged from $1,200 to $20,000 and provided matched funds at ratios that ranged from 0.5:1 to 7:1 (Richards & Thyer, 2011). In one evaluation study, IDA programs were shown to help participants increase their confidence, financial independence, and feelings of pride; improve their future orientation; and promote a positive outlook on their future (Shobe & Christy-McMullin, 2005). However, other studies have reported mixed results, with some demonstrating that IDAs were not effective in improving the participants' long-term financial well-being (Richards & Thyer, 2011).

Some domestic violence organizations have used IDAs with survivors to help women increase their financial independence and become more financially secure (Sanders, 2014). For example, IDA programs have been used with domestic violence survivors by the Kentucky Coalition Against Domestic Violence (KCADV) and REAP in St. Louis, Missouri. Although evaluation studies of these programs failed to assess any sustained impact over time, the studies have shown that the programs produced positive results. The evaluation of REAP's IDA program found that almost two-thirds of the women participating in the program were able to save money and use matched savings to purchase assets (Sanders, 2014). For example, the average participant saved $1,310, which was increased to $3,014 using matched funds (Sanders, 2014). Similarly, KCADV reported that survivors who enrolled in their 4:1 matched savings IDA program were able to save money and use those savings to purchase cars or homes (KCADV, https://kcadv.org). Unfortunately, as funds became more limited, the matching ratio shrank to a 1:1 match. Other statewide coalitions such as the Florida Coalition Against Domestic Violence (http://fcadv.org) have also embarked on matched savings programs through support from the Purple Purse Campaign at The Allstate Foundation (http://purplepurse.com).

Job Assistance Programs. Providing job assistance is another strategy used to help individuals with limited income to become self-sufficient. Most of these programs are directed to individuals on welfare, and most provide case management and assistance for individuals struggling to find work. One such program, based in Portland, Oregon, participated in the National Evaluation of Welfare-to-Work Strategies (NEWWS) project; the Portland program showed promise with regard to the size and consistency of earnings over time. The program credited this success to several strategies that differed from those used by other welfare-to-work programs. For example, the Portland program counseled participants that instead of taking the first job offered, they should continue their job search until they found a job that paid at least 25 percent more than the minimum wage and offered stability. The Portland program also partnered with community colleges to create a custom-made program designed to encourage program participants to advance their education. Unfortunately, the evaluation did not assess the impact of college participation on participants' income; however, other studies have demonstrated that education is a strong factor in lifting individuals and families out of poverty (Hamilton, 2002). As far as the impact of welfare-to-work programs on participants' financial well-being goes, the program in Portland was the exception and not the rule. Hamilton (2002) synthesized the existing studies on welfare-to-work programs and found that although participants increased their earnings through better employment and decreased their welfare participation, most did not increase their earnings enough to lift them out of poverty.

Education. Another example of asset-building programs is those that focus on increasing an individual's education level (ideally postsecondary education) as a way to increase their access to employment opportunities and jobs that offer higher wages (i.e., to obtain a living-wage job; Zhan & Schreiner, 2005). Most experts agree that attaining a higher education can promote stronger financial security in the modern world. Indeed, one study examined a sample of women who were receiving welfare while attending college; most of the respondents reported that their postsecondary training gave them greater opportunities for better jobs, higher pay, and more stable employment (Butler & Deprez, 2002). Notably, twenty-seven states that participate in IDA programs for people living below the poverty line allow saved funds to be used for education costs, including vocational education; however, only eleven of these states allow IDA savings to be used for the costs of postsecondary education (Pandey et al., 2000).

Most of our knowledge around linking survivors' increased education to reduced risk of further victimization is more theoretical than evidence based. For example, dependency theory posits that improving survivors' access to resources, with such access often improved through education, would be expected to decrease their dependency on their partners (Kalmuss & Straus, 1990). Dependency theory also suggests that if women have greater opportunities for education, they might delay family formation, which in turn might lead to higher occupational prestige and greater earnings, thereby making women less dependent on a partner.

Unfortunately, existing research on the link between education and domestic violence has yielded mixed results. Findings of some studies have suggested that pursuing higher levels of education (i.e., secondary and postsecondary) put survivors at risk of further abuse, whereas other studies have suggested that pursuing education decreased the likelihood of a woman experiencing abuse (Peterman et al., 2015; Vyas & Watts, 2009). However, a few recent studies conducted with non-U.S.-based samples found that increased levels of education reduced women's current and lifetime experiences of physical, psychological, and sexual violence (Peterman et al., 2015; Shiraz, 2016; Weitzman, 2018). More research is needed to fully understand whether increased education helps women avoid and escape abuse or puts them at greater risk of violence.

In sum, having assets can help survivors exert greater control over their own financial standing and become economically secure (Sanders, 2014). Indeed, having access to resources (e.g., savings, home or car ownership, steady employment, higher education) not only increases survivors' opportunities but also supports their efforts to become financially independent from an abusive partner. However, determining whether such independence leads survivors to safety is critically important, and the answer remains unknown at this time. Further evaluation of asset-building approaches is needed to know how best to safely support survivors in gaining access to resources and building assets without increasing their risk of abuse and further victimization.

Microloans and Microenterprise

Microfinance-based interventions are another common financial empowerment intervention used primarily for individuals who have lower incomes. These interventions share a common goal of lifting individuals out of poverty by giving them small loans or other financial services (Khandker, 2005; Swain et al., 2008). Women have often been the recipients of these interventions, with the rationale that improving women's financial standing will in turn improve the well-being of their children and the overall well-being of their families (Mayoux, 1998; Weber & Ahmad, 2014).

Microfinance interventions have recently been used with domestic violence survivors, but these programs have yielded mixed results. Some research has indicated that survivors' involvement in microfinance increased their empowerment (Deininger & Liu, 2013; Kim et al., 2007; Orton et al., 2016), and a few studies have demonstrated that microfinance interventions lessened survivors' risk of further experiences with domestic violence (Gupta et al., 2013; Kim et al., 2009; Yoo, 2012). However, other microfinance programs have reported that survivors' participation in the programs led to initial increases in domestic violence that subsided with time but did not lead to long-term reductions in abuse (Ahmed, 2005). Still other research has shown that microfinance interventions either had no effect on abuse (Bajracharya & Amin, 2013; Kim et al., 2009) or, worse, increased survivors' risk of experiencing further domestic violence (Dalal et al., 2013; Green et al., 2015; Murshid, 2016). However, when researchers combined microfinance interventions with gender-transformative interventions such as training programs to reshape gender norms, attitudes, or power dynamics between men and women, they found that the combined programs had a positive effect toward reducing exposure to abuse (Gupta et al., 2013; Pronyk et al., 2006).

Studies conducted more recently have examined the effects of microfinance-based interventions on economic abuse as a specific type of abuse (Gupta et al., 2013; Ranganathan et al., 2019). Researchers in South Africa identified several risk factors that increased economic abuse, such as a woman receiving a new loan or being in a relationship with a partner who did not value the woman's contribution (Ranganathan et al., 2019). One possible explanation for the increase in abuse is offered by the backlash theory, which posits that male partners feel threatened by women's stronger financial standing and power; hence, men use violence to regain the power they believe they have lost or believe women have taken from them (Guarnieri, 2018; Macmillan & Gartner, 1999).

Conversely, researchers in rural Côte d'Ivoire in West Africa conducted a controlled experiment in which they compared two groups of women; the control group saved money only, whereas the treatment group saved money *and* received training on gender norms (Gupta et al., 2013). Study findings indicated that women in the treatment group experienced a significant decrease in economic abuse (although not significant decreases in physical or sexual abuse). On the basis of these findings, the researchers concluded that the combination of an economic intervention (savings) with gender-norm training supported the household bargaining theory, which holds that women's participation in microfinance activities (e.g., savings program) can reduce their exposure to abuse. The decreases in abuse are believed to result from the women's newfound financial independence and economic opportunities that help balance the power dynamic between partners, recalibrating the dynamic to a more equal distribution of power between the couple (Aizer, 2010; Guarnieri, 2018; Gupta et al., 2013; Kim et al., 2009).

Another common approach to financial empowerment uses cash transfers, with this strategy most frequently used in low-income countries to target interventions for poor women. Notably, several research studies have documented the potential of cash-transfer programs to reduce IPV rates (Buller et al., 2018; Hidrobo & Fernald, 2013; Hidrobo et al., 2016). Using the randomized rollout of the Ecuadorian government's cash-transfer program to mothers ($N = 1{,}254$), Hidrobo and colleagues (2016) found that the effect of the cash transfer (i.e., income) on domestic violence varied by the women's education level. For women whose education was greater than primary-school level, the cash-transfer programs significantly decreased psychological abuse. However, in households in which the woman's education level was equal to or higher than her partner's education, the cash transfer significantly increased rates of emotional abuse.

Research findings remain inconclusive regarding whether microloans and microenterprise interventions help or hurt survivors of domestic violence. Most of the studies examining such interventions have been carried out in countries other than the United States, within distinct contexts with different cultural norms and expectations. To better address the needs of survivors in the United States as well as survivors in other countries, microfinance-based interventions will require further testing to determine how best to financially empower survivors in each country and context. Increasingly, scholars are calling for greater attention to be given to the potential of financial empowerment as a pathway for reducing domestic violence. This call to examine the impact of financial empowerment on domestic violence is reflected in the following statement: "Prevention response such as development of a comprehensive micro-enterprise or small- and medium-business ventures by women to help themselves out of the cycle of violence should be supported" (Fawole, 2008, p. 174).

Employee Assistance Programs

As of May 2019, more than 75 percent of U.S. men and 60 percent of U.S. women were employed (U.S. Bureau of Labor Statistics, 2019). Given the large percentage of the U.S. population engaged in work, workplace programs such as employee assistance programs (EAPs) are an effective strategy for helping employees who are struggling with problems affecting their work and personal lives. The 2016 National Study of Employers reported that more than 75 percent of all U.S. employers have EAPs available to their employees. These EAPs provide valuable resources and deliver preventive services to all employees of these firms, which includes survivors of domestic violence (Pollack et al., 2010). However, the biggest challenge for EAPs is employers' lack of awareness that domestic violence is a major problem among the workforce and, ultimately, a major problem for the workplace (Lindquist et al., 2010).

EAPs can enhance several levels of support for survivors, provided by their workplace supervisors (Perrin et al., 2011). For example, on a basic level, it is crucially important that EAP staff and workplace supervisors treat survivors as equal to other workers. Higher levels of support are provided under the label of the "support in every way," which includes all forms of emotional and tangible support (e.g., referrals for housing, economic assistance, and legal aid) as well as safety considerations such as a security guard to escort survivors to their cars or other transportation. Additionally, it is important for EAP staff and supervisors to maintain strict confidentiality when an employee discloses that she is experiencing domestic violence;

keeping such disclosures confidential is especially important when related to the employee's requests for time off to attend to the outcomes of domestic violence, such as medical appointments or court hearings.

Furthermore, the patterns of desired support vary across employees, and such variation might reflect the different stages that survivors move through while in an abusive relationship or during the process of leaving an abusive relationship. What constitutes desired support might change from limited support to support in every way possible, depending on the needs of individual survivors. Imposing services or specific supports and mandating that a survivor take certain actions (e.g., getting a restraining order or pressing charges) not only has the potential to alienate the survivor but also might create a less supportive attitude among the EAP staff and work supervisors if the survivor refuses to follow through with a "required" action. The survivor's decision whether to follow through on a recommended action must be supported by EAP staff, especially those who might function as an advocate with the work supervisor (Perrin et al., 2011).

EAP staff should also be well informed on financial abuse and familiar with the tactics abusers might use to sabotage the survivor's work efforts. These financial abuse tactics include making harassing phone calls or sending harassing texts during work hours, frequently showing up at the survivor's workplace, or causing a public scene at the survivor's workplace. In addition, an abuser might sabotage the survivor's work efforts by turning off her alarm clock, destroying her work clothing, or canceling child care or transportation arrangements without the survivor's knowledge. These tactics are not only designed to prevent the survivor from attending work but also intended to leave the survivor feeling humiliated and embarrassed—or, worse, believing that terminating her employment is the best solution. Additionally, employers and workplace supervisors might not realize that a survivor's poor performance (e.g., coming to work late, being inappropriately dressed, having frequent work disruptions) might be due to an abusive partner's attempts to sabotage the woman's employment efforts. EAP staff should be aware and mindful of such tactics while providing support to the survivor-employee and educating workplace supervisors about financial abuse and abusers' tactics.

EAPs can play an important role in screening employees for domestic violence and providing interventions for survivors-employees. Given the critical role of EAPs, an emerging need exists to raise awareness of domestic violence, to improve the use of screening and interventions for all employees, and to develop workplace policies that address domestic violence (Lindquist et al., 2010; Pollack et al., 2010).

Macro-Level Interventions

Although it is crucially important to provide survivors of domestic violence with the supports and interventions necessary to increase their access to and control of assets, it is equally crucial to ensure that the larger systems (i.e., banks, workplaces, and criminal justice systems) are aware of their roles in supporting survivors' efforts to become financially independent. Policies and programs promoting individual economic sufficiency have been instituted by various government agencies, corporate entities, and community-based services. These efforts align with our society's ideology that individuals must pull themselves up by their bootstraps in order to succeed. However, these same entities also need to acknowledge and take responsibility for their actions as larger forces in communities. "It is not only economic independence, but also freedom from violence and the creation of conditions to secure long-term safety that need to be the objectives of policy and institutional interventions" (Seith, 2001, p. 810). In this section, we discuss three distinct systems and the ways in which a self-examination of their policies could lead these systems to implement interventions that would help individuals as well as society. Specifically, systems could increase access to financial institutions, provide employment protections in the workplace, and address financial abuse in the criminal justice system.

Increasing Access to Financial Institutions

Survivors' comments clearly indicate the ways in which access to mainstream financial tools such as checking and savings accounts helps them in achieving their financial goals:

> And when I have my money in checking, . . . well, I do this: . . . this is for the rent, this is for the telephone. What is left over, I take out, and I put it in savings. Now I feel sure that I don't have a reason to touch even a cent in the checking . . . because I have it in savings. That is one way to also pressure yourself so that you feel that you don't have money there. I have it in savings. I can't touch anything, because if I touch it, it's in savings. So what I had in checking, now I don't have a cent, because what I spent was to pay my things that I had to pay: . . . my rent, my telephone, an example. And in the end, for what am I going to take out fifty dollars? To buy myself a purse that I don't need? Instead, if I would have had it there, all of a sudden, I would have taken it. But since I have it in savings, I feel like, "No, I don't have money." It is one way that I manage myself also.

> More than anything, how to do a bank account, that I could . . . so you can save. That motivated me a lot, because sometimes I think that it is easier to save having an account, because . . . having money in your hand, . . . because you spend it faster. (Hoge & Postmus, 2014, p. 3)

In 2017, over fourteen million adults in the United States were unbanked, meaning that they did not have a savings or checking account at an insured institution (Federal Deposit Insurance Corporation, 2017). Rates of the unbanked population are disproportionately high among marginalized populations such as Black and Latinx households as well as households of working-age individuals with disabilities. Without access to mainstream financial institutions, unbanked households tend to use risky methods to manage their money (Federal Deposit Insurance Corporation, 2017). For example, as compared with 75 percent of banked households that deposit their money in savings accounts, a majority of unbanked households (66.8 percent) keep savings in their home or leave money with family or friends for safekeeping. In addition, unbanked households receive income in a variety of ways, with the most prevalent form being a paper check or a money order, followed by cash and direct deposit onto a prepaid debit card. Two-thirds of unbanked households prefer to use cash to pay monthly bills, with the remaining third using nonbank money orders and prepaid cards for bill payments. Although no official statistics exist regarding the number of survivors who are unbanked or underbanked, banking services can be considered the foundation for survivors to build their financial security (Boyce et al., 2014). Accordingly, abusive partners often control the woman's access to and use of cash and prepaid cards, which leads to unbanked survivors experiencing higher risk of being economically abused.

To address this problem, banks could be more attentive to greater inclusion in the mainstream banking system by using situated learning strategies (Buckland, 2014). Specifically, banks should focus on developing relationships with potential customers by reaching out to those who are currently excluded from banking (e.g., those who are excluded by policies requiring minimum balances) and by providing tools and incentives to encourage individuals to become banked. For example, relationships between banks and the unbanked could be strengthened if bank employees received training to have a more inclusive perspective of bank customers. If an unbanked person thinks that bank employees are willing and able to help them, then that person might be more willing to participate in that relationship. In essence, "a person is more likely to ask questions and learn about new financial service options in a context in which staff are friendly, polite, and inviting. If mainstream banks place more branches in low-income neighborhoods, then they are signaling that they plan to work in those neighborhoods and that they are a part of the community" (Buckland, 2014, p. 22). As one survivor stated in research conducted by Hoge and Postmus, "Yes, I save sometimes. . . . I don't have a bank account because it makes it difficult that the bank charges you and charges you, and when you come to see, they close it on you if you don't continue depositing. . . . But yes, I can say that each month, I save at least a little, sometimes $50, sometimes $75" (2014, p. 4).

Although financial institutions, like many other institutions, interact with both the survivors and perpetrators of domestic abuse, only limited research exists regarding how financial institutions respond to domestic violence or economic abuse. Survivors' interactions with financial institutions are often negative or inconsistent (Sharp-Jeffs, 2015b). Because of limitations set by current fiduciary regulations, survivors who use banks might experience barriers when trying to close a joint bank account or open a new bank account (Boyce et al., 2014). The consequences of economic abuse for survivors' access to financial institutions make it more difficult for survivors to access banking services when they are trying to establish economic safety or economic independence. For example, if a survivor closes a joint account, the bank might choose to liquidate the account by issuing a check for the remaining funds. However, a survivor might lose access to that check if it is mailed to the joint holder's (i.e., abusive partner's) address on file. In turn, this check would alert the abuser that the woman had closed the account, putting her at increased risk of further abuse (Boyce et al., 2014). Additionally, given the current address-verification rule, survivors might be unable to open a new bank account because safety precautions prevent survivors from providing the address of shelters, temporary residences, or post office boxes, because that information would allow perpetrators to locate the survivors. Most, but not all, states have an Address Confidentiality Program (ACP) that masks a survivor's address; however, financial institutions are not mandated to participate in ACP protections.

One way to increase survivors' access to financial institutions is to enhance guidelines for customer due-diligence programs to better codify, clarify, and strengthen expectations of financial institutions (Boyce et al., 2014). Additionally, the ACP protections could be expanded, and all financial institutions could be mandated to comply with ACP. The U.S. Treasury's Financial Crimes Enforcement Network has established that the ACP substitute addresses are valid for banking purposes. Finally, financial institutions can promote "second-chance accounts," which are a financial product that some financial institutions offer to serve as an entry point into banking for individuals who would otherwise be excluded from access to transaction accounts. Most important, facilitating direct relationships between domestic violence organizations and financial institutions is beneficial to creating pathways for survivors to work with financial institutions.

Employment Protections

Domestic violence is not isolated within the home, and its spillover can be a major problem in the workplace. Domestic violence researchers have estimated that 36–75 percent of abusers harass their victim at her workplace (Swanberg et al., 2005). The consequences of domestic violence not only affect work performance but also pose a risk to public safety in the workplace, the safety of employers, and the safety of the survivors' coworkers. In particular, as compared with employed women who had not experienced domestic violence, employed women who had experienced domestic violence had lower earnings (Pollack et al., 2010); twice the rate of work absenteeism (Hensing & Alexanderson, 2000); decreased productivity and increased errors, higher turnover, and more time spent away from work (Swanberg et al., 2005; Wathen et al., 2015); and more frequent on-the-job harassment (Showalter, 2016). In each workplace, the average annual costs associated with domestic violence include $2,400 for absenteeism, $4,300 for workplace distraction, and $80 for tardiness (Reeves & O'Leary-Kelly, 2007). Across U.S. employers, the consequences of nonfatal domestic violence result in annual losses of $900 million (Centers for Disease Control and Prevention, 2003). In 2016, homicides accounted for 10 percent of all fatal occupational injuries in the United States; of these, approximately 2 percent of male victims but 40 percent of female victims were killed in the workplace by a relative or an intimate partner (U.S. Bureau of Labor Statistics, 2018).

Survivors find that working for pay not only benefits their economic security but also provides a level of physical safety and improves their mental health (Rothman et al., 2007). Survivors often feel physically secure in the workplace because of the presence of police, safety precautions, and security protocols. Employed survivors are more likely to disclose their plight to a coworker than to their work supervisors, EAPs, or human resource personnel (Kulkarni & Ross, 2016). Thus, coworkers can play a crucial role in providing direct support, referrals, and resources for survivors. However, a survivor's relationships with coworkers and employers are also complicated by the abuser's sabotaging efforts, which make the woman late to arrive, forced to leave early, having to lie to cover for her abuser, or being distracted at work (Alsaker et al., 2016), all of which can make the survivor feel shame and guilt while causing some coworkers to resent the survivor's poor work performance.

Domestic violence impacts employers' bottom line not only by adding extra organizational costs but also by affecting work productivity of women experiencing such violence (Reeves & O'Leary-Kelly, 2007; Swanberg et al., 2005). Not surprisingly, as compared with women who are not experiencing domestic violence, survivors (with either current or lifetime experiences of domestic violence) have higher estimated organizational costs of absences, tardiness, and work distractions. Moreover, these organizational costs include costs beyond production costs, such as added medical costs of employed survivors and secondary victims (e.g., coworkers, supervisors, or customers), administrative costs (e.g., duty shifts, hiring, training), and legal liability costs (e.g., creating a safe working environment; Swanberg et al., 2005).

By law, employers are required to create a safe work environment for all employees. However, in one study, which analyzed 369 state-level employment protection policies for domestic violence survivors—including work-leave policies, antidiscrimination employment policies, and workplace awareness and safety policies—no state had comprehensive policies covering all of these areas (Swanberg et al., 2012). Nationwide, only thirty-seven states have policies guaranteeing work leave for court appearances. In 2007, Oregon passed the Violence, Harassment, Sexual Assault or Stalking Protections Act, which makes provisions for "reasonable and unpaid leave" for all employees who work for an employer with more than five employees. Under the provisions of the act, an employee can use leave to seek medical treatment, counseling, or legal assistance, to attend court hearings, or to relocate without fear of loss of employment. Despite the employment protections in this act, the policy has no provisions for making employers or survivors aware of these protections. Three years after implementation of this act, a research team interviewed a sample of work supervisors and county-level employees who had experienced IPV in the past year. Of this sample, 74 percent of participants did not know the work-leave policy existed, and 65 percent of the IPV survivors reported that they would have used the provisions for work leave if they had known about the act. However, survivors who were aware of the policy reported being reluctant to use the work-leave provisions because of (a) fear of job loss, (b) lack of paid time off, and (c) stigma (Laharnar et al., 2015). Accordingly, paid leave will increase the use of such work-leave protections. The best way to advocate for change is to pass specific laws that address employment protections of survivors and to ensure that employees are aware of their employment protections. In addition to meeting the legal standard, employers are expected to create a culture of a zero tolerance of violence in the workplace, which includes domestic violence (Katz et al., 2017).

Response of the Legal System to Domestic Violence

Historically, domestic violence was not considered a crime but rather a personal and private issue between a couple. It was not until the 1970s that domestic violence was treated as a serious legal offense. The responses of the legal system to violence against women have focused primarily on physical abuse and sexual assault, with the aim of holding the perpetrators accountable. For example, to provide survivors protection from further abuse, civil law provides means for survivors to obtain civil protection orders. The criminal justice system has sought to protect survivors by emphasizing consequences for perpetrators, carried out through policies such as mandatory arrest, court-mandated treatment, and no-drop prosecution policies (i.e., the state prosecutor will not drop charges in a domestic violence case solely because the victim refuses to participate in the case). At the federal level, the U.S. Office on Violence Against Women provides grant funding for programs working to improve criminal justice responses to domestic violence, dating violence, sexual assault, and stalking. However, little is known about the extent to which the criminal justice system treats financial abuse as a serious violation, given that current policies exclude the consideration of financial abuse between intimate partners as a legal offense. Only elder abuse policies include financial abuse as a punishable crime (i.e., it is typically treated as financial exploitation of an elder person).

Unfortunately, law enforcement and prosecutor involvement is often limited in elder exploitation cases, especially when compared to physical abuse and neglect cases (Jackson & Hafemeister, 2011). Prosecutors find it difficult to prosecute elder abuse cases in general and even more difficult if the charge is financial exploitation (Jackson & Hafemeister, 2011). As a result, staff working in adult protective services are less likely to investigate financial exploitation; instead, APS staff focus more on physical abuse, since such abuse is easier to investigate and substantiate and it is easier to get law enforcement and prosecutors to take the case (Jackson & Hafemeister, 2011).

Survivors of IPV frequently interact with the criminal justice system through the civil and the criminal courts. In the criminal courts, these interactions focus on criminal proceedings related to the abuse, such as the survivor providing testimony at the abuser's trial. In civil court proceedings, the interactions are typically related to obtaining protection orders or orders for separation, divorce, and child support. Unfortunately, survivors find the legal system complex and difficult to navigate; therefore, most survivors require substantial assistance from legal professionals, which in turn often leads to survivors reporting a lack of personal agency or control over the legal processes (Wright & Bertrand, 2017).

Notably, civil proceedings around separation and divorce do not take financial abuse into account when making determinations on behalf of survivors. When it comes to debt, the courts view couples as one financial entity; hence, survivors who experience coerced debt through financial abuse often have to share an equal burden of resolving that debt even when the debt was accumulated by the partner (Littwin, 2012; Smallwood, 2015). Of course, new policies could shift the law in a similar way to other changes in the legal perspective of marital unity. For example, the courts have shifted from viewing a married couple as a unit to treating each of the partners as an individual in cases related to assault, rape, ending pregnancies, and granting restraining orders (Littwin, 2012). Until the new policies are enacted, the courts still have options to use protection orders not only to deal with debt and small property issues that arise in cases of domestic abuse but also to improve the available legal and financial remedies for survivors (Smallwood, 2015). Additionally, law enforcement could be more aware and interested in the consequences of financial abuse or even stopping such abuse (Smallwood, 2015). To address these much-needed changes, survivors, advocates, and professionals in the IPV field will need to establish close working relationships with law enforcement and the courts to create greater awareness of the prevalence and impact of financial abuse on the lives of survivors.

Emerging Issues

Among the array of services to support survivors of domestic violence, service providers need to give top priority to programs designed to financially empower survivors, thus equipping survivors to improve their financial knowledge, enhance their access to resources and assets, strengthen their economic self-efficacy, and improve their financial behaviors. A wide range of micro and macro interventions are available that service providers can incorporate into existing services. Although providers working with survivors have demonstrated an increased awareness of financial abuse, this awareness still needs to be put into action by prioritizing survivors' financial recovery and empowerment as a primary component of IPV interventions (King et al., 2017). Achieving this goal requires a commitment from providers and organizations serving survivors of domestic violence. Providers need to commit to ensuring that interventions include financial services to address both the short- and long-term financial challenges survivors face in creating a safe, financially independent life. The leaders of IPV organizations must be willing to make an organizational commitment to revise their core services, train their staff, advocate at the state and federal level for policies to address economic abuse, and secure funding for financial empowerment services for survivors (Stylianou, 2018b).

These recommendations are hardly new, especially given that domestic violence service providers and survivors have long recognized that economic issues pose one of the major barriers that prevent women from leaving their abusers. Both providers and survivors are also aware of the divergence between what survivors say they need and want and what service providers are able to provide (VonDeLinde & Correia, 2005). However, it is imperative that domestic violence service providers and advocates receive the specialized financial training and support they need to incorporate financial empowerment interventions into their work with survivors. Service providers need to be able to screen for financial abuse and assist survivors with creating financial safety plans. They need to know the best way to help survivors access resources and expand their assets along with other employment or job-training needs (Silva-Martinez et al., 2016; Stylianou, 2018b). Therefore, domestic violence organizations should invest in providing financial empowerment programs for survivors as well as invest in training and support for service providers and advocates delivering those interventions. Ultimately, the service providers' and advocates' improved financial knowledge and economic self-efficacy will improve the financial empowerment services provided to survivors (Postmus, Silva-Martinez, et al., 2013).

The potential for gaps to exist in service providers' financial knowledge was underscored in the study that evaluated the impact of the *Moving Ahead* curriculum (Postmus, Silva-Martinez, et al., 2013). In addition to interviewing survivors who received the financial education, the research team also interviewed the advocates who implemented the curriculum. The researchers learned that the advocates learned as much from the curriculum as the survivors did. Comments from a few advocates summarized the comments of many regarding the impact of *Moving Ahead* on advocates' financial knowledge and behaviors:

> I had to remind myself, "Remember that what you are teaching you also have to apply. You must apply it personally." . . . You talk a lot and say many things that women must do, but it is difficult to apply it yourself.

> So I found out that even though I didn't think I was a victim of domestic violence, in reality, when it came to financial, I was.

> Because of the curriculum, I am actually . . . budgeting makes more sense to me now, and I actually opened a savings account. I don't have a lot in it, but I opened a savings account.

> One of the things I did was open two checking accounts. . . . I probably would not have done that if I had not trained on this curriculum.

> I think over all the curriculum was great. . . . There were many things that I didn't even know for myself. . . . I learned a lot of things like having a good score. I didn't know that, you know.

Revising and revamping core services can seem daunting, but collaborations and resources are available to help with such efforts. For example, service providers can collaborate with community agencies that provide financial education or tangible support, including welfare organizations. Providers could also collaborate with local banks, insurance companies, or financial advisers (Silva-Martinez et al., 2016; VonDeLinde, 2002). These types of collaborations connect survivors with financial experts to get customized financial counseling and support while staying linked with domestic violence service providers who can focus on financial, physical, and emotional safety.

In addition to assessing the impact of *Moving Ahead* on the advocates' financial knowledge, the research team also asked advocates to identify challenges they faced when implementing the curriculum as part of their workload. The advocates reported feeling overworked because they did not have enough time to facilitate the financial empowerment groups while maintaining normal standards for meeting the needs of individual clients:

> In terms of time, making it [the curriculum] compatible with my job, it was terrible, Unfortunately, because of the nature of working over at shelter, there's just always a crisis. I always intended to make time, but you know, if there's a new family coming in and they're coming straight from their abuser's arraignment, I have to put the fire out, the fire in front of me.

> I feel, I think that it was difficult because of the fact that every department here is so—has such a workload that they often are unable to see outside of what their particular crisis is at the moment with their particular client.

> Ideally, I think that rather than taking staff who have full-time roles, it might have been nice to use someone who is part-time and have that be a project that they work on or to have someone who's per diem or on call—maybe train them because that [*Moving Ahead*] would be their project. (Postmus, Silva-Martinez, et al., 2013)

As financial empowerment programs continue to grow and expand in the IPV field, it is critical that these programs are developed in collaboration with

IPV survivors and tested with large samples of IPV survivors representing varied backgrounds and experiences. Financial empowerment programing needs to be reconceptualized for diverse IPV populations, including victims residing in rural areas; Native American and Asian victims; victims who are male, lesbian, gay, bisexual, transgender, and queer/questioning-identified; victims with disabilities; immigrant victims; and victims of diverse socioeconomic backgrounds.

Although substantial efforts have done much to improve financial empowerment interventions at the micro and macro levels, much work remains to ensure that such services are available and customized for survivors from diverse backgrounds. In particular, more work needs to be done to customize financial empowerment interventions for survivors who are immigrants, live in low-income communities, or are excluded from the financial mainstream. In serving these highly vulnerable groups, more attention must be given to ensuring that survivors have access to banking services; adequate transportation, especially to improve employment opportunities; affordable, quality child care; and access to the internet and other technological resources related to survivors' self-sufficiency. Equally important, to ensure that survivors (and others) are not exploited by predatory lending practices, the IPV field and advocates need to work with policy makers to ensure that unfair and predatory lenders receive greater scrutiny from regulators. Financial empowerment programming stands as an integral tool for service providers working with survivors to address the financial challenges they face on the path to a life free from violence.

CHAPTER 5

Specific Strategies on How to Financially Empower Survivors

A Practitioner Perspective

Jolynn Woehrer

"Economic dependence is one of the reasons that traps women in situations of violence. Providing opportunities for women helps them get to their full potential as human beings and as members of a society. Economic empowerment is key for any woman to be able to make her own choice regarding her own body, her future, and the way she wants to live her life."

—Milica Gudović, Citizens Association for Combating Trafficking in Human Beings and All Forms of Gender Based Violence

---

In recent years, the field and study of domestic violence have evolved to address financial abuse as a distinctive form and have fostered awareness of the often insidious and indelible impacts this form of abuse has on those who are injured by it. Financial support and resources have become increasingly allocated to this issue, contributing to a rise of financial empowerment programs and initiatives in domestic violence organizations. Throughout the field, growing numbers of direct-service organizations have accepted the challenge not only to target financial abuse directly but also to incorporate financial empowerment into their core services.

No standard, one-size-fits-all approach exists for this work. Each organization and the community it serves are a distinct ecosystem, uniquely interconnected within ever-evolving social, economic, and political landscapes. Both organizations and practitioners attempting the shift toward supporting survivors' long-term financial empowerment will experience growing pains throughout the transformation. Rather than assuming the position of expert, this work carries far greater potential when organizations and practitioners approach financial empowerment as enthusiasts and center survivors throughout the process.[1]

When I first began domestic violence work in 2001, financial empowerment advocacy was relatively uncharted territory. Only a few general empowerment models existed, much less a model for domestic violence programs. Upon my introduction to the concept of financial empowerment, I personally had few tools and little direction to help guide me in how to put it into practice. I had little idea of best practices to follow at the time. I also lacked financial know-how. My own financial picture was incoherent, and my awareness of money matters was limited. However, I was also unsaddled by preconceived notions or expectations of what this work should look like. Had I attempted to become a financial expert or relied solely on books to steer my path, I probably would have experienced far fewer successes and learned far fewer lessons of value to share now. Instead, I learned to approach this work with the spirit of an enthusiast, bringing my heart as well as my head, along with open-minded curiosity, passionate humility, a commitment to my own growth, and a resolve to enhance empowerment opportunities for survivors of domestic violence. If I could give only one piece of advice in this chapter, it would be to take this approach.

It is my hope that in sharing my journey, along with its trials, tribulations, and successes, I can assist others who are interested in traversing the terrain of financial empowerment advocacy. I draw from over twenty years of experience working primarily within domestic violence organizations committed to meeting the needs of victims who are still vulnerable to abuse while offering opportunities for healing and empowerment in the aftermath of trauma. I bring the unique insight of having witnessed domestic violence organizations struggle to stretch their existing scope of services to comprehensively address financial abuse and to grow financial empowerment opportunities. I have had the privilege of overseeing the design, implementation, and management of financial empowerment programs and then witnessing the transformation of organizations that elevate their response to domestic violence by actively committing to both social and economic justice. I can attest to the invaluable impacts of these organizations' growing pains, ultimately witnessing countless survivors achieve financial independence, obtain economic self-sufficiency, access opportunities for professional and personal growth, and gain leadership skills.

Within such organizations, I cultivated skills in training advocates on financial abuse and financial empowerment strategies. My most significant responsibilities specific to financial empowerment practices have included facilitating large-scale educational workshops and one-on-one sessions with survivors on economic, professional, and personal empowerment tools; cultivating relationships with community partners and volunteers; and coordinating mentorship programs for women along their journeys to independence. My most rewarding endeavors in this field have included enhancing women's options in the areas of financial empowerment, employment, education, and leadership—in essence, helping women to achieve economic self-sufficiency and to participate in civic engagement opportunities. What I have found to be true, as discussed in depth in chapter 3, is that cultivating opportunities for empowerment is just as valuable to a survivor's ongoing safety as ensuring her access to resources.

Over the trajectory of my career, I have worked with domestic violence organizations that were just starting to navigate the shift to incorporate financial empowerment interventions beyond traditional safety intervention services. In these roles, I experienced a variety of ways in which agency-wide initiatives were implemented to respond to financial abuse and to embed financial empowerment interventions at every level of the organization's services, from initial crisis interventions to longer-term support, advocacy, and education efforts. In doing so, these agencies expanded not only their concepts of safety but also their scope of services to better enhance self-efficacy for survivors attempting to escape the cycles of both violence and poverty. Although I had the privilege of working with solid leadership teams taking the necessary first step of committing to enhance financial empowerment efforts, the process of putting these intentions into practice was neither simple nor straightforward.

My practitioner's perspective on introducing financial empowerment in domestic violence organizations, to programs, staff, and survivors, complements the other chapters of this book. This chapter explores various considerations inherent in advancing survivors' empowerment within the context of direct-service organizations that have historically been focused on prioritizing immediate safety services over longer-term interventions. In laying the groundwork for financial empowerment, I discuss integrating financial empowerment into existing support and education programs designed to support survivors' overall healing and empowerment. Drawing from my professional experiences, I identify a life skills framework as a potential program model in which to develop and facilitate financial education and empowerment programs with survivors, to enhance survivors' long-term empowerment, and to support the integration of financial empowerment into core advocacy services. I examine factors to consider when working with survivors in a variety of financial empowerment capacities and incorporate personal experiences in doing so. I approach challenges—particularly resistance expressed by front-line advocacy teams—as opportunities not only to identify financial empowerment strategies embedded within existing advocacy practices but also to anchor these strategies more deeply and deliberately into broader organizational principles, processes, and plans. I highlight the importance of engaging survivors in financial empowerment education as active agents capable of guiding their own lives and this work. Finally, I conclude with a call to expand financial empowerment efforts to include interventions with men and youth.

Shifting from Safety to Empowerment

Historically, financial empowerment advocacy has not existed as a core component of most domestic violence organizations. This absence is understandable considering that the majority of domestic violence service models originated to intervene on behalf of individuals victimized by gender-based violence or seeking safety from abusive partners. Often, victims of domestic violence arrive at direct-service organizations with significant safety concerns and initially request assistance with emergency medical, housing, and legal needs. Consequently, core domestic violence services primarily address survivors' most pressing and immediate safety needs, including receiving medical assistance, accessing emergency shelter, safety planning; changing locks, obtaining restraining orders, navigating the court system, and taking the time and space to process, cry, and receive emotional support. These interventions, which primarily focus on foundational safety needs and system interventions, are vital and valuable—and the resources to maintain such services are essential.

However, these traditional direct-service crisis-response models have primarily positioned people on the front line as short-term interventionists tasked to help, sometimes even rescue, individuals who are presumed to be dependent on these front-line workers. In the context of domestic violence, this is not to say that such approaches do not result in survivors' empowerment. They do, but an empowerment outcome is more of a by-product rather than a guiding principle of the overall process. A more unfortunate, although unintentional, consequence of these traditional approaches is the potential to disempower survivors, relegating them to passive roles as recipients at the periphery of service networks rather than actively including them in leadership capacities at the center of them.

Unlike the crisis-response model, empowerment models theoretically assume that survivors are capable of independently harnessing their own power and, thereby, support their long-term change and growth processes. As discussed in chapter 3, empowerment processes expand the concept of safety to improve a survivor's quality of life; these processes include individual, interpersonal, sociocultural, and political interventions that enhance survivors' human capabilities. In general, empowerment frameworks carry the radical potential for survivors to challenge systemic roots of violence, to liberate themselves and others from the trappings of the victim stereotype, and to emerge as active leaders in social, economic, and political endeavors. Rather than simply mitigating the effects of abuse, initiatives emphasizing survivors' empowerment extend the potential to disrupt, and even end, cycles of violence.

When empowerment is applied to domestic violence interventions, I find it helpful to envision it as a complex network of highway systems designed for survivors. In these systems, survivors are given the support to occupy the driver's seat in their lives, to self-determine their destinations and travel plans, and to navigate the routes and timelines they choose. In this analogy, empowerment practitioners occupy support roles, tasked with not only helping prepare survivors to anticipate detours and challenging road conditions but also providing survivors with the resources and tools to ensure that their journeys are safe and successful. Leadership supporting the transition to integrate empowerment models within domestic violence organizations is vital in formalizing the design and construction of such networks as well as in safeguarding the continued maintenance and expansion of them.

Life Skills Program Model: Building Financial Empowerment into Existing Support and Education Services

Although organizational change processes require systematic shifts over time within staff cultures and intervention strategies, opportunities to embed financial empowerment can often be found within existing programs and practices, particularly in support and education groups and services. Through support and education programs, many domestic violence organizations routinely offer a range of services such as counseling, parenting assistance, intervention classes, support groups, and family-focused opportunities. The majority of my work in such programs has been to facilitate access to information, resources, and opportunities for individuals and families seeking safety, healing, and empowerment. In this capacity, I have occupied a variety of roles within a "life skills" framework to support the psychosocial competency of survivors and to comprehensively integrate financial empowerment efforts within a range of interventions aimed to bolster survivors' human capabilities.

The terms "financial" and "economic" are often used interchangeably, but the life skills model purposely differentiates them. Sharp-Jeff's proposal, discussed in this book's introduction, helps to distinguish between the term "financial" empowerment (i.e., relating to micro-focused issues of finances and money) and the term "economic" empowerment (i.e., relating to macro-focused resource-generating avenues such as employment, education, or civic participation). Returning to the image of empowerment as a complex network of highway systems, financial empowerment can be conceived as a specific lane by which survivors can access information and tools for the purpose of accessing financial resources as well as their own financial independence and security. On the other hand, economic empowerment serves as a broader multilane highway designated for survivors to navigate and access a wider variety of resources, information, and tools to benefit them in ways that are not limited to monetary outcomes. Economic empowerment also contains tracks for survivors to gain skills, strengthen abilities, access resources, grow connections, and navigate opportunities to achieve greater social and political empowerment, in addition to employment and education avenues. A life skills framework can encompass these many diverse pathways to economic and financial empowerment.

The delivery of life skills can entail a specific set of topical interventions within existing support and education services and, thus, is often the best arena to introduce financial empowerment education. However, life skills can also exist as a programmatic umbrella, encompassing a diverse range of empowerment-focused opportunities, including support and education among other services. A life skills program model offers survivors opportunities to navigate systems by facilitating their access to these avenues and providing survivors with the tools and support necessary to be successful. In addition to an emphasis on financial literacy and economic self-sufficiency, the range of life skills services extends to family and parenting support, formal and informal education assistance, comprehensive wellness initiatives, employment coaching, and survivor leadership development. These varied interventions empower survivors to self-determine their overall goals; to access a variety of supportive tools and resources; and to gain personal, interpersonal, and political power in a multitude of contexts.

From my perspective in developing, coordinating, and delivering financial empowerment programs, a comprehensive life skills model offers a viable strategic approach for organizations to enhance micro- and macro-financial empowerment interventions (defined in chapter 4), as well as to promote financial empowerment as a process, an intervention, and an outcome (discussed in chapter 3). Additionally, such a range of services collectively responds to both interpersonal and intrapersonal consequences of economic abuse (chapter 2), including financial, health, family, and life consequences, and also bridges connection and expands access to a wide variety of empowerment channels at the same time. By designing a life skills program to be as flexible and responsive as possible in its delivery, organizations can meet the most pressing social, economic, and interpersonal needs central to the well-being of the individuals and communities they serve. This adaptable approach allows for a broad, evolving scope of interventions to address the effects of domestic violence, trauma, and poverty, including the unique risks, barriers, and needs identified by those who are seeking assistance.

The life skills program model requires at least one designated full-time staff member (working in partnership with facilitation staff, advocates, and volunteers) to manage program operations and provide comprehensive life skills support and education to survivors both individually and in group settings. When the life skills model is given programmatic standing, it also has greater capacity to influence internal organizational priorities, practices, and culture. Moreover, life skills programs can bridge organizational efforts with external partners to leverage relationships and resources *as well as* to enhance financial empowerment opportunities that are responsive to the needs of survivors. The life skills model also makes the most sense for sustainable funding of services because of its adaptivity to respond to a variety of ongoing issues facing survivors.

Harnessing the Power of Groups

Whether within a life skills program or not, existing support and education programs are accessible routes of intrapersonal, interpersonal/interactional, and behavioral empowerment (discussed in chapter 3). Such programs provide a means by which practitioners can engage individuals and families in a wide variety of empowerment avenues and on topics ranging from coparenting safety considerations to asset-building opportunities. Support and education groups can help survivors access critical social supports and financial resources. Vital aspects of empowerment include emotional health, safety, social support, and sense of belonging (explored in chapter 3); therefore, infusing financial empowerment into supportive group environments has immense potential to also support survivors' skills and abilities, self-confidence, and access to resources. A safe and trusting group environment enables women to learn from one another, to consider perspectives different from their own, and to create a network of support and accountability.

Support and education groups generally consist of survivors who are navigating various stages of empowerment and regularly committing time and attention to their own healing and empowerment in a comfortable and safe space. Some participants might still be in relationships with abusive partners, whereas others might be years out of an abusive relationship. Support-group participants typically represent a cross-section of survivors who are navigating a range of specified service channels, including shelter, legal clinics, personal advocacy, counseling, family support programs, or other community organizations. Providing free child care and transportation assistance (e.g., vouchers) removes barriers to access for women with children or limited financial resources. Specific groups can be diverse or culturally specific (e.g., LGBTQ+, age sixty-plus, dual domestic violence / sexual assault, or non-English-speaking). Trauma-informed empowerment interventions can respond distinctly to risks faced by survivors who are marginalized by systems of power and oppression, including undocumented immigrants, women who have been negatively impacted by the criminal justice system, and mothers who are navigating child protective services.

One strategy to experiment with program practices addressing a range of topics, such as financial management, credit basics, goal setting, interviewing skills, and scholarship opportunities, is to integrate financial education into ongoing support groups on a consistent basis (e.g., monthly or even quarterly), depending on program capacity and number of groups held. Focusing even a small amount of time for participants to share information and resources with each other during regular support-group sessions can do much to advance the empowerment process. In the context of support and education groups, financial education is not limited to a specific end goal of improving survivors' knowledge about money matters and financial management skills. In such settings, financial education enhances participants' self-efficacy in a process designed to support them in developing self-confidence and overcoming obstacles, including personal fears and limiting beliefs, to successfully put their new knowledge and skills into practice and successfully follow through on their goals.

Exploring Personal Attitudes and Beliefs around Money in Financial Education Endeavors

When advocates and practitioners work with survivors of domestic violence, financial education must not only deliver information to raise survivors' economic self-efficacy and self-sufficiency but simultaneously provide survivors with a supportive environment in which they can heal, grow, and evolve throughout the process. Providing this supportive environment is crucial because money matters are often emotional matters. For most people, talking openly about finances is an uncomfortable and vulnerable experience. Feelings about finances can include guilt, embarrassment, fear, and shame; these difficult feelings can affect if, and how, a person is capable of making certain financial changes. Feelings about money are often bound up with deep-rooted beliefs about human nature, relationships, gender roles, and even self-worth. Talking openly about such matters can have a positive influence on the financial socialization of survivors in these processes, as well as counteract the consequences of economic abuse (discussed in chapter 2).

Becoming aware of personal financial beliefs can inspire deeper healing and changes, increasing an individual's capability to make empowered choices. I can attest to experiencing personal growth in my own experience of receiving financial education. I was once given the opportunity to identify my personal financial beliefs by completing the statement, "People with money are . . ." My initial response was that people with money were different from me, had more than me, and had the capacity to be especially unkind. These first thoughts surprised me because I did not consciously agree with them. Although I would never publicly proclaim such beliefs—especially because I did not consciously think these things were true—the fact that these ideas were the first unfiltered thoughts to come to mind was worth examining.

I found the origins of this belief in my early financial socialization process, particularly in my childhood experiences during elementary school. I grew up in a home where religious education was deeply valued, and my parents prioritized their limited financial resources so that my brother and I could receive such instruction at a local private school. As a result, we had little money for much else beyond the basics. We pinched pennies in our home, and it showed. My classmates rudely remarked on it regularly, especially egregiously on the mornings our mom drove us to school. They took to publicly dubbing my mom's yellow clunker of an automobile as the "garbage truck" and my brother and me as "white trash." Unknowingly, these foundational experiences directly contributed to my financial beliefs and influenced my behaviors. I learned to avoid money-related matters, to my detriment, as a protective coping mechanism. Exploring the origins of my money story has helped me loosen the hold of limiting beliefs and make space to form more empowered beliefs, enhance my capabilities to set and achieve financial goals, and heal and transform the heart of the matter with my pocketbook.

My evolved awareness benefits me personally and pushes me to become a better financial empowerment practitioner. My personal process of unpacking my relationship with money freed me from bringing my unconscious baggage and biases into my professional work with others. Instead, I have grown to develop a solid belief in the value of integrating trauma-informed financial empowerment throughout domestic violence interventions. I have also grown comfortable talking with key financial professionals and funders about the importance of financial empowerment strategies directed at individuals and families working to break cycles of violence and poverty, and I can do so with conviction.

I find that when practitioners share their own personal growth experiences relating to financial education, it often fosters deeper engagement and connections in group processes. Given that learning is an endless adventure, I have embraced a standard practice of approaching each financial education session I hold as both an informed facilitator and a fellow student navigating the tricky terrains of continuous growth and development. When I facilitate workshop series, I purposefully and deliberately challenge myself to take ownership of working toward specified financial goals throughout the process so that I model the vulnerability necessary to navigate the inevitable challenges along any financial empowerment path. I intentionally draw from my own embarrassing financial blunders, such as the ramifications of not reading the fine print of a rental agreement or my frustrating attempts to resolve delinquent accounts blemishing my credit report. I normalize learning curves and growing pains. Financial empowerment becomes something we navigate together.

Providing financial education to survivors is not a by-the-book endeavor. Rather than simply facilitating a transfer of information and tools, practitioners delivering financial education need to intentionally provide opportunities for survivors, in community with one another, to rebuild their human capabilities. For this reason, although structured financial education curriculums (see chapter 4) provide valuable roadmaps to deliver tools and information for survivors, these curriculums are often limited to a sole focus on the intrapersonal and financial consequences of financial abuse and, thus, need to be supplemented with opportunities for building human capabilities.

How service providers tailor the delivery of financial education specifically for domestic violence survivors is important. Financial education needs to simultaneously address the impact of various forms of financial abuse along with *both* interpersonal and intrapersonal consequences experienced by survivors and their families (discussed in chapter 2). To fully address the impacts of financial abuse, the delivery of financial education should be inclusive of opportunities for survivors to connect financial consequences to consequences in their parenting, in their well-being and quality of life, and within their families. Financial education offers significant potential for survivors to put their newly acquired financial skills into practice when it integrates personal reflection and connects with participants' lived experiences.

Individuals develop their own unique relationships with money matters. Survivors' relationships with money will often be complicated by the lingering effects of abuse and can influence how a woman perceives her financial capabilities and how she chooses to navigate her empowerment. Delivering financial education from a trauma-informed lens provides survivors with opportunities to apply the tools they receive to their own unique lives and experiences. Broadening the focus of financial education to incorporate experiential opportunities and generate deeper self-discovery and awareness (e.g., exploring personal beliefs about money matters or identifying financial fears) can help survivors gain financial knowledge, enhance internal resources, and increase self-confidence. In these contexts, survivors not only increase financial knowledge and internal tools within safe and supportive group communities but also explore and reflect on personal financial beliefs, values, and behaviors. Financial education programs designed to examine both interpersonal and intrapersonal learning consequences can yield greater visible engagement and more positive outcomes, as reported by survivors.

With repeated practice delivering financial education curriculums to diverse groups and in different settings, practitioners can learn to anticipate issues that are commonly experienced during the process and transform potential learning hurdles into opportunities for teachable moments. For example, after teaching numerous multiweek financial empowerment series and providing survivors with multiple expense-tracking tools and an assignment to track all their expenses for one week, I noticed a common trend. Many participants would initially not complete, or sometimes not even start, the expense-tracking assignment. At first, I could not understand why so few people completed, or even started, the task. I thought I had anticipated every potential hiccup to ensure that survivors had every tool at their disposal to put this piece into practice. I had sent everyone home with various expense-tracking tools, including pocket-sized notebooks, calculators, envelopes, and wallets to store every receipt. I demonstrated how phones could be used to track expenditures. I folded up an expense-tracking form very small to illustrate how easily it can be kept in a sock, a shoe, a pocket, and even a bra! If I had supposedly done everything I could, what was the hang-up?

Eventually, I became curious, and rather than jumping straight to the next module on budgeting, I devoted most of the class time to discussing the survivors' experiences with the expense-tracking process. As survivors shared their internal processes, they identified many factors and emotions that contributed to why they did or did not put these new tools into practice. A few survivors said that they felt shame or guilt about their spending habits and did not complete the assignment to avoid facing their spending habits. A few other survivors did not track their expenses and reported that the act of tracking was unsettling because it brought back painful memories of abusive partners demanding they account for every dollar they spent. One survivor was so afraid of spending money that she was able to mentally account for the few purchases she had made during the week. Another woman admitted that she was embarrassed because her purchases would expose her hard-to-kick smoking habit, and she was afraid of possible judgment from others. A small number of women had started or completed the tracking assignment; however, all reported at least some level of discomfort in tracking their spending habits. This discussion included tears, laughter, and a few hugs; most important, the discussion provided everyone with significant reassurance and relief. Near the end of class, one participant recommended that they all try again to complete the expense-tracking activity during the coming week, and the entire group committed to doing so. By the following session, every survivor had successfully tracked her entire past week's expenses and was fully on board and ready to move on to budgeting.

I advocate for practitioners to ensure that participants have space and time to share emotional processes and that this critical element of space and time be intentionally integrated as a core component of financial education with domestic violence survivors. For many survivors, dealing with past credit issues will often summon difficult memories, and many may have avoided dealing with debt to avoid dealing with uncomfortable feelings. For survivors with children, budgeting goals are likely to be challenging if they have developed habits of buying their children things they cannot afford because of feeling guilt around what their children have experienced. Some survivors will dismiss financial planning to avoid potential disappointments in setting goals—especially if important goals set in the past were sabotaged by an intimate partner. Other survivors might not have recognized financial abuse as abuse before these conversations. For these survivors, being able to recognize how they have been harmed in yet another way, and being able to name it as abuse, will summon a complex array of emotions to sort through. Survivors need to have opportunities not only to discuss these issues but also to receive validation and support in their struggles. When financial education is presented in a manner that encourages space for such intimate conversations, survivors often realize that they are not alone with their struggles and can process difficult emotions or fears that might be holding them back from putting financial tools into practice. Repeatedly, I have found that such conversations help survivors to connect deeply with financial tools as well as to become more confident in their own capabilities.

When domestic violence organizations strive to deliver this type of healing-focused financial empowerment intervention, they introduce survivors to a more complete process of empowerment (see chapter 3). These financial education efforts expand beyond addressing survivors' personal safety needs to also provide the following:

- Individual empowerment (i.e., gaining individual knowledge, self-efficacy, self-confidence, and self-sufficiency)
- Interpersonal empowerment through social connection and financial socialization
- Environmental empowerment (i.e., connecting to resources to enhance their financial empowerment)
- Enhanced development and practice of beneficial financial behaviors

In this regard, more comprehensive financial education approaches yield the most comprehensive financial empowerment.

Individualizing Financial Empowerment Support Strategies

In the context of the life skills model, a significant portion of participants attending educational workshops seek opportunities to receive individual support and resources specific to their personal goals. These individualized sessions help survivors develop personal empowerment plans to anticipate and navigate potential barriers, to access appropriate community resources, and to identify tangible, manageable action steps they are willing to commit to within a determined time frame.

Most often, survivors who engage in ongoing support and education programs are motivated and ready to focus on their empowerment goals. Because they often have established relationships with program staff, they also have a higher rate of attendance in individualized settings. However, a word of caution is warranted. Although infusing financial empowerment education into existing groups and following up with individualized support is an incredibly effective way to engage survivors in both financial education and long-term empowerment, this approach can be a victim of its own success, and demand for individualized support can quickly surge beyond a program's limited capacity. To accommodate a potential growth in demand for individualized interventions, practitioners will need to actively recruit volunteers before launching financial empowerment education efforts, as well as to create a staggered schedule for empowerment workshops and education groups.

Like group education endeavors, working individually with survivors on financial empowerment goals is rarely a straightforward process and will often play out in unexpected ways. Initially, some survivors might seem entirely ready and motivated to tackle their finances but will not be as ready to prioritize financial empowerment in action. I have worked with women who have scheduled and rescheduled individual appointments for months before actually attending an appointment. Survivors are navigating complicated circumstances and will show up for individual support when they are ready. When they do show up, survivors might seek individualized support to work on financial matters that practitioners have not anticipated. For example, when I first began providing individualized financial empowerment support, I was surprised how often survivors came to these one-on-one appointments with boxes of unopened envelopes from bill collectors and financial institutions: they just needed support opening the envelopes. Quite a few times, I have sorted through and added up piles of wadded receipts with survivors who were having a tough time reining in their spending. In these cases, they wanted an "accountability buddy" to face the reality of their spending habits—as a practitioner, I acted as that buddy.

I quickly learned to let survivors guide their own empowerment process and to meet them on their own terms and without imposing my own expectations, process, or judgments. Although this can be a challenging posture for practitioners, it is of utmost importance to remain both neutral and responsive to survivors' unique intentions and behaviors. A practitioner can help a survivor increase her intrinsic motivation to accomplish her goals by first eliciting the survivor's own experiences, perceptions, and values. Practitioners also need to ask survivors about their immediate goals and follow up with future-oriented questions such as, "Where would you like to be a year from now?" and "What kinds of support would you find helpful in reaching your goals?" Asking such questions will help practitioners respond to the issues that the individual sees as a priority, rather than the practitioner prioritizing issues for them. Additionally, asking future-oriented questions invites survivors to imagine what their empowerment process could look like. These questions can also help the practitioner in linking survivors to the best-suited external resources. This future-oriented approach creates opportunities for survivors to determine their goals and accomplish goals at their own pace and on their own terms.

Empowerment plans are most effective when they are designed for a survivor to develop incrementally in ways that help her achieve or maintain financial stability while working toward her long-term goals. For example, a mother with small children who has lost her job due to domestic violence might simultaneously desire new employment while also needing to access public assistance resources (e.g., food benefits, child care, Medicaid) until she finds a new job. This mother might very well jump at the first job offered, even if it is a lower-wage job opportunity that could potentially decrease the level of benefits she is eligible to receive. If she is unable to access affordable child care, she might face challenges to maintaining her new job. Similarly, a mother who is already relying on limited public assistance to supplement her income from low-wage work might be successful in obtaining a higher-paying job, only to find that her increase in income renders her ineligible for certain public benefits. If this wage increase is not enough to cover the lost benefits, then rather than gaining empowerment, her overall financial health declines. The process of financial empowerment planning needs to be responsive to the needs identified by the survivor and her decisions impacting her and her family. Individualized interventions help each survivor approach empowerment in a manner that helps her both achieve and maintain financial safety while accessing the resources she needs for personal financial empowerment without jeopardizing her autonomy or progress.

Practitioners need to apply a strengths-based approach when working with survivors, being well informed of accessible, culturally appropriate, and substantive resources to help individuals meet their needs and attain their self-determined goals. I see it as the practitioner's responsibility to create positive, safe contexts that foster accountability, honesty, learning, and personal growth. Partnering with survivors throughout the financial empowerment process helps each individual to take ownership over her process, choices, and goals. Practitioners who actively listen to survivors, ask open questions, and respond with empathy are effectively inviting survivors to problem-solve for themselves and determine their own paths. Rather than practitioners assuming the position as expert-teacher in the context of financial empowerment education, they should instead presume that survivors' essential resources primarily come from deep within the person; the survivor must guide her own process.

Employment Support as Financial Empowerment

Typically, individuals navigating domestic violence need financial income and employment. A life skills model can respond to this need by offering professional-development and job-readiness resources, workshops, and support. In my experience, a significant portion of survivors' requests for individualized support is for employment assistance at various stages in the job-search process. When engaging with survivors, practitioners should anticipate working with individuals with limited, inconsistent, or nonexistent employment histories due to repeated victimization. Such histories can present challenges in crafting job-search tools with survivors, especially with chronologically ordered résumés.

However, survivors possess internal tools obtained through life experiences that also translate to qualifications and skills that employers often value. Given the impacts of financial abuse (especially considering financial gender norms), to align survivors' job seeking with their intended employment outcomes, it is important for practitioners to develop creative strategies to reframe survivors' skills and abilities, such as their skills used within the context of unpaid labor. This reframing is especially pertinent in working with survivors to create résumés and cover letters as well as to practice interviewing skills. Rather than a chronological format for a résumé, a functional format often offers the best approach to construct a strong résumé for a survivor whose employment history might be minimal or inconsistent. With a functional résumé format, a survivor's unpaid labor in the context of domestic housekeeping and maintenance skills might translate to relevant professional qualifications on a résumé, such as, "Skilled in performing quality assurance inspection to ensure high standards of cleanliness, maintenance, and upkeep (including dusting, vacuuming, sweeping, mopping, laundry, cleanliness of rooms, high and low dusting, scrubbing, sanitization, and special area cleaning)."

In reframing child-care and youth-engagement abilities inherent in active parenting roles, employment qualifications might translate as one or both of the following:

- Innovative and detail-oriented in employing a variety of interactive educational tools to accommodate different learning styles.
- Experience coordinating and preparing play and learning materials, setup of the children's learning environment, and guiding children's behavior and social development.

Even the skills that survivors develop in navigating conflict and abuse in their intimate relationships can be reframed as beneficial qualities in employment contexts, including abilities to multitask, work effectively under time constraints, and quickly respond and/or adapt to sudden changes in environment or circumstance. Creative approaches in the creation of employment-related empowerment tools can reflect the internal qualifications survivors possess, validate survivors' strengths, and support survivors' economic self-efficacy and self-confidence.

Cultivating a volunteer network of professionals and students can increase a program's capacity to offer individualized employment assistance to survivors. Often, survivors need support in creating email accounts, crafting résumés and cover letters, conducting effective job searches, applying for employment, and preparing for interviews. Volunteers can work individually with survivors to create a résumé and/or cover letters and to offer survivors opportunities to learn helpful job-search techniques or practice interviewing skills. If space is available, furnishing small working areas with computers capable of running office-related software and internet searches will provide room for survivors to work independently or with assistance from program staff or volunteers.

Connecting Survivors to Financial Empowerment Resources and Opportunities

Linking survivors with community resources can provide them with crucial information and skills to make confident, informed decisions about the economic and emotional well-being of their family, enabling survivors to participate in the local economy more fully. When delivering financial education, partnering with bank representatives, financial advisers, and insurance or real estate agents on related activities will generate useful community-based financial tools and connect survivors with local resources they can access on their own in the future. Within the life skills model, financial education is just one pathway to empowerment; as such, survivors will often benefit from accessing a variety of financial empowerment avenues. Practitioners need to forge connections throughout their communities with a diverse range of empowerment resources such as educational/job-readiness programs, microenterprise opportunities, business loan resources, credit counseling services, home-ownership advocacy, foreclosure prevention services, and asset-building opportunities.

Connecting survivors to financial empowerment resources and opportunities can be facilitated in several ways. Survivors can benefit from even simple organizational efforts to create accessible resource areas in waiting areas or lobbies, stocked and up-to-date with relevant pamphlets and brochures from allied community organizations. Another option is to invite community partners to spend designated blocks of time to meet with survivors at the location of the domestic violence agency or emergency shelter; this option has been popularly received by both community partners and survivors. With this approach, survivors sign up for appointment slots or come on a drop-in basis to complete an initial consultation with a community organization, such as with credit counseling services or employment assistance programs. In my experience, survivors significantly benefit from such facilitated opportunities to connect with independent insurance agents and financial advisers. Without the concern of obligation to provide personal contact information or sit through uncomfortable sales pitches, survivors often report feeling safer to access and engage these financial professionals within the context of the domestic violence program setting.

I found tremendous success in partnering with local home-ownership advocacy programs to deliver financial education series. Staff are generally eager to work with survivors and increase their program's reach in the community. Many of these programs provide additional asset-building opportunities such as matched-savings accounts, fee waivers, or individual development accounts (IDAs), and they are often willing to partner with groups that can enhance their program's impact.

Organizations can forge alliances with staffing agencies and workforce development programs to enrich survivors' access to employment-related financial empowerment resources across a community. Through such collaborations, I have seen ideas and efforts creatively combined across diverse sectors to support the overall empowerment of women overcoming domestic violence (like the empowering relationships discussed in chapter 3). In one circumstance, working with a corporate staffing agency to hold a day-long employment seminar provided more than one hundred survivors with job-seeking strategies and direct connections to employers. Because of the success of this initial event, the employment seminar has since continued as an annual event and, over the past decade, has expanded to include a fashion show that highlights the "dos and don'ts" of professional attire and provides vouchers for women to receive clothing that is appropriate for professional interviews. Resource and job fairs, as well as employment seminars, present excellent opportunities to enhance collaborative relationships and leverage resources to connect survivors to financial empowerment experiences.

Working in collaboration with corporate partners (e.g., financial institutions, corporate staffing agencies) to best support the financial empowerment of domestic violence survivors will undoubtably entail a learning process for all vested parties. These collaborative efforts also offer opportunities for domestic violence organizations to train industry professionals and inform community partners regarding how to understand, address, and respond to issues that survivors often face. For example, domestic violence organizations can help financial institutions develop protocols to minimize opportunities for someone to use their systems to perpetrate financial abuse, whether through coerced loan applications or by controlling joint accounts (see further discussion in chapter 6).

Professionals working in employment contexts can benefit from training on identifying the signs of domestic abuse and developing supportive policies and practices to ensure the safety of survivors and their coworkers. When employers are responsive to domestic violence, they are well positioned to help individuals seeking to leave abusive relationships by working with their payroll systems to help victims save portions of their paycheck for future needs. Moreover, employers can also use security measures to prepare responses in the case of an abusive partner disrupting the survivor's workplace or harassing the survivor. If a company operates several worksites in varied locations throughout a community, they can offer to relocate a survivor to a safer worksite, keeping the location confidential. Employers play a vital role in the safety and empowerment of survivors and their families.

Expanding Organizational Capacity to Advance Financial Empowerment

The life skills model presents far more opportunities than challenges to delivering financial empowerment, but it also exists in a particular bubble at a distance from core advocacy services. Generally, only a small percentage of survivors participating in support and education groups also receives ongoing assistance from advocates. An unspoken assumption seemingly exists among many advocates that holds that a survivor is ready to participate in support groups only when she is no longer in crisis; in other words, once survivors are no longer actively working with advocates, then survivors are ready to move on to support and education groups. As a result, the life skills model has limited reach. Without front-line advocates adopting the life skills model, they lose the ability to actively address financial abuse and economic factors with survivors who are initially seeking safety, independence, or empowerment due to an immediate crisis.

The life skills model is also at risk of existing in a programmatic silo. Without intentional collaboration with a substantial cross-section of the entire organization, this model does not reach far enough to influence broad organizational cultures, practices, or services as a whole. On its own, the life skills model is limited in its ability to advance overall empowerment for survivors navigating the entirety of the organization. The life skills model is best for promoting financial empowerment through existing education and support programs and can be substantially expanded from this vantage point to address a broad range of financial empowerment avenues. However, it is necessary to engage advocates working on the front lines to integrate financial empowerment into core services if organizations are going to be successful in their efforts to include financial empowerment interventions as a standard practice.

Domestic violence organizations seeking to expand their scope of services to prioritize both safety *and* empowerment will need to achieve a cultural shift for such an evolution to be possible, much less a success. Given the inherent emphasis on safety over empowerment ingrained in the architecture of most domestic violence organizations, it is reasonable to expect some resistance to shifts toward adopting financial empowerment interventions. Rather than meeting resistance as challenges to be fought or overcome, accepting and acknowledging areas of resistance as potential opportunities will help practitioners and their organizations to smoothly traverse unanticipated learning curves. Engaging multiple stakeholders in the organizational change process can help to identify the areas within an organization in which financial empowerment is already happening and build on existing efforts to influence the organization's future practices.

Understanding Advocates' Resistance as a Growth Opportunity

Front-line advocates work directly with a high number of survivors to address a variety of issues and in diverse contexts, including shelters, legal and personal advocacy, and family support programs. Advocates are enthusiastic about the general idea of empowerment: they want to see survivors become empowered, and therefore, advocates frequently become deeply invested in the overall well-being of the survivors and the families in their programs. Advocates receive great satisfaction when survivors achieve safety and readily celebrate survivors' strengths, accomplishments, and successes. However, front-line advocates can also generate powerful tides of resistance in organizations that are working to integrate financial empowerment practices into their existing services.

Areas of resistance are not barriers. Rather, areas of resistance offer excellent places in which to anchor empowerment work. I have grown to love a quote I have heard often attributed to Louise Hay: "Resistance is the first step to change." This statement wonderfully speaks to the value of engaging resistance—not as an obstacle but as a vital component of the change process, especially in the early stages. I found that in the initial stages of introducing financial empowerment in organizations, it was vital to regularly attend different department meetings, experience diverse support groups, shadow advocates assisting survivors in various contexts, participate in cross-training opportunities, and—most important—listen to the insights and concerns of front-line advocates. Knowing the terrain of the organization, including its programs and practices, is a foundational step in mapping the necessary groundwork for financial empowerment efforts to take root and grow.

Skilled but overextended advocates might initially be hesitant to adopt financial empowerment strategies simply because they might find the idea of making large changes daunting. Most advocates are underpaid despite working long hours, and most take the mental and emotional loads of their work home with them. I have heard many advocates who were feeling overwhelmed themselves voice their fear that addressing too many issues beyond immediate safety concerns might overburden their clients as well as overwhelm their caseloads. Such worries are backed by advocates' good intentions and sound reasoning, as well as their concerns that survivors moving through recent or ongoing traumatic experiences are not ready to address their finances, much less their empowerment goals.

Advocates' skepticism might be rooted in their own insecurities about their finances or their lack of knowledge regarding financial tools and resources available in the community. Advocates might even fear that they are ultimately ineffective in supporting the financial empowerment process of survivors. In addition, advocates' earlier training experiences might have been rooted in the traditional direct-service crisis models, which taught them to prioritize short-term crisis interventions for survivors who are immediately seeking safety and assistance, rather than envisioning these efforts in context with survivors' empowerment goals. All of these factors are important to address.

Engaging advocates' resistance with curiosity will help organizations reframe conceptualizations of financial empowerment in light of existing strategies and practices commonly shared among advocates. Moreover, this open approach will lay the groundwork to firmly anchor financial empowerment in existing service areas. Practitioners should adopt a strengths-based approach and welcome resistance as an opportunity to listen to concerns from front-line staff and identify the supportive resources advocates need to feel willing and able to incorporate financial empowerment into their practices and services. This approach affirms advocates' capacities, capabilities, and qualities to practice financial empowerment advocacy. This approach also includes advocates' input and feedback in the design and development of adaptations in service delivery. When those who are working on the front lines are empowered to contribute in processes of designing and developing larger organizational programs, practices, and policies, the outcomes are likely to be more responsive to the unique cultural and practical realities in their communities.

Identifying Existing Financial Empowerment Advocacy Practices

I have consistently found that advocates take financial abuse and financial safety into account (at least to some extent) as a standard component of the safety-planning procedures they do with survivors. Advocates are keenly aware that survivors experience financial abuse as part of domestic violence and are at risk of losing access to whatever financial resources or support they might have had (see chapter 1 for a discussion of this risk). Advocates know that a survivor's efforts to regain personal power might lead to an escalation of abuse by a partner seeking to maintain or regain control over her.

During the safety-planning process, advocates often draw from a survivor's experiences of various forms of abuse to identify uniquely tailored safety strategies. Advocates take into consideration the extent of a survivor's financial dependency on her abusive partner as well as factors affecting the survivor's physical, emotional, and financial safety. Throughout the safety-planning process, advocates commonly help survivors anticipate or navigate obstacles erected by partners who refuse financial support for children, withdraw funds from joint bank accounts, withhold payments of shared financial obligations, or sabotage the survivor's employment. Advocates can work with survivors over long periods to help them establish independence; however, advocates recognize that abuse can continue even when an abusive partner no longer has direct contact or access to a survivor. Advocates also understand that finances are a common resource manipulated by abusive partners to coerce survivors into dropping a restraining order, not cooperating with criminal court proceedings, or returning to the abusive relationship. In addition, advocates often help connect survivors to basic financial empowerment resources such as child care, affordable housing, and job-readiness programs.

Advocates already listen for financial factors, including financial abuse, as central components informing the specific strategies and resources they choose to use with each individual survivor. Determining the financial resources a survivor can access as well as the extent of control the abusive partner has over such resources will influence an advocate's intervention strategies. Whether a survivor is currently employed or if she has concerns about being able to safely maintain employment due to harassment or stalking will affect an advocate's approaches to safety planning and referral processes. When survivors disclose circumstances in which a partner is refusing promised child care or using child protective services or custody disputes to perpetuate further hurt and harm, advocates factor this information into how they problem-solve issues, from helping to secure safe child-care arrangements to navigating systems or court processes.

Advocates can guide the process of formalizing an organization's procedural standards to assess for financial abuse, develop financial safety plans, and incorporate financial empowerment practices that are already used in their routine advocacy efforts with survivors. For example, while assessing survivors, advocates frequently prefer to ask particular questions and pose them in a specific order; by adding questions about financial abuse, advocates can gain a fuller understanding of a survivor's financial strengths, resources, and vulnerabilities without overwhelming survivors or overstepping their boundaries. Questions such as, "How does your partner impact your financial situation?" or "How has your financial situation with your partner, or anyone else, impacted your safety?" can be gentle exploratory inquiries to help assess for potential financial abuse. Advocates know the questions to ask that will inadvertently open the door to elicit sensitive details from survivors: advocates also know which questions might shut down the conversation or could be culturally inappropriate to even ask. For example, open-ended questions such as, "How do you feel about your money situation?" or "What are your biggest financial concerns?" might be received as less intrusive inquiries regarding a survivor's financial resources than asking questions directly related to income, such as, "What are your sources of income?" or "How much money do you currently make?" Developing standards for advocates to ask survivors about their immediate goals while following up with future-oriented questions (e.g., "Where would you like to be a year from now?" and "What kinds of support would you find helpful in reaching your goals?") can help advocates to better respond to the issues the survivor has prioritized and to assist survivors in imagining what their empowerment process could look like (see additional screening and assessment strategies in chapter 1).

Advocates routinely connect survivors to resources to minimize the survivors' dependency on abusive partners and increase their financial independence. Frequently, as a part of their advocacy practices, advocates make the case for financial assistance on behalf of survivors. In their pleas for financial assistance for survivors, advocates often highlight survivors' strengths and hopes, the financial resources they might or might not have access to, the survivors' current financial picture and budget, any ongoing patterns of financial abuse they might face, and the reasons why assistance will be of vital benefit. Advocates also work to identify long-term strategies for survivors to independently secure financial resources in the future. Advocates often come together to troubleshoot options and share strategies and resources so that survivors can feel prepared and empowered in accessing financial resources or navigating systems on their own.

Frequently, financial empowerment advocacy is something advocates are already doing in practice, often informing the processes by which they do advocacy. Celebrating the creative and compassionate ways advocates already engage in the practice of financial empowerment can prepare fertile groundwork for organizations to build on the principles, practices, and protocols that are already embedded and sown into their existing service models.

Including Advocates in the Design of Standardized Assessment Tools and Response Protocols

Organizations shifting to incorporate financial empowerment interventions into core advocacy services will need to formalize assessment tools to identify survivors' experiences with financial abuse and develop response protocols to address safety risks (including financial risks) impacting survivors. Throughout the process of creating standard procedures, documents, and staff training protocols, it is constructive to ask advocates about the strategies they regularly use to identify and respond to financial factors in all stages of their work with survivors. Engaging advocates in the design of formalized assessment tools will help incorporate standard organizational or program practices for gathering information pertaining to financial abuse, as well as identify survivors' financial strengths, resources, and vulnerabilities. This approach will guide organizations to integrate financial empowerment into key service provisions while acknowledging the best practices of their front-line advocates.

Interfacing with front-line advocates throughout various programs within an organization helps to identify and amass pertinent information that is valuable for survivors who are navigating specific services or systems:

- Advocates gain unique insights into the challenges survivors often face in accessing supportive resources.
- Advocates are aware of the eligibility requirements to access particular financial resources and can steer survivors away from the resources they will not be eligible to receive, which can save time and frustration.
- Advocates often prepare survivors to anticipate a range of specific questions they are likely to be asked when applying for financial assistance, what the process entails, and how long the process might take. In this context, advocates empower survivors to become their own advocates.

- Advocates help formalize referral processes and develop tools to connect survivors with direct routes to access specific services.
- Advocates develop working relationships with direct-service providers to ultimately help empower survivors to effectively advocate for themselves.
- Advocates direct informal referral processes by pooling the names and individual contact information of key persons who can directly assist in particular matters.

Advocates' collective insights benefit survivors as well as advocates because, rather than individual affinities, the relationships that advocates build with key persons in their local area become shared community alliances. By asking advocates to assess their current knowledge and to share their insights regarding financial empowerment resources available in the community, organizations can prioritize and strategize future partnerships.

Empowering Advocates with Financial Education

Organizations working to become increasingly responsive to financial abuse will need to mandate comprehensive education for advocacy staff on the various forms and consequences of financial abuse (see chapter 1), including economic control, employment sabotage, and economic exploitation. In addition, organizations should identify assessment tools they will use or draw from to illuminate trends among the survivors they serve and to identify strategies to best respond to those trends. Such measurement and assessment tools can help advocates and programs identify the unique financial issues that individual survivors face. This process can also help organizations identify life-generated risks (e.g., poverty, discrimination, health issues, negative environmental conditions, inadequate system responses) that are uniquely facing individual survivors and ensure that standard practices are inclusive of culturally sensitive intervention strategies.

Most of us in this field do not have finance or business degrees. Financial empowerment—having the knowledge, skills, and access to resources to support oneself and one's family—is something every human being deserves, including advocates. Because advocates are often compensated more with a sense of purpose than they are with paychecks, it is crucial that domestic violence organizations take the time and resources to address the financial awareness and the economic health and well-being of the individuals they employ. The majority of advocates I have worked with have expressed financial concerns of their own, often feeling ill equipped to manage their own economic well-being and long-term goals. As emphasized earlier, advocates do not need to be financial experts. However, without receiving additional instruction related to financial empowerment, advocates will be limited in how well they can incorporate financial empowerment strategies.

It is difficult, if not impossible, for anyone to educate or empower another without being first educated and empowered with the very tools they are expected to pass on. Some financial skills, especially budgeting and saving strategies, are tools that can benefit anyone. As suggested in chapter 4, introducing advocates to financial tools can help empower them professionally and personally. Because advocates often have busy and chaotic schedules, organizations can promote financial self-efficacy of their staff by regularly inviting financial professionals to speak at staff meetings on issues such as insurance, retirement, or long-term investment strategies. Occasional lunch-and-learn sessions can focus on exploring a wide range of topics from couponing to employee benefits. The organization's leadership can invite external service providers across a variety of sectors to host in-service training sessions to help empower staff to practice, as well as pass on, financial empowerment strategies.

Financial empowerment need not be daunting or burdensome to advocates. Creating opportunities for staff and advocates to formally or informally come together to share financial information, skills, and resources can be an effective means to promote financial empowerment practices across the organizational culture. Once advocates are more attuned and confident in navigating the economic challenges in their own lives, this confidence can strengthen their ability to support the financial empowerment of the survivors they encounter.

Crafting Cross-System Partnerships

Crafting partnerships with diverse entities, specifically with organizations providing services addressing the economic realities facing survivors, strengthens both direct-service staff and survivors. These partnerships often help advocates wrap community supports around survivors to assist them with their immediate needs and long-term goals. When supported by formal partnerships, front-line staff are more likely to feel confident encouraging clients to access additional support from community agencies matched to their needs. In working in conjunction with partnering services, advocates are able to support survivors in obtaining safety and achieving financial security, without overwhelming themselves in the process. Such partnerships promote financial empowerment on the macro level and serve to support survivors' financial self-sufficiency on the micro level (identified in chapter 4). To increase financial empowerment on both micro and macro levels, organizations can work with specific programs focusing on asset building and saving, job assistance, education, or microloans and microenterprise opportunities, or they can work with larger financial institutions, criminal justice systems, or government-funded human service agencies.

Partnerships with government-funded human service agencies ultimately assist survivors to better access and navigate these systems. Collaborations create opportunities to increase advocates' understandings of local and state policies affecting survivors' eligibility or requirements to access resources. These formal organizational relationships also have the potential to yield larger system interventions, to increase access for survivors, and to create survivor-sensitive policy changes.

For example, domestic violence organizations that partner with agencies overseeing the federally funded TANF program will find many benefits for survivors from this partnership. To receive public benefits and financial assistance, federal law requires applicants with children to cooperate with child-support enforcement programs. However, individual states are allowed to craft their own specific policies and practices to exempt survivors from this requirement if they fear their safety will be jeopardized or they will be put at increased risk. Each state has the ability both to develop domestic violence assessment tools and to modify participation requirements so that domestic violence survivors are not penalized for prioritizing their safety and/or the safety of their children over adherence to program requirements. When domestic violence organizations collaborate with state-level policy makers and administrators, these organizations are well positioned to directly influence their state's specific policies and practices by advocating for those whom they serve.

When advocates are informed about state-specific policies affecting survivors applying for public benefits, the advocates are better equipped to advocate for survivors and empower survivors to advocate for themselves. In the case of TANF, case managers are allowed to modify service plans to include domestic violence services in lieu of work activities, lifting time limits and adjusting activity requirements to include participation in support groups, time spent obtaining medical or mental health care, and attending required court appearances. To qualify for such modifications, domestic violence survivors must provide documented proof of the abuse, such as police reports or orders of protection. However, advocates are permitted to help survivors draft sworn statements or complete a Domestic Violence Verification Form on behalf of survivors to confirm that they are participating in a domestic violence program as proof of their status to qualify for any exemptions. When survivors know what they need to navigate public benefit programs, they are able to avoid unnecessary sanctions that can sabotage their efforts toward safety and financial security.

Most important, cross-system partnerships present organizations with opportunities to increase awareness of domestic violence as well as to institutionalize safe interventions on the behalf of survivors. Through partnerships, such as in the case with TANF, direct-service professionals can deepen relationships across systems, especially during coordinated meetings or cross-training opportunities. Building relationships between case managers and advocates ensures that survivors can more easily access these programs and are prepared to advocate for themselves in the process. Further, cross-system partnerships facilitate opportunities for service providers in various systems to team up on behalf of the survivors navigating those systems.

Organizations can formalize partnerships with fellow service providers by crafting service agreements such as a memorandum of understanding and drafting release forms for survivors to permit advocates to coordinate with external partners on their behalf. These partnerships can run the gamut of collaborations that aim to increase and ease survivors' access to resources relating to a variety of economic needs, including food, clothing, housing, health care, employment support, and legal advocacy. I have also found that formalizing partnerships both facilitates survivors' access to resources *and* leverages resources to support survivors in obtaining their intended outcomes; formalized partnerships have been particularly beneficial for survivors seeking to access to asset-building opportunities, microenterprise programs, employment assistance, and financial services. For example, domestic violence organizations can partner with local financial institutions to create matched-savings programs and to raise funds to provide ongoing support for such efforts as well as to facilitate survivors' access to financial tools and services (e.g., banking and checking accounts). Not only do these partnerships increase opportunities for survivors to increase self-sufficiency, but they can also simultaneously build community alliances that are committed to leading the way in advancing financial empowerment efforts on behalf of those who are victimized by domestic violence.

Engaging Survivors to Lead Financial Empowerment Efforts

Listening to Survivors to Guide Organizational Practices and Priorities

Organizations should ensure that efforts to enhance financial empowerment are responsive to the specific realities survivors face and include survivors in strategic planning processes. Survivors will provide valuable perspectives, and their insights should help inform the practices, programs, goals, and funding priorities of organizations responding to domestic violence. Survivor-responsive organizations and interventions can better meet the multifaceted needs of survivors with varied experiences and diverse backgrounds. Survivor-responsive strategies prevent the risk of domestic violence organizations unintentionally eclipsing the voices, experiences, and needs of marginalized persons. When informed by diverse domestic violence populations, survivor-responsive financial empowerment strategies can be customized for and delivered to survivors from diverse backgrounds and within specific communities (as discussed in chapter 4). Together with survivors, organizational leadership can engage in the challenge of addressing inequalities within the domestic violence movement itself and work toward developing inclusive, dynamic programming and organizational leadership policies, practices, and structures with greater racial/ethnic, cultural, linguistic, and developmental diversity.

Listening to survivors will also help organizations gain a greater understanding of the terrain of available financial resources that are most frequently accessed in the community and identify which resources are most beneficial, most challenging to access, or seemingly nonexistent. Understanding how survivors navigate available community resources along with their interactions with specific programs will help organizations illuminate where service gaps exist or where they can avoid service duplications. Survivors' insights will help organizations illuminate their programmatic strengths, limitations, and areas for growth or improvements. Asking survivors to identify how well current services are meeting, or are failing to meet, their immediate economic needs, which are vital to safety, can help organizations adapt their programs and practices to increasingly address financial factors in their front-line interventions. Inquiring how services can be improved to support survivors' long-term goals will be valuable in guiding the development of financial empowerment programs.

Organizations can also engage survivors not only to assess what information, skills, and resources are common knowledge among survivors but also to identify misinformation or misperceptions that might be circulating in their community. Such insights will help service providers educate survivors on financial matters and teach survivors how to access and utilize community supports to their best advantage. These insights can also guide organizations to identify needed community partnerships and to comprehensively address both the economic and safety needs of the survivors they serve.

Survivors' voices can be captured in a variety of ways and should be factored in at each level of programming to identify interventions that are best matched to each specific domestic violence service area. Financial empowerment in the context of a shelter environment will probably look different from the way it looks in the context of legal advocacy. Mechanisms to gather survivors' perspectives can range from needs-assessment surveys to focus groups. These opportunities should be voluntary and must ensure participants' safety and confidentiality for survivors to speak truthfully and openly.

Supporting Survivor-Led Financial Education

Given that one in four women experience physical violence at the hands of an intimate partner and nearly half of women in the United States experience psychological aggression by an intimate partner (see chapter 1), it is likely that some financial professionals will also identify themselves as survivors of domestic violence. By focusing volunteer recruitment strategies on professionals in the finance sector who also willingly identify as survivors, organizations can further incorporate survivor leadership as a central component in the delivery of their financial education programs.

Early on in my efforts to provide financial education in groups, I spent an afternoon calling various financial institutions to recruit banking professionals who were willing to present on financial resources available in the surrounding neighborhood. After being repeatedly directed to leave voice messages, I was eventually connected directly to the vice president of a locally owned bank, an African American woman who enthusiastically agreed to present to one of our groups. The night this bank executive came to present, our area was on the tail end of a snowstorm, so participants were arriving later than usual and it was a challenge to get the group settled. At the time, we had just started to hold financial education in groups once a month, and the group members had not yet taken to the idea of turning their attention to a stranger; they needed time to discuss pressing personal issues and connect with one another. (I learned, over time, to always hold space for this process and invite guest speakers to come thirty minutes after the start of group.)

While everyone was busy talking, I noticed our presenter quietly at the edge of the room with a reserved energy I originally mistook for annoyance. The longer the group talked, the more worried and guilty I felt, imagining that we were disrespecting the precious and valuable time of this important person. When everyone finally settled, she began her presentation and surprised every single person in the room. She shared that, in stark contrast to the annoyance I had mistakenly perceived, she had been during those past minutes deep in reflection about her own empowerment origins. She spoke on budgeting and banking and her own journey from bankruptcy to building a successful career in banking, but in her story, she also shared her own journey through domestic violence. She discussed her specific experiences of financial abuse, as her husband not only controlled the finances but, without her knowledge, made significant financial decisions that bankrupted their family. After leaving her husband, she focused her efforts on developing savviness in investing and real estate strategies to increase her personal assets, and she committed to pay her empowerment forward. She eventually became vice president of a bank in the neighborhood where she grew up, to help increase access to banking services and tackle economic discrimination in her community. She also dedicated herself to women's financial empowerment and economic justice efforts, eventually leading a foundation that supports initiatives advancing equity for women and girls. In transforming her pain into power, she shared how she became a "thriver" as well as a survivor. After the session, she expressed how much it meant to share her journey with survivors who were just at the beginning of their own paths to transformation.

Survivors who are just beginning to navigate the initial stages of empowerment should, whenever and as often as possible, be presented with stories of what becomes possible when survivors are empowered. When survivors are allied in financial empowerment education and efforts, they model what is possible and provide hope for other survivors. When participants in financial empowerment opportunities relate personally to the financial professionals speaking to them, the participants are more likely to retain information and connect with new knowledge in meaningful ways. Centering survivors as leaders in financial education interventions helps transform financial empowerment as a channel for individual and collective empowerment, yielding inspiring outcomes.

Centering Survivors in Civic Engagement and Economic Justice Efforts

It is those who are actively working to break out of and put an end to cycles of violence, voicing their personal truths and demonstrating courageous fortitude, who truly carry the empowerment movement. Their stories hold valuable insight and highlight courage, heart, resilience, and hope. Domestic violence organizations should work to develop the leadership capabilities of survivors as allies and leaders in economic efforts on local, state, and national levels. Centering survivors as leaders guiding financial empowerment advocacy in the context of these social, political, and economic systems tasks people in leadership positions to make structural and systemic changes in policies and practices both in partnership with and responsive to survivors.

Organizations should support leadership development, enhance access to civic engagement opportunities, and center survivors and their perspectives in discussions pertaining to financial empowerment and economic justice. Organizations can seek to develop opportunities for survivors to develop, practice, and execute leadership skills in a variety of capacities. Mentoring programs can match volunteer professionals with survivors on the basis of survivor-identified personal, financial, and professional goals. Advisory councils, led by survivors, can be founded by organizations to ensure that survivors influence the current trajectories within the domestic violence movement. Organizations need to include survivors in training opportunities to represent and speak for themselves regarding their experiences with financial empowerment. Conference presentations should include survivors as panelists when possible, to engage survivors in the conversations leading financial empowerment advocacy efforts throughout the field.

Survivors should also be encouraged and prepared to address current legislative issues impacting survivors through ongoing public speaking and policy trainings at local and state levels. On both state and national levels, I have witnessed the powerful impacts of survivors using their stories as dynamic mechanisms to advocate for legislative protections for survivors. I have had the privilege of accompanying survivors throughout this process, and I can attest that these leadership opportunities are deeply healing and tremendously empowering experiences for survivors who are beginning to hear the power of their own voices again. Infinite possibilities exist for hope, healing, and creative innovation when survivors are centered as leaders in social, economic, and political justice efforts.

Expanding Interventions beyond Adult Survivors of Domestic Violence

Addressing financial empowerment from multiple vantage points expands opportunities not only to increase awareness of financial abuse as a form of domestic violence but also to identify the effect of financial abuse, break its intergenerational cycles, and ultimately enhance economic equality and justice. In addition to working with adult domestic violence survivors, I have acquired extensive experience working with children who have witnessed abuse and men who have been court ordered for domestic violence intervention services. The intersections of these particular vantage points have illuminated my understanding of the profound intergenerational impacts of domestic violence and the crucial importance of interventions aiming to interrupt cycles of abuse. This perspective has challenged me to expand my vision of financial empowerment efforts not only to educate and empower survivors but also to engage men and youth as part of these efforts.

A significant gap exists when it comes to engaging more men as allies and active change agents in efforts to eradicate domestic violence and its many forms, including financial abuse. Domestic violence practitioners need to involve men who have perpetrated abuse and promote strategies to help these men understand the short- and long-term effects of abuse on the lives of their partners and/or children, as well as to provide them with new insight and compassionate practices to interrupt their own abusive behavioral patterns and cycles of violence. Interventions need to engage men to reflect on their use of economic power and control within relationships as well as to learn healthy financial relationship behaviors, to commit to economic equality with partners, to support women's safety and financial empowerment, and to advocate for social, political, and economic justice.

Traditional gender roles are informed by patriarchal assumptions and expectations around who is responsible for providing financially in heteronormative households and who is responsible for domestic work, caregiving, and education (often in the form of unpaid labor). As I write this chapter two years into the COVID-19 pandemic, it is apparent that these assumptions still exist today. Gender socialization practices reinforce these norms. When masculinity is equated with the responsibility to financially provide for families and an entitled authority in decision-making, interventions with men will also have to challenge men's beliefs around gender roles and finances. Such efforts will have to interrupt gendered expectations tethering manhood to the ability to financially provide, rather than wholeheartedly nurture and care, for their children and families. Men need to come to value the nonmonetary ways they can contribute, to recognize the equal worth of various forms of labor both within and outside the home, and to practice shared decision-making in partnerships and equitable responsibility for duties in their households.

As part of the recovery efforts following this pandemic, men will be needed as allies to support policies and practices (e.g., paid leave, paid sick days, support for pregnant workers, family leave, affordable child care, etc.) that support women and working families. According to a McKinsey analysis of the Current Population Survey, conducted jointly by the U.S. Census Bureau and the U.S. Bureau of Labor Statistics, when schools resumed during the pandemic in September 2020, many of them with remote learning, 80 percent of the 1.1 million people (about the population of Montana) who exited the workforce were women. Combined with less pay and more expectations to manage domestic responsibilities, economic gender disparities have deepened in lockdown conditions, to the detriment of women. The pandemic has also exacerbated existing societal inequalities and amplified disparities upheld by systemic racism. Economic and social justice efforts will need to prioritize cisgender and transgender women and align with demands for racial justice to address the inequalities faced by Black people, indigenous people, and people of color and other marginalized communities. Justice efforts must be intersectional and comprehensive.

Financial empowerment interventions also need to include children and youth. I have heard the distress of countless survivors struggling to make ends meet or achieve financial goals that are in conflict with the desires of their children. Practitioners can work with survivors, along with their children, in family-led financial goal-setting activities and incorporate age-appropriate financial education in the process. Educating youth on financial literacy, including lessons on economic abuse, relationship equality, and how to have conversations about money, will prepare them to make safe and informed decisions for the benefit of themselves, their families, and their future relationships.

Although the shift toward financial empowerment has fortified strategies protecting women's rights to safety, well-being, and self-determination, more needs to be done beyond direct interventions with survivors. The continued growth of financial empowerment throughout the field of domestic violence depends on innovative interventions forged across a vast spectrum of populations, perspectives, programs, and positions. Creative and strategic collaborations can serve to challenge inequalities and advance philosophies and practices to cultivate justice and inspire positive personal and collective transformations. As practitioners increasingly come together in collaboration and creative innovation not only to listen and respond to the needs of survivors and their families but also to generate groundswells of support to address these needs, the possibilities for positive social, economic, and political change become endless.

CHAPTER 6

Call for Action

"Two of the women who were living with their abusers were surprised: They said, 'Wow I didn't know I could actually financially support myself and leave him because of these additional benefits that are coming in to support my children.'... It was kind of like a light bulb going off, it almost opened more doors for them, more choices so they felt like they weren't stuck."

—advocate (Postmus, Silva-Martinez, et al., 2013, p. 14)

Financial abuse, which makes survivors increasingly dependent on abusers, is a key tactic abusers use to exert power and control over their victims and trap the women in the relationships. This type of abuse is carried out through various strategies, ranging from economic control (i.e., a situation in which the abuser controls all financial decisions regarding the survivors' income and how household monies are spent) to economic exploitation (i.e., a situation in which the abuser exploits the financial standing of survivors, such as ruining her credit rating by not paying bills or by making late payments). Additionally, abusers use other strategies to hinder survivors' ability to support themselves financially, including causing disruptions in survivors' ability to work, sabotaging their work efforts, harassing them at their places of work, or preventing them from going to work or attending classes.

Various organizations have launched efforts to address financial abuse and to empower survivors by increasing their financial knowledge, economic self-efficacy, and economic self-sufficiency and also by assisting them to develop and expand assets as a pathway to financial independence from their abuser. Domestic violence organizations have led the efforts to financially empower survivors; however, other organizations and systems should step up and assume leading roles in efforts to empower survivors with financial knowledge and asset-building skills. It is critically important to expand the responsibility for financial empowerment to criminal justice systems, financial institutions, and the banking and housing industries because professionals and staff of these systems and industries are likely to encounter survivors of intimate partner violence in the course of their work. This chapter calls out to domestic violence organizations as well as other organizations and systems and provides recommendations on ways to financially empower survivors.

Call-Out to Domestic Violence Organizations

Domestic violence organizations have made great strides in incorporating financial empowerment strategies into their usual services for survivors; however, such efforts are still hampered by a number of barriers. A requisite first step in even coming close to providing financial empowerment for survivors demands that domestic violence organizations also give priority to the social and economic justice needs of survivors (Silva-Martinez et al., 2016). Such considerations include securing economic power at the individual and collective levels. Additionally, domestic violence organizations need to recognize the unique nature of their service provision, in that they not only provide immediate and short-term services such as crisis hotlines and emergency housing but also provide long-term services such as transitional housing, legal advocacy, and support groups. Delivering this spectrum of services is made even more complex given that services are frequently provided to survivors who have low incomes and are from diverse populations (i.e., racial/ethnic, immigrant, LGBTQ+, and abilities communities).

Research examining survivors' help-seeking behaviors has found that most survivors first seek help from informal sources such as family and friends and then turn to formal sources of help, including the following:

- Criminal and civil justice system (e.g., law enforcement, lawyers or paralegals helping with restraining orders)
- Social service agencies (e.g., counseling for the survivor or therapeutic play groups for her young children)
- Medical services, including medications for physical injuries or behavioral issues stemming from IPV experiences)
- Crisis counseling and support groups

- Mental health services
- Spiritual leaders (e.g., clergy, rabbis, imam, tribal faith leaders; Gordon, 1996; Postmus et al., 2009).

Unfortunately, many survivors have reported that formal services were not helpful and felt revictimized by having to recount their abuse history multiple times or felt that staff blamed them for some part of the abuse. The services that survivors most frequently perceived as helpful were those focused on material needs (e.g., child care, welfare, housing, food, job training, education; Bonica, 2000; Postmus et al., 2009). Although domestic abuse and its associated trauma impose emotional and cognitive challenges that survivors must address, these challenges are perhaps most effectively addressed after a survivor's physical, financial, and environmental needs are met. However, one study with domestic violence service providers found that survivors' financial challenges were not given priority or even given equal attention to other challenges (Bonica, 2000). Specifically, the study found that advocates reported that 40 percent or less of their time involved attention to financial empowerment, with only half of that time focused on helping survivors secure employment (Bonica, 2000).

Developing a new mind-set among domestic violence organizations to bring financial empowerment to the forefront, including greater attention to asset development and economic justice, will probably involve developing a protocol for identifying economic service needs (e.g., housing, employment, child care), finding appropriate and available services in the community, and addressing potential barriers survivors might encounter (Bonica, 2000). Other tasks might include collaborating with financial institutions, financial planners, financial consultants, and community-based organizations involved with programs that provide financial products (e.g., IDAs, microloans) or assistance with credit repair (Bonica, 2000; Silva-Martinez et al., 2016).

In the midst of addressing the financial challenges of survivors, domestic violence organizations must remember that their staff, service providers, and other advocates might be facing their own economic hardships and might need to be financially empowered as well (Silva-Martinez et al., 2016). Those who work in these organizations might also face ongoing struggles with balancing their own financial concerns while providing safety, emotional support, and financial empowerment to survivors. Therefore, in addition to identifying interventions that providers and advocates can use to financially empower survivors, it is also critically important to identify resources and supports for providers and advocates to use in their own process of achieving financial empowerment.

"We run, run, run, run, run. So you don't have a whole lot of time that you can sit down and really get more into it because the phone is always ringing, someone's coming in." —advocate (Silva-Martinez et al., 2016, p. 117)

Shifting an organizational culture from a strong focus on cognitive behavioral change to a focus on economic justice and financial matters presents additional challenges. The greatest challenge might be getting advocates to embrace the idea of change if they are already feeling overwhelmed with maintaining large caseloads, which forces advocates to operate in a "reactive" mode of crisis interventions (Silva-Martinez et al., 2016). For example, a research team asked advocates about their experiences with implementing The Allstate Foundation's *Moving Ahead through Financial Management* financial empowerment curriculum;[1] this sample of advocates reported that they were given the substantial responsibility of delivering the *Moving Ahead* curriculum without a reduction in their other responsibilities (Silva-Martinez et al., 2016).

Nevertheless, Silva-Martinez and colleagues (2016) found that advocates reported benefiting personally from their engagement with the financial empowerment curriculum, which provided advocates with the opportunity to role-model changes in their own financial behavior. Several advocates embraced the *Moving Ahead* content on a personal level and reported having conquered their own financial fears. Existing anecdotal evidence also indicates that when survivors shared their experiences while receiving the curriculum, they were also teaching the advocates. On numerous occasions, advocates stated that the information in the financial curriculum should be not only disseminated to survivors of IPV but also made widely available to all women. This thought was echoed repeatedly, underscoring the need to acknowledge financial literacy and economic empowerment as a tool for addressing a multiplicity of dimensions around economic equality for women, including those who work with survivors of IPV.

"I looked at my credit. I looked at my debt and stocks. I recognized I did have fears around money." —advocate (Silva-Martinez et al., 2016, p. 118)

Although the financial curriculum provided an opportunity for advocates to role-model positive financial behavior, many advocates also found that being a financial role-model was especially challenging because they lacked financial knowledge and were concerned and anxious about their personal financial status. To overcome their personal challenges, advocates turned to a key strategy of collaborating with other advocates or community members from the financial industry.

"If I wasn't sure about something they [survivors] were asking us, I'd say, 'You know what? I need to get back to you.'... If I had to, I called the bank and say, 'Okay, I had this come up, what do we do?'"

—advocate (Silva-Martinez et al., 2016, p. 118)

"We are going to be bringing in some professional people to talk about investments. I don't know enough about that myself to feel like I can share with anybody. If the women want, I've talked to a couple of local bankers, and they're more than willing to come in and work with us on that."

—advocate (Silva-Martinez et al., 2016, p. 118)

However, not all advocates shared the same positive reaction to implementing a financial empowerment curriculum as a primary service for survivors. Silva-Martinez and colleagues (2016) found that a few advocates expressed resistance to implementing financial empowerment services. Specifically, these advocates reported believing that a financial empowerment curriculum was irrelevant to the survivors' hierarchy of needs, especially survivors in crisis, because the information was not needed during a crisis point. However, these advocates did not articulate their perception of a survivor's hierarchy of needs, particularly if financial literacy was not an urgent need. Instead, these advocates reported relying on their experience and personal beliefs about what survivors need.

"Women in crisis—it [the curriculum] is too much because they are not at a point in which they can begin with this information. Once out of the crisis and they are settled, then we can begin on this information, . . . when they are transitioning out of the shelter."

—advocate (Silva-Martinez et al., 2016, p. 120)

Other barriers to shifting financial empowerment to the forefront of domestic violence services include obstacles that could be resolved if the domestic violence organization provides additional resources. For example, providing on-site child care during financial classes might help with survivors' ability to attend and be attentive to the presentations. Additionally, advocates also identified challenges that arise when survivors have been involved with the criminal justice system and have been incarcerated. A history of incarceration can create added layers of barriers, especially related to housing and employment. These additional barriers can substantially increase the difficulty of financial empowering survivors who have been incarcerated.

"Women who have been incarcerated, their biggest concern is how to get a job, plus restitution and court fees, bill, and some kind of charge. Even talking about money, they get mad. They can't even talk about it because they don't have anything. . . . They are discouraged."

—advocate (Silva-Martinez et al., 2016, p. 120)

Another reason for advocates' mixed feelings about the curriculum, which contributed to variance in implementation of the modules, was rooted in advocates lacking a depth of knowledge around certain financial management topics. Not surprisingly, these deficits in financial knowledge created anxiety for advocates tasked with delivering the content to survivors, and in turn, advocates tended to avoid these topics. Although many advocates said they were comfortable with the content, when further pressed about the content delivered, it became clear that advocates were teaching certain fundamental issues (e.g., budgeting) but were not teaching more complex topics (e.g., stocks and bonds, education funds). Avoiding complex topics is understandable given that many advocates are underpaid or receive fairly low wages (Behounek, 2011). Hence, many advocates not only have personal financial situations that might not be much better than their clients but also might have limited experience with those more complex topics.

Findings from the advocate interviews corroborated an existing need to promote financial literacy as a strategy for economic empowerment with survivors and also to encourage financial literacy for all women in general, including advocates. One way to promote financial literacy is through collective identification because empowerment for individual women depends on collective efforts, particularly in regard to financial empowerment (Fraser, 1989). In essence, domestic violence organizations can promote financial empowerment for the women receiving services as well as for the women providing services. This approach requires organizations to include financial education for both advocates and survivors in all facets of their programming, including shelter, nonresidential services, and transitional housing.

What is the bottom line? Domestic violence organizations should expand traditional domestic violence services to include financial empowerment for both survivors and staff. Given the acknowledged low wages and high turnover rates of staff working in community-based nonprofit domestic violence organizations, these organizations should provide financial literacy education to all staff as an employment benefit. Indeed, in our discussions with advocates, several reported that in delivering the financial empowerment curriculum to survivors, they became aware of their own deficits in financial management skills, especially around budgeting, savings, and credit scores.

"Because of the [financial management] curriculum, . . . budgeting makes more sense to me now, and I actually opened a savings account. I don't have a lot in it, but I opened a savings account."

—advocate (Postmus, Silva-Martinez, et al., p. 23)

"I think it was like I wasn't interested. I was like, 'It is fine. It should be fine.' You know, 'I'm good, don't worry.' And I actually, after I did the [financial management] curriculum, . . . I went into the website and got my credit score, and there was actually something that I should not have had. I didn't know that it was there, and I had to take care of those two things. And I did it. They are gone now. . . . Well, actually, I never got my credit report before."

—advocate (Postmus, Silva-Martinez, et al., p. 23)

Call-Out to Personal Financial Management and Banking Industries

Financial abuse exacts an emotional and financial toll from survivors. In particular, survivors are often left with crushing debt, low credit scores, and few or no assets to start life away from the abuser. Despite the prevalence of financial abuse, the financial industry has shown limited awareness of the challenges that survivors face, with many survivors reporting that their interactions with people in the financial industry have been unhelpful and unproductive (Smallwood, 2015). The negative effects of these unhelpful interactions can be compounded if survivors have limited knowledge of their financial rights during and after leaving abusive relationships. At the same time, the financial industry has shown little willingness to support survivors in recovering from financial abuse; instead, the industry insists on its right to enforce joint debts, putting survivors at greater risk of limited financial recovery (Smallwood, 2015).

Although domestic violence organizations will always have the lead role in supporting survivors emotionally and teaching financial management skills, the efforts of these organizations should receive support through collaborations and partnerships with banks, credit unions, and other sectors of the financial industry. Collaborative strategies include financial abuse training for all employees of financial institutions, with the aim of improving awareness and understanding of financial abuse and equipping a vast army of employees to detect financial abuse and respond appropriately by linking survivors with domestic violence organizations. Moreover, the financial abuse training should increase the cooperative attitude among the financial industry so interactions with survivors are more productive toward strengthening survivors' credit and providing data for criminal and civil cases.

Understanding and Detecting Financial Abuse

It is imperative that the financial industry has a strong understanding of all forms of domestic violence—especially financial abuse—and awareness of signs that someone might be experiencing abuse. First, the financial industry should not assume that financial abuse in an intimate relationship is the same as elder abuse, identity theft, or financial fraud. The key to differentiating financial abuse from other types of financial fraud is the abuser's intent in using this tactic. Financial abusers may not be primarily focused on taking a partner's money for personal gain but rather intent on using financially abusive tactics to control, exploit, or sabotage the financial standing of an intimate partner as a means of keeping the partner dependent on the abuser and, thus, trapped in the relationship.

Second, the financial industry should ensure that employees at each level are kept aware of changes in the laws regarding domestic violence. Although the United States has yet to make financial abuse a crime, several countries have proposed revisions to domestic violence laws to be more comprehensive and include financial abuse as a criminal act. For example, the United Kingdom passed a coercive control law that covers multiple types of abuse, including financial abuse. Although the U.S. financial industry does not have to comply with UK laws, financial institutions often have a global presence, with divisions located in the United Kingdom or other countries with similar comprehensive domestic violence laws. In countries with such laws, financial institutions could be involved in court cases addressing financial abuse, providing evidence of financial abuse, or answering inquiries regarding their knowledge of ongoing abuse and efforts to prevent escalation of financial abuse.

Finally, the financial industry should consider expanding work to identify survivors and give them the tools to become empowered. Survivors are customers of financial institutions, and therefore, helping survivors not only is good customer service but also projects a positive image of the institution as a good community member guided by a moral compass.

With this understanding of the role that financial institutions need to take, the employees of these institutions are well positioned to identify the signs of potential financial abuse as part of their routine interactions with their customers. Signs of potential financial abuse can include the following:

- A customer reports restricted spending and limited access to finances.
- A couple shows evident problems around joint finances, whether earnings or savings, as well as when one partner takes complete control of the accounts (e.g., removes the other partner's name from accounts; Telford, 2020).
- A customer applies for credit cards or loans in the other partner's name.
- A customer accumulates debt in suspicious ways (i.e., the other partner is unaware of the debt).
- A customer shows unusual shopping behaviors with unexplained charges.
- A customer has a sudden change in work habits or locations.

These signs are possible indicators of financial abuse but do not automatically mean that financial abuse is happening in a customer's relationship. For example, many reasons could explain a sudden shift in work location or unusual shopping behaviors. Indeed, credit card companies have instituted security protocols that flag suspicious spending and alert customers to such charges. However, sometimes the activity or behavior is an indicator of financial abuse. As such, a first step for financial institutions is to develop a guide for front-line employees with customer contact who are likely to observe the signs of financial abuse. This resource would help front-line employees develop greater awareness of the signs of financial abuse and know how to respond to and support customers who might be experiencing financial abuse (current and postseparation; Sharp-Jeffs, 2015b). To be an effective resource, the guide should include definitions of financial abuse, examples of the strategies and tactics abusers use in financial abuse, the ways this type of abuse can impact survivors, and what customers can do if they or someone they love might be a victim of such abuse.

The only way to determine if financial abuse is happening is to ask a potential victim. Asking about abuse seems like a straightforward approach to determining if such abuse exists; however, this question is difficult for the individual doing the asking and for the person being asked. Moreover, it can be equally difficult for an employee in a financial institution to find an appropriate time and setting to ask a customer this question. Advocates have suggested some best practices when asking difficult questions, which include asking about potential abuse in direct and indirect ways. Direct ways of asking include questions such as the following:

"Do you believe you are in control of your money?"
"Are you part of decisions being made around money?"
"Do you feel safe in your home? Do you feel safe around how money is spent?"

With difficult questions, it sometimes helps to contextualize the question, such as, "Many women experience all forms of abuse in this country, so I routinely ask these questions." However, those who are asking these questions must remember that financial abuse is not widely understood as a form of abuse and that many survivors are unaware that they are being abused in this way. Asking, "Are you a victim of financial abuse?" is likely to result in many answers of "no." Instead of a direct question about financial abuse, a better approach is to talk about the different ways abusers control their partners around financial management.

Advocates consulting with organizations toward developing guides to understand and detect financial abuse can help identify indirect ways of communicating information about abuse. For example, some organizations hang posters or pictures defining financial abuse in clearly visible places in the building. Some leave brochures on financial abuse in multiple places in public areas as well on the desks of employees with customer contact. Additionally, some companies post information regarding financial abuse on their websites, which can be a valuable source of information for customers who rarely come into a brick-and-mortar bank branch. By letting customers know that the financial institution and its employees understand financial abuse and care about their customers' safety, this guide will help financial institutions (and related businesses such as accountants and tax preparers) provide a "safe zone" for customers to talk about abuse as well as be a resource to refer survivors to domestic violence organizations or other services.

Most importantly, advocates working with financial institutions will need to emphasize—repeatedly—that a survivor's safety is always a primary concern. Guides on detecting financial abuse should include a cautionary note for financial institutions and employees: be careful of the setting and context in which you ask about abuse. If in person, make sure that you are alone with the customer and do not ask about potential abuse in front of the partner. If online, ensure that the website design includes safety strategies such as a safe exit button that immediately closes the website and removes it from the browsing history. Finally, develop a protocol to guide the response of individuals and the organization when a customer reports financial abuse; such protocols should specify immediate action steps to direct the customer to trained staff or teams who specialize in handling cases of financial abuse and ensuring the customer's safety (Sharp-Jeffs, 2015a).

All efforts toward understanding and detecting financial abuse constitute the first step for the financial industry to support its customers dealing with such abuse. The next step is to partner with domestic violence organizations.

Partnering with Domestic Violence Organizations

What happens if a bank manager learns that a customer is experiencing financial or other forms of abuse? Because people in the financial industry are highly likely to encounter victims of domestic abuse in the course of their routine duties, especially front-line employees with substantial customer contact, the best strategy for financial institutions is to partner with domestic violence organizations. Such partnerships should be established at the national and local levels. These partnerships are crucial, given that banking customers might tell bank employees about financial abuse experiences, and therefore, all bank staff will need to know where and to whom they should refer a customer who discloses possible financial abuse or other forms of domestic violence. Partnering with a local domestic violence organization not only can give financial institutions access to advocates who can provide staff with education on financial abuse but also can establish a safe network for referring customers who are experiencing abuse.

Additionally, domestic violence organizations need support from the financial industry. As a partner with a domestic violence organization, financial institutions can provide financial education and other financial empowerment services to advocates and survivors. For example, domestic violence organizations and financial institutions might partner in information-sharing seminars, with staff from each partner organization teaching their expertise. Staff from domestic violence organizations can share information on financial abuse and other forms of abuse, and in turn, staff of financial institutions can share information on financial management practices as well as support advocates' efforts to provide survivors with financial education and financial counseling.

Strengthening Survivors' Credit

Once a partnership is established, the next step involves working with survivors around specific financial matters, especially those related to credit and debt. Survivors experiencing financial abuse will probably have poor credit histories and large debt and, therefore, will need guidance and support in repairing their credit and might need financial hardship support. Survivors might be struggling under the burden of coerced debt, in which force, fraud, or misinformation was deliberately used to financially trap the survivor in the relationship (Littwin, 2012). In addition, financial institutions can strengthen survivors' individual capacity building by providing information to educate and help survivors change their attitudes and build confidence in their financial management skills (Office of Manhattan Borough President, Sakhi for South Asian Women, & The Worker Institute at Cornell ILR, 2012). The following examples illustrate some of the services or programs financial institutions could offer to help survivors build capacity and recover from financial abuse:

- Help survivors build assets using loans, matched savings, or other strategies with proven outcomes that support survivors
- Provide one-on-one financial counseling to address bad credit and develop workable plans to reduce outstanding debt
- Offer hardship assistance, ensuring that survivors' requests are kept confidential
- Waive requirements for minimum account balances and fees such as monthly account maintenance fees, late fees on loan payments, overdraft fees on debit cards, or fees tied to credit cards, loans, and transaction accounts

In essence, financial institutions should develop financial hardship policies and ensure that the public is aware of the policies and is able to easily access information regarding how to request hardship assistance. In addition, such hardship policies should focus on all forms of domestic violence, with special emphasis on financial abuse as a cause of such hardship (Smallwood, 2015).

Providing Data for Criminal and Civil Cases

Whether working independently or in partnership with domestic violence organizations, financial institutions are well positioned to advocate not only for change in industry policies to better address financial abuse but also for civil and criminal law to be more comprehensive. Given that financial abuse is not a crime under current U.S. law, perpetrators can use joint debt to continue abusing partners. Unfortunately, survivors have little, if any, legal recourse to sever joint liabilities (Smallwood, 2015). Financial institutions could consider releasing survivors from liability for joint debts if the survivor can demonstrate that the debts were the result of financial abuse (Smallwood, 2015).

How to Incorporate Financial Abuse Recovery Strategies

The strategies outlined thus far in this section—understanding and detecting financial abuse, linking victims to and partnering with domestic violence organizations, strengthening survivors' credit, and providing data for criminal and civil cases—can be collectively referred to as *financial abuse recovery strategies*. Taken together, these are sound strategies for financial institutions to use toward supporting their customers who are experiencing financial abuse. So how can financial institutions best incorporate financial abuse recovery strategies into their routine practices and business models?

First, and of greatest importance, is keeping in mind that safety is paramount. It is imperative to keep customers and staff safe from further financial, physical, or emotional abuse.

Second, several UK-based financial institutions have developed a Financial Abuse Code of Practice (UK Finance, 2018), which includes a commitment to the following:

- Raise awareness of financial abuse among customers and encourage disclosure
- Train colleagues to understand and detect financial abuse
- Identify possible financial abuse and respond appropriately
- Minimize the need for victims/survivors to repeat their story
- Help survivors regain control of their finances
- Refer survivors to others (e.g., domestic violence organizations, legal services)

Third, financial institutions should change policies and procedures to support survivors (HSBC UK, 2019; National Australia Bank, 2020). Revised or new policies should include provisions for the following:

- Helping survivors get safe online access to statements and correspondence
- Assisting survivors with changing personal identification numbers (PINs), account security settings, and other passwords

- Setting security notification on accounts to send text message alerts of unusual activity and to require two-factor authentication on account access
- Ensuring that survivors are asked if they want to keep their address confidential
- Changing signatory requirements for joint accounts, mortgages, or personal loans from "anyone to sign" to "all to sign"
- Encouraging survivors to close joint accounts and open an individual holder account, so they have access to assets if they have to leave home suddenly (Telford, 2020)
- Ensuring that the survivor's documents (e.g., bank card, account statements) use an untraceable national sort code, so account information cannot be traced to a particular bank branch (HSBC UK, 2019)
- Offering to appoint a trusted representative to deal with the finances on the survivor's behalf, if necessary

Such policy provisions and protections can provide banks and other financial institutions with effective means to provide support and service to their customers who are experiencing financial abuse.

Call-Out to Human Service Organizations

Domestic violence organizations and financial institutions are not the only entities that need to answer the call to action to address financial abuse in their communities. Staff from human service organizations also interact with survivors and should provide support that financially empowers their clients. These include staff from human service fields, public welfare agencies, and child welfare organizations. Typically, domestic violence organizations collaborate with such organizations and provide training on identifying domestic violence and referring clients for IPV services. However, the existing training protocols for these staff might not include information on financial abuse, given that most of the organizations have historically focused on recognizing signs of physical, emotional, or sexual abuse. However, it is imperative that this broad range of health and human service organizations also understand financial abuse, indicators of this type of abuse, and how best to support clients with referrals and services. Similar to financial institutions, health and human service organizations should partner with domestic violence organizations to share information, to provide training, and to develop a strong referral network to meet the needs of clients who are experiencing financial and other forms of abuse. Additionally, similar to advocates in domestic violence organizations, staff of these human service organizations are also likely to benefit personally from receiving financial management training, and in turn, they can incorporate that training in their work with clients.

Staff of welfare organizations or other human services organizations that focus on providing financial support to clients should be especially sensitive to the possibility of financial abuse. Women receiving cash assistance through the TANF program, also known as "welfare," have reported high levels of past and current domestic violence (Tolman & Rosen, 2001). During welfare reform in the late 1990s, advocates and key lawmakers ensured that domestic violence survivors would be eligible for waivers from the newly created restrictions for receiving cash assistance, such as time limits, work requirements, and cooperation with child support enforcement. Such waivers, provided under the Family Violence Option, are available in almost all states and Washington, DC (Holcomb et al., 2017). Adoption of the Family Violence Option requires states to confidentially screen individuals receiving TANF benefits for domestic violence, refer them for services, and waive program requirements (P.L. 104-109, 402(a)(7)).

During the early days of welfare reform, one study conducted focus groups with welfare workers regarding whether they routinely screened and assessed for domestic violence (Hagen & Owens-Manley, 2002). The researchers found that instead of the workers screening universally for domestic violence—and basing decisions regarding waivers on their domestic violence assessment—they often based waiver decisions on their own perceptions, beliefs, and attitudes such as whether survivors were credible, their own experiences with survivors in general, the severity of the physical abuse, or the impact of the abuse on children. Other workers reported that they were often skeptical about reported abuse because they believed that welfare recipients often manipulate the system to gain additional benefits (Hagen & Owens-Manley, 2002). These findings align with those of a later study, conducted in Maryland, that found that welfare workers based their decisions about waivers on factors such as the severity of abuse or if the survivor fled from another state (Hetling, 2011). These findings provide empirical evidence of the ways in which caseworkers' beliefs about the dynamics of abusive relationships (e.g., the severity of physical abuse) and attitudes toward welfare recipients can influence their interactions with survivors and, thereby, effect a survivor's ability to access resources and supports needed to recover from financial abuse.

Since caseworkers may be more familiar with physical abuse, women who experience such abuse are more likely to receive additional services to support their efforts to become economically self-sufficient. If caseworkers include screening for financial abuse, they may also develop distinct plans of actions for survivors. Some research has shown that giving particular attention to integrating social support and financial literacy with employment-oriented self-sufficiency programs might slightly increase women's financial independence and empowerment (Alfred & Martin, 2007; Gregoire & Snively, 2001).

In addition to welfare organizations, child welfare organizations also need to understand, screen for, and address financial abuse among their clients. As many as thirty million children are exposed to domestic violence before the age of eighteen (Hamby et al., 2010). Given the high prevalence of domestic violence within families involved with the child welfare system, it is essential for child welfare organizations to coordinate efforts with domestic violence organizations. One challenge of this collaborative-service approach is the divergence of the missions of these systems (Potito et al., 2009). The child welfare system's mission focuses on children's safety, whereas the mission of domestic violence organizations is to safeguard adult survivors (Jones & Gross, 2000). Staff working within these organizations also have their own characteristics and experiences with domestic violence (Waugh & Bonner, 2002). Studies have found that characteristics of staff as a whole and of individual staff members, such as demographics, training, length of employment, and personal experiences with domestic violence, can influence the staff's attitudes and responses to families (Magen et al., 2000; Pecnik & Bezensek-Lalic, 2011; Postmus et al., 2011; Postmus & Merritt, 2010; Postmus & Ortega, 2005; Saunders & Anderson, 2000; Yoshihama & Mills, 2003). One recent study found that child welfare workers' attitudes toward survivors of domestic abuse were positively influenced by factors such as the workers' gender, place of employment, type of education, personal feelings of being affected by domestic violence, and domestic violence training (Nikolova et al., 2021). Moreover, workers' attitudes were influenced by feelings of being impacted by domestic violence without having personal experience with it.

Little, if any, information is available regarding the role that financial abuse plays in families involved with child welfare systems or how systems respond to the presence of financial abuse. At the time of the previously mentioned studies examining child welfare caseworkers' attitudes toward survivors, few of the study surveys addressed financial abuse. However, as noted in chapter 2, financial abuse affects family formation and parenting practices (Huang, Postmus, et al., 2013; Postmus, Huang, & Stylianou, 2012). Hence, it is vital for child welfare organizations to understand and screen for all forms of domestic violence, especially financial abuse, because it can be the most hidden and secretive type of abuse. It is also vital for these organizations to collaborate with domestic violence organizations to ensure that the entire family is kept safe from further abuse at the hands of the perpetrator.

All health and human service organizations should increase training opportunities to put a spotlight on financial abuse and its impact on self-sufficiency, families, and survivors. All staff of these agencies should have an adequate understanding of domestic violence, including financial abuse, the issues and obstacles that survivors of financial abuse encounter before and after leaving an abusive relationship, and how all priorities should coalesce to empower survivors and progress toward self-sufficiency.

These organizations also need to consider using co-located advocates from domestic violence organizations to support the survivor throughout the welfare or child welfare process. Having an advocate on-site allows these agencies to provide an immediate response to the survivor, to identify the needs of the individual, and to begin rapid establishment of support services. The ability for a survivor to immediately begin working toward a strategy for regaining control of her life helps to validate the individual's disclosure and should serve as a foundational step in reintroducing self-determination into the life of the survivor.

Finally, to make co-located services work well and have the desired impact on survivors and their families, organizations will need to develop strong communication systems, mutual training, and agreed-on protocols across organizations to prevent confusion and improve outcomes for survivors. The goal of the ultimate empowerment and self-sufficiency of the survivor remains, yet there must be collaboration to maximize the supports available within the confines of the welfare and child welfare program.

Call-Out to Corporate and Other Work Environments

Millions of women in the United States and across the globe suffer from current and past abuse. Many of these same women provide financial support for their families through work in corporate and other work environments. Indeed, survivors need employment to improve their financial standing, increase their self-esteem, improve social connectedness, provide mental respite from the home, and provide motivation to keep surviving (Rothman et al., 2007). These work environments should play a key role in supporting their employees and staff in their struggles to survive.

Domestic violence frequently spills over from the home into the survivor's work environment, with abusers harassing survivors at work (see chapter 4). Workplace harassment impacts survivors through lower earnings, higher absenteeism, decreased productivity, increased errors, and increased turnovers, negatively affecting both the survivor and the workplace (Hensing & Alexanderson, 2000; Laharnar et al., 2015; Pollack et al., 2010; Reeves & O'Leary-Kelly, 2007; Swanberg et al., 2005; Wathen et al., 2015). Prior to

2020, almost 60 percent of survivors of IPV lost their jobs as a result of such abuse, and 77 percent of survivors reported that their abuser had interfered with their employment (Ruiz et al., 2020). Over one-third of all female homicides that occurred in the workplace were committed by an intimate partner (U.S. Bureau of Labor Statistics, 2013). In one systematic review study (Showalter, 2016), each of the twenty quantitative studies reviewed found that women experiencing domestic violence also experienced workplace disruptions caused by their abuser.

Domestic violence also affects the fiscal health of the organization, with U.S. businesses reporting a $900 million loss in annual revenue because of lost productivity related to workers' experiencing IPV; survivors of severe violence lose nearly eight million days of paid work because of their IPV experiences (Centers for Disease Control and Prevention, 2003). The same CDC study reported that businesses lost a combined $5.8 billion. Given that the CDC study was completed almost twenty years ago, the amount of losses that businesses attribute to IPV has probably doubled or possibly tripled since then. At least 25 percent of large, private businesses (with one hundred or more employees) experienced at least one incident of domestic violence in 2006 (Mollica & Danehower, 2014).

Currently, no federal laws exist to protect victims of IPV in the workplace or to prohibit employment discrimination due to domestic violence (Swanberg et al., 2012). However, several laws, including Title VII of the Civil Rights Act of 1964, the Americans with Disabilities Act, and the Family and Medical Leave Act, all provide some level of protection for victims of IPV if employers take action that can be considered illegal discrimination (Mollica & Danehower, 2014). As such, when companies deny employment to a survivor or dismiss an employee because of their experiences of IPV, those companies might be putting themselves at risk of lawsuits and face legal liability for discriminatory employment practices. However, companies might also be legally liable for injuries and deaths that occur in the workplace (Mollica & Danehower, 2014).

Going to work every day gives survivors a break from their abuser for at least some hours of the day. For work settings that have security and safety precautions in place, survivors can feel physically safe. Additionally, coworkers can lend a hand in helping with safety of survivors through providing support, referrals, and resources (Kulkarni & Ross, 2016). Hence, the call to action for corporations and other workplace settings is to develop policies and protocols for identifying domestic violence, including financial abuse, and assisting survivors at work. These policies can create a safe haven for survivors to disclose their abuse and get support without stigma. Further, these policies can provide education for all employees and staff to be active bystanders and know what to do if they see or even suspect abuse and harassment by significant others.

By law, employers are required to create a safe work environment for all employees. However, one study analyzed 369 state-level employment protection policies for domestic violence survivors (including work-leave policies, antidiscrimination employment policies, and workplace awareness and safety policies) and found that no state had comprehensive policies covering all of these areas (Swanberg et al., 2012). Currently, thirty-seven states have work-leave policies that prevent employers from dismissing employees for taking leave because of court appearances. (For example, see chapter 4 for discussion of Oregon's Violence, Harassment, Sexual Assault or Stalking Protections Act.) However, a gap often exists between a policy being enacted and employers and/or employees being aware of the policy. Employers, especially small- to midsize employers, are often unaware of policy changes related to work-leave policies and other workplace protections. Moreover, many, if not most, survivors are unaware of employment protections made available through policy-level changes. Increasing employers' and employees' awareness of policy changes will increase the use of such employment protections. The best way to advocate for change is to pass specific laws that address employment protections of survivors, such as paid time off to attend court hearings. In addition to meeting the legal standard, employers are expected to create a culture of zero tolerance of violence in the workplace, which includes domestic violence (Katz et al., 2017).

Employers could also implement a variety of workplace security measures, ranging from having on-site security staff to physical security measures (e.g., locked doors) to electronic security measures (e.g., metal detectors, alarms, surveillance cameras) to prevent violence in the workplace. A study reported by the U.S. Bureau of Labor Statistics (2006) found that the majority of workplaces (72 percent) had at least one form of security, especially among larger employers with more than one thousand employees. However, only 66 percent of smaller employers (between one and ten workers) had some form of workplace security.

Finally, corporate and other workplace settings should develop comprehensive policies that recognize the seriousness of domestic violence as a problem that is likely to spill over into the workplace and, therefore, needs to be addressed by workplace policies (Mollica & Danehower, 2014; Niolon et al., 2017). Such policies should include training programs for managers, supervisors, and all employees to equip them with the knowledge to recognize domestic violence, respond appropriately, and make connections to workplace supervisors and domestic violence organizations (Laharnar et al., 2015; Mollica & Danehower, 2014). Employers should have policies and protocols that can increase awareness about domestic violence, help recognize and support victims, and demonstrate commitment to workplace safety. Putting such policies in place can do much to improve survivors' and their coworkers' feelings of safety, to reduce tolerance of violence, and to help facilitate a positive workplace climate (Niolon et al., 2017).

Summary

The organizations discussed in this chapter—domestic violence organizations, financial institutions, health and human service organizations, and corporate and workplace settings—all encounter survivors during routine operations. Whether the survivor is a client, consumer, or employee, all experiences of IPV will affect the organization through loss of revenue or other funding, staff turnover, and even employee death. All are called to understand domestic violence, including financial abuse, to understand its impact on their own setting, to know how to identify and screen for such abuse, and to know what to do when survivors disclose abusive relationships. All of these organizations need policies and protocols to screen for domestic violence, to provide support to survivors, and to link survivors to appropriate services. Further, these organizations need to join in public-awareness campaigns through training, workshops, fliers, and social media to ensure that all members of their organizations have an understanding of domestic violence and know how to respond.

Ideally, all organizations would practice empowerment interventions for physical, sexual, psychological, and financial abuse. Such empowerment techniques (Levy-Simon, 1994) could include the following:

- Individualize one's responses to the expressed preferences of survivors.
- Ensure that responses are convenient and accessible without undue emotional or financial costs
- Insist that the organization be as dedicated to "solving" the problem as it is to asking survivors to resolve the problem
- Focus on the survivors' strengths rather than their problems or challenges
- Be flexible and nimble in creating policies and protocols that respond to individual survivors' situations and needs
- Make leadership development a constant priority
- Be patient with survivors and the organization, given that empowerment takes substantial time and continuity of effort to achieve
- Connect with and make use of other organizations whose knowledge can support your organization's efforts

In essence, all organizations should provide a safe work climate for all and a workplace in which victims can get the support they need to become survivors. The challenge, of course, is that most of the limited research on domestic violence in various organizational settings focuses on physical violence and stalking; more research and intervention strategies are needed to understand how financial abuse affects organizations of all sizes.

CHAPTER 7

The Future of Financial Empowerment

The work of financial empowerment is critical not only to ensure the long-term safety of survivors but also to assist survivors in gaining long-term economic stability. Curiously, little of the research on domestic violence has sought either to fully understand the impact of financial abuse or to determine which intervention strategies are most effective toward the financial empowerment of survivors. This book addresses this critical knowledge gap by providing those who work directly or indirectly with survivors of domestic violence with practical knowledge on how to empower survivors' financial well-being and stability. Specifically, screening survivors for economic abuse, developing financial safety plans, and implementing or referring survivors to financial empowerment programs are the responsibility of every practitioner, human service provider, criminal justice practitioner, financial manager, and corporate supervisor. Those who have the financial knowledge and skills to assist with financially empowering survivors are well positioned to assist survivors to become free from abuse.

We present the next steps in the future of financial empowerment as a three-stage process of research, policy advocacy, and building community awareness and support. Our discussion includes practical suggestions for teaching financial empowerment strategies to advocates and practitioners. We also outline how to advocate with policy makers and to educate the public about economic abuse and financial empowerment. We discuss a range of implications of financial empowerment for researchers, academics, and students in professional education programs to encourage them to screen for economic abuse and incorporate financial empowerment strategies in their work. Last, we examine how survivors in the United States and around the world can use the information in this book to help rebuild their lives, restore their financial security, and recover their well-being.

Next Steps for Advocates and Practitioners

Advocates and practitioners are in the unique position of working directly with victims and survivors of domestic violence regardless of their work context. These "front-line bureaucrats" (Lipsky, 1980) often have the discretion to determine how and when to screen for IPV; how to ask about financial abuse; and which resources, interventions, and referrals to offer to survivors. Though usually trained on screening for physical abuse, these workers must also increase their understanding of financial abuse and its impact so that they can adequately screen for and intervene with a survivor experiencing such abuse. As a survivor once told one of our research assistants, she had been asked about all forms of abuse but never realized that her partner could be using her finances and credit standing as a weapon to trap her in the relationship.

To be successful in practicing financial empowerment with survivors, advocates must first become empowered themselves. Ask for financial education for you and your team at your organization; if not available, seek out programs that are available in your community. Turn to The Allstate Foundation's curriculum online and learn the content yourself. Become empowered to manage your own financial situation and improve your assets.

Next, when working with survivors, it is critical to screen for employment sabotage, economic control, and economic exploitation with survivors, if only to alert them to these types of abuse that they may encounter in addition to the "more common" types of abuse (i.e., physical, emotional, and sexual). Advocates and practitioners must be able to provide practical tools to survivors to financially empower them to gain financial knowledge, increase their economic self-efficacy, improve their economic self-sufficiency, and increase their assets. Such tools may include the following:

- Assisting them in locating and analyzing their credit report
- Helping them identify any hidden assets of their partner
- Developing financial safety plans to protect their assets and their financial standing
- Providing financial education to improve their financial management skills
- Supporting them in repairing and strengthening their credit

- Helping them develop their assets through matched savings, individual development accounts, microloans, or other types of asset-development strategies

Additionally, advocates and practitioners should partner with other organizations and businesses to support their efforts to financially empower survivors. They can start with staff in the personal financial and banking industry to team up with to provide financial education for survivors as well as to improve their own knowledge about financial management. Advocates and practitioners can also team up with corporations to provide training and referral opportunities while perhaps also benefiting from support from these corporations.

Third, advocates and practitioners should examine the micro-focused and macro-focused interventions outlined in chapter 4. Perhaps there are interventions to try at the organization? Or perhaps, by collaborating with other organizations, it makes sense to apply some macro-focused interventions? Such interventions could include ways to increase survivors' assets, such as matched savings or microloans. Interventions could also include supporting survivors in their efforts to secure and maintain employment. Even if the agency or organization in which the advocates work does not have such programs available, they can still connect to programs in the community that are available.

Next Steps for Researchers

Though financial abuse has been a part of the Power and Control Wheel for decades and has been recognized by advocates, researchers have only recently embarked on studying it. With one study completed in Australia recently, researchers still need to conduct a prevalence study on financial abuse in the United States. Some existing domestic violence prevalence studies may include a question or two on financial abuse, but the nuanced differences on the types of financial abuse is lost. Researchers must determine what the prevalence of experiencing and perpetrating financial abuse is in the United States.

In addition to prevalence studies, researchers should continue testing financial empowerment programs to determine their effectiveness in improving the financial and emotional well-being of survivors. Such testing should include access to resources and the availability of securing assets. Researching financial empowerment should also include samples that include a wide array of survivors—from those not connected to domestic violence organizations to those from different racial or ethnic backgrounds to those who have recently immigrated to the United States to those from LGBTQ+ populations. Of course, survivors from underrepresented and marginalized communities may be part of multiple cultures. Such intersectionality must also be studied to determine how best to adapt interventions for any survivor seeking financial empowerment.

Finally, researchers should test to see if financial empowerment puts survivors at greater risk of further abuse or if empowerment decreases the experiences of abuse. How lasting are financial empowerment interventions over time? Do they function as a buffer from experiencing more abuse at the hands of a current or future partner? Can financial empowerment be used to prevent financial abuse—and other forms of abuse—among youth and young adults prior to their being abused? Researchers are in the unique position of partnering with advocates and practitioners to answer some of these questions and to provide the evidence needed to keep survivors safe—physically, emotionally, and financially.

Next Steps for Policy Makers

Policy makers—or those who create policies at the local, state, and national levels—also play a role in financially empowering survivors. First, the Violence Against Women Act (VAWA), first passed in 1994, provides comprehensive financial support to organizations (i.e., domestic violence organizations, law enforcement, and prosecutors) to respond to domestic violence, sexual assault, dating violence, and stalking. Every five years, VAWA must be reauthorized by Congress to renew the act and provide financial support for its services. The act was reauthorized in 2000, 2005, and 2013, but Congress stalled the reauthorization process in 2018 under the Trump administration, with concerns about specific provisions in the act (e.g., gun control with perpetrators and services to transgender victims). Under the Biden administration, VAWA was finally reauthorized in March 2022. In this newest version of VAWA, economic justice responses have been added to include helping survivors access unemployment insurance, creating protections from employment discrimination due to experiences of violence and abuse, and providing community awareness around economic abuse. This is the first time such language addressing financial empowerment or economic justice has been included in VAWA. Unfortunately, the inclusion falls short of providing additional funding to service providers to include financial empowerment services in their core practices with survivors. Nor does VAWA include any recommendation on encouraging banks or the financial industry to address financial abuse in their practices, nor does it include any funding to support asset development through individual development accounts, job assistance programs, or microloans.

In addition to federal policy makers' role in reauthorizing VAWA, state policy makers also play a role in addressing financial empowerment and financial abuse in their own policies. For example, economic abuse is not a crime in the United States, nor can a married survivor find justice in the civil courts when her partner exploits or controls her finances or sabotages her employment efforts. Some countries (e.g., the United Kingdom) have passed measures regarding "coercive control" as a reframed way of identifying all types of abuse used by perpetrators to trap survivors in relationships, including the use of economic abuse. "Coercive control," a term coined by Evan Stark (2007), includes threats, humiliation, monitoring, and isolating victims and may or may not include physical or sexual abuse. Such controlling tactics leave survivors with little recourse through the criminal justice systems or civil courts and can even persist after the relationship has ended. Yet evidence exists, such as phone records, social media accounts, emails, and testimony from family, friends, and coworkers, to establish a pattern of behavior and to help substantiate that such controlling tactics exist and can leave devastating consequences on survivors.

State-level policy makers should examine the coercive control policy in England, Scotland, Wales, and Ireland to learn what works and to identify ways to adapt it for their particular state. Other countries, such as Australia and New Zealand, are considering changing their domestic violence laws to include coercive control. Several states (New York, Texas, and California) are in the very early stages of introducing such legislation. Unfortunately, under the Trump administration, the Office of Violence Against Women narrowly defined violence as felony or misdemeanor crimes of violence, with a strong emphasis on physical and sexual violence. Such definitions led to states diminishing their efforts to consider other types of violence and abuse, including financial abuse, as a crime.

Financial abuse fits into coercive controlling strategies since the intent is to control the victim and trap her in the relationship. In England, policy makers are considering revising the Domestic Abuse Act to recognize, define, and raise awareness about economic abuse. If passed, England will create a national advice service for banks in working with survivors and provide resources for those that are supporting victims of economic abuse to be self-sufficient (Surviving Economic Abuse, 2021). Other states have focused on addressing employment practices that protect survivors. For example, in 2013, New Jersey passed the SAFE Act (Security and Financial Empowerment Act) to provide relief to employees who are experiencing physical or sexual violence. Such relief includes getting paid leave for seeking medical attention for physical or psychological injuries or participating in criminal or civil court proceedings related to their experiences with violence. Creating policies that provide opportunities for victims to get help securing their assets, repairing any credit problems, and becoming financially empowered will provide a path toward recovery for women seeking to become economically self-sufficient.

Next Steps for Community Members

Finally, it is crucial that community members gain greater awareness around financial abuse and help family and friends understand the signs of such abuse and know what steps to take to support the victim to take control of her financial life. Ask those close to you how they define financial or economic abuse, and chances are, they would describe such abuse as being perpetrated by an employer toward an employee or by the financial industry taking advantage of their consumers. Those who live side by side with survivors and victims need greater awareness of the types of financially controlling and exploitative tactics that can destroy one's credit and future financial standing. They need to advocate for support for their family members and friends who are experiencing such abuse and advocate for policy changes that create greater protections and opportunities to ameliorate the effects of financial abuse.

Minimally, community members should be able to talk about economic abuse with their loved ones, especially those living in abusive relationships, since these loved ones may not be familiar with economic abuse or the controlling or exploitative tactics that their partner may use to financially trap them in the relationship. Indeed, even during our own research with survivors who are acutely aware of the controlling strategies used by their partners, we surprised many of them by describing this "additional" abuse that they had never heard of or thought of before being asked. As one survivor indicated, "I never realized that he could abuse me in this way. I knew about all of the other ways but never even thought of how he controlled me with money." Survivors themselves can use the information from this book to help rebuild their lives following financial abuse experiences. Naming the abuse and understanding the different forms of economic control, economic exploitation, and employment sabotage will bring additional awareness of the variety of tactics used by abusers and create a sense of urgency to identify and protect assets.

Additionally, educational systems—including secondary and postsecondary systems—should be teaching financial literacy to all students and include the signs of financial abuse. Taking control of one's own finances is an important skill that all should possess but especially those who are emerging from their families as young adults entering into the workforce and becoming self-sufficient. Understanding the signs of economic abuse can only bolster one's knowledge of managing finances by being able to identify if someone is attempting to manipulate, control, or exploit one's standing.

Financial education should be included as a core part of financial empowerment efforts with survivors, advocates, human service professionals—the list is exhaustive and should include everyone. As advocates increase their own knowledge, confidence, and skill in helping survivors navigate complex financial and safety concerns, these advocates will be able to enhance the empowerment of the survivors they serve. In addition to advocates, other professionals need to attend to their own financial education and understanding of financial abuse and other tactics used by abusers to trap survivors in abusive relationships. Professionals working in an array of settings ranging from human service agencies to the criminal justice system are likely to encounter survivors in their everyday practice and, thus, should remain mindful of addressing the financial capabilities of survivors. Similarly, professionals in financial fields, although knowledgeable about financial literacy, are likely to need a better understanding of financial abuse and the tactics abusers use to control and trap survivors of domestic violence. Last, managers and supervisors working in corporate settings need to gain a thorough understanding of the various tactics used by an abuser to sabotage a survivor's work efforts and then ensure that their organizations have policies and protocols in place to help survivors be safe at work.

Specifically, every practitioner, human service provider, criminal justice practitioner, financial manager, and corporate supervisor should be screening the women they encounter for economic abuse, and when such abuse is found, they should then work with the women toward developing financial safety plans and refer survivors to financial empowerment programs to assist them to become free from abuse. Only then will survivors gain long-term economic stability.

Acknowledgments

Postmus

My path to understanding and studying financial abuse and empowerment was not a direct path but one that started decades ago when I was an executive director of a shelter program for survivors. I learned so much from conversations with the survivors and staff around housing and employment struggles and how their financial needs were so overwhelming that becoming self-sufficient seemed like a dream. That experience nudged me toward pursuing a PhD, in which I focused on evaluating the Family Violence Option as part of the Temporary Assistance for Needy Families policy that was intended to support and protect survivors seeking financial relief from the state. I had not yet connected the attention to economic justice and focus on the financial needs of survivors until I met Jennifer Kuhn from The Allstate Foundation. She described the foundation's new financial literacy program, developed with the National Network to End Domestic Violence, as one that needed an academic partner to evaluate its effectiveness. After piloting the first study, I realized just how important financial education, group and individual counseling support from advocates, and a deep commitment by domestic violence organizations can be in supporting survivors reach their own financial independence. From listening to survivors and advocates, I learned what works and what does not and what is missing in such interventions. I connected with organizations across the country and Puerto Rico, which all were struggling with just how to financially empower survivors. This book is a result of those years of examining, listening, and analyzing the work being done.

Hence, I dedicate this book first to all of the survivors who struggle to make ends meet, support their children, and survive in a world that may seem to be against their every step. I encourage each of you to find the support you need to be financially empowered and free from abuse. I also dedicate this book to the advocates working on the front lines with survivors and who may not have enough money themselves to feel financially empowered. My hope for you is to advocate within your organization and community for the support you need. I dedicate this book as well to the many supporters including organizational partners, staff, students, and faculty. This journey would not have happened without you and your unfailing support of this work. Specifically, I am grateful to my coauthor, Amanda Stylianou, who has been with me throughout most of this journey as an MSW student, PhD student, and colleague. She breathed life into this book when I was not even sure I could make this become a reality. Finally, I dedicate this book to my partner, Geri Summers, and her dogged determination to keep me grounded, motivated, and passionate about this work. This book would not be a reality without her unfailing love.

Stylianou

After listening to survivors of domestic violence across our country, it became evident that what injures women more than physical violence is when abusive partners impact their ability to care for their children. Economic abuse deeply harms survivors and their children, leaving short- and long-term scars that are often not addressed through our criminal justice system or our domestic violence services. As our financial system in the United States becomes more complex, an abusive partner's access to create financial harm has only expanded. It is the voices of women throughout our country that have given life to this book. I thank them for sharing their stories with us. I acknowledge your pain and frustration, your strength and courage. This book is dedicated to you.

I am deeply grateful for the work of Judy Postmus in addressing economic abuse among survivors of domestic violence. I began my career working as a research assistant for Dr. Postmus, and our journey in this field continues today. She has forever been a mentor and adviser, a feminist and advocate, a colleague and friend. Through years of writing, researching, traveling, growing and laughing, I will always be thankful for our time working together.

I am also forever thankful for my family: my grandfather, grandmother, father, mother, sister, husband, and three beautiful daughters. It is my family that taught me to think critically and love deeply, fight for what I believe in, and never give up. And to my three daughters, Brianna, Emily, and Alexis, may we continue to build a better world for you.

Notes

Notes to Introduction

1 All names in this book are pseudonyms created to protect the privacy and safety of survivors.

2 Although violence occurs across all types of relationships—with male, female, cis- and transgender victims and perpetrators and among heterosexual and LGBTQ+ relationships—women are disproportionately the victims of intimate partner violence, while men are disproportionately the perpetrators of physical, sexual, and other forms of abuse. Hence, we refer to victims/survivors as women and perpetrators as men. This terminology is not intended to minimize the experiences of male victims or to absolve females of violence that they might inflict on others.

Notes to Chapter 5

1 The phrase "center the survivor" refers to an empowerment principle that holds that survivors are capable of independently harnessing their own power and, thereby, determining their long-term change and growth processes. Empowerment models actively include survivors as valued contributors and leaders at the center or hub of the service network.

Notes to Chapter 6

All illustrative quotes presented in this chapter are from advocates involved in delivering financial empowerment interventions to survivors. Advocates' names have been removed to protect their confidentiality. All quotes are from Postmus, Silva-Martinez, et al., 2013; or Silva-Martinez et al., 2016.

1 "The Allstate Foundation *Moving Ahead Curriculum* is a 5-module program that has been academically validated to help prepare survivors as they move

from short-term safety to long-term security" (The Allstate Foundation, 2021). The curriculum includes lesson plans for advocates, who deliver content on financial abuse, fundamental financial literacy, credit basics, creating a financial foundation, and long-term financial planning.

References

Acs, G., & Loprest, P. (2007). *Final report: TANF caseload composition and leavers synthesis report*. U.S. Department of Health and Human Services, Administration for Children and Families, Office of Planning, Research, and Evaluation.

Adams, A. E., & Beeble, M. L. (2019). Intimate partner violence and psychological well-being: Examining the effect of economic abuse on women's quality of life. *Psychology of Violence, 9*(5), 517–525. https://doi.org/10.1037/vio0000174.

Adams, A. E., Beeble, M. L., & Gregory, K. A. (2015). Evidence of the construct validity of the Scale of Economic Abuse. *Violence and Victims, 30*(3), 363–376.

Adams, A. E., Bybee, D., Tolman, R. M., Sullivan, C. M., & Kennedy, A. C. (2013). Does job stability mediate the relationship between intimate partner violence and mental health among low-income women? *American Journal of Orthopsychiatry, 83*(4), 600–608. https://doi.org/10.1111/ajop.12053.

Adams, A. E., Greeson, M. R., Littwin, A. K., & Javorka, M. (2019). The Revised Scale of Economic Abuse (SEA2): Development and initial psychometric testing of an updated measure of economic abuse in intimate relationships. *Psychology of Violence, 10*(3), 268–278. https://doi.org/https://doi.org/10.1037/vio0000244.

Adams, A. E., Littwin, A. K., & Javorka, M. (2019). The frequency, nature, and effects of coerced debt among a national sample of women seeking help for intimate partner violence. *Violence Against Women, 26*(11), 1324–1342. https://doi.org/10.1177/1077801219841445.

Adams, A. E., Sullivan, C. M., Bybee, D., & Greeson, M. R. (2008, May 1). Development of the Scale of Economic Abuse. *Violence Against Women, 14*(5), 563–588. https://doi.org/10.1177/1077801208315529.

Adams, A. E., Tolman, R. M., Bybee, D., Sullivan, C. M., & Kennedy, A. C. (2012). The impact of intimate partner violence on low-income women's economic well-being: The mediating role of job stability. *Violence Against Women, 18*(12), 1345–1367. https://doi.org/10.1177/1077801212474294.

Afifi, T. O., MacMillan, H., Cox, B. J., Asmundson, G.J.G., Stein, M. B., & Sareen,

J. (2009). Mental health correlates of intimate partner violence in marital relationships in a nationally representative sample of males and females. *Journal of Interpersonal Violence, 24*(8), 1398–1417.

Ahmed, S. M. (2005). Intimate partner violence against women: Experiences from a woman-focused development programme in Matlab, Bangladesh. *Journal of Health, Population and Nutrition, 23*(1), 95–101.

Aizer, A. (2010). The gender wage gap and domestic violence. *American Economic Review, 100*(4), 1847–1859. https://doi.org/10.1257/aer.100.4.1847.

Ajzen, I. (1985). *From intentions to actions: A theory of planned behavior*. Berlin: Springer.

Ajzen, I., & Fishbein, M. (1970). The prediction of behavior from attitudinal and normative variables. *Journal of Experimental Social Psychology, 6*(4), 466–487.

Alcalde, C. M. (2006). Migration and class as constraints in battered women's attempts to escape violence in Lima, Peru. *Latin American Perspectives, 33*, 147–164.

Alexander, P. C. (2011). Childhood maltreatment, intimate partner violence, work interference and women's employment. *Journal of Family Violence, 26*(4), 255–261. https://doi.org/10.1007s10896-011-9361-9.

Alfred, M. V., & Martin, L. G. (2007). The development of economic self-sufficiency among former welfare recipients: Lessons learned from Wisconsin's welfare to work program. *International Journal of Training and Development, 11*(1), 2–20.

Allstate Foundation. (2020). "What We Do: End Domestic Violence." https://allstatefoundation.org/what-we-do/end-domestic-violence/.

Alsaker, K., Moen, B. E., Baste, V., & Morken, T. (2016). How has living with intimate partner violence affected the work situation? A qualitative study among abused women in Norway. *Journal of Family Violence, 31*, 479–487. https://doi.org/10.1007/s10896-016-9806-2.

Anderson, M. A., Gillig, P. M., Sitaker, M., McCloskey, K., Malloy, K., & Grigsby, N. (2003). "Why doesn't she just leave?": A descriptive study of victim reported impediments to her safety. *Journal of Family Violence* 18:151–155.

Anitha, S. (2019). Understanding economic abuse through an intersectional lens: Financial abuse, control and exploitation of South Asian women's productive and reproductive labours. *Violence Against Women, 25*(15), 1854–1877. https://doi.org/10.1177/1077801218824050.

Antai, D., Oke, A., Braithwaite, P., & Lopez, G. B. (2014). The effect of economic, physical, and psychological abuse on mental health: A population-based study of women in the Philippines. *International Journal of Family Medicine, 2014*. https://doi.org/10.1155/2014/852317.

Australian Bureau of Statistics. (2013). *2012 personal safety survey*. https://www.abs.gov/au/ausstats/abs@.nsf/lookup/4906.0chapter1002012.

Bachman, R., & Saltzman, L. E. (1995, August). *Violence against women: Estimates from the redesigned survey*. U.S. Department of Justice. https://www.ojp.gov/ncjrs/virtual-library/abstracts/violence-against-women-estimates-redesigned-survey.

Bader, D., Doherty, D., Dumont-Smith, C., Guruge, S., Nepinak, J., Porteous, T., Campbell, M., Straatman, A. L., & Dawson, M. (2019). *Creating safety plans with vulnerable populations to reduce the risk of repeated violence and domestic homicide: domestic homicide (6)*. Canadian Domestic Homicide Prevention Initiative. http://cdhpi.ca/sites/cdhpi.ca/files/Brief_6-Online_0.pdf.

Bajracharya, A., & Amin, S. (2013). Microcredit and domestic violence in Bangladesh: An exploration of selection bias influences. *Demography, 50*(5), 1819–1843. https://doi.org/10.1007/s13524-013-0226-0.

Bandura, A. (1997). *Self-efficacy: The exercise of control*. Freeman.

Banyard, V., Potter, S., & Turner, H. (2011). The impact of interpersonal violence in adulthood on women's job satisfaction and productivity: The mediating roles of mental and physical health. *Psychology of Violence, 1*(1), 16–28. https://doi.org/10.1037/a0021691.

Becker, A. B., Israel, B. A., Schulz, A. J., Parker, E. A., & Klem, L. (2002). Predictors of perceived control among African American women in Detroit: Exploring empowerment as a multilevel construct. *Health Education & Behavior, 29*(6), 699–715.

Behounek, E. K. (2011). "No help for the weary": An ethnographic examination of factors impacting burnout among domestic violence and sexual assault advocates. Open SIUC, Research Papers (Paper 50). http://opensiuc.lib.siu.edu/gs_rp/50.

Belsky, J. (1984). *The determinants of parenting: A process model*. Wiley-Blackwell.

Berk, R. A., Newton, P. J., & Berk, S. F. (1986). What a difference a day makes: An empirical study of the impact of shelters for battered women. *Journal of Marriage and the Family, 48*, 481–490.

Bernasek, A., & Bajtelsmit, V. L. (2002). Predictors of women's involvement in household financial decision-making. *Financial Counseling and Planning, 13*, 39–47.

Black, M. C., Basile, K. C., Breiding, M. J., Smith, S. G., Walters, M. L., Merrick, M. T., Chen, J., & Stevens, M. R. (2011). *The National Intimate Partner and Sexual Violence Survey (NISVS): 2010 summary report*. http://www.cdc.gov/violencePrevention/NISVS/index.html.

Blood, R. O., & Wolfe, D. M. (1960). *Husbands and wives: The Dynamics of married living*. Free Press.

Bograd, M. (1999). Strengthening domestic violence theories: Intersections of race, class, sexual orientation, and gender. *Journal of Marital and Family Therapy, 25*, 275–289.

Bonica, T. (2000). *Supporting battered women's economic development: One community's effort*. National Resource Center on Domestic Violence.

Bonomi, A. E., Thompson, R. S., Anderson, M., Reid, R. J., Carrell, D., Dimer, J. A., & Rivara, F. P. (2006). Intimate partner violence and women's physical, mental, and social functioning. *American Journal of Preventive Medicine, 30*(6), 458–466. http://www.sciencedirect.com/science/article/B6VHT-4JYSD9C-2/2/2580dff0414ed3366615bda76eee91c7.

Borchers, A., Lee, R. C., Martsolf, D. S., & Maler, J. (2016). Employment maintenance and intimate partner violence. *Workplace Health & Safety, 64*(10), 469–478.

Bornstein, R. F. (2006, September). The complex relationship between dependency and domestic violence. *American Psychologist, 61*(6), 595–606. https://doi.org/10.1037/0003-066X.61.6.595.

Bowie, S., & Dopwell, D. (2013). Metastressors as barriers to self-sufficiency among TANF-reliant African American and Latina women. *Affilia, 28*, 177–193.

Boyce, C., Koliner, S., Koplin, L., Sun, S., Trifone, D., & Wong, J. (2014). *Barriers to building financial security for survivors of domestic violence*. Financial Clinic, Workshop in Public Affairs. https://lafollette.wisc.edu/images/publications/workshops/2014-abuse.pdf.

Brabo, L. M., Kilde, P. H., Peskek-Herriges, P., Quinn, T., & Sanderud-Nordquist, I. (2003). Driving out of poverty in private automobiles. *Journal of Poverty, 7*(1/2), 183–196.

Brandwein, R. A., & Filiano, D. M. (2000). Toward real welfare reform: The voices of battered women. *Affilia, 15*(2), 224–243.

Braunstein, S., & Welch, C. (2002). Financial literacy: An overview of practice, research, and policy. *Federal Reserve Bulletin, 88*(11), 445–457.

Breiding, M. J., Black, M. C., & Ryan, G. W. (2008). Chronic disease and health risk behaviors associated with intimate partner violence—18 US states/territories, 2005. *Annals of Epidemiology, 18*(7), 538–544. https://doi.org/10.1016/j.annepidem.2008.02.005.

Breitkreuz, R. S., & Williamson, D. L. (2012). The self-sufficiency trap: A critical examination of welfare-to-work. *Social Service Review, 86*(4), 660–689.

Brewster, M. P. (2003). Power and control dynamics in prestalking and stalking situations. *Journal of Family Violence, 18*(4), 207–217. https://doi.org/10.1023/A:1024064214054.

Brooks-Gunn, J., Garfinkel, I., McLanahan, S. S., & Paxson, C. (2011). *Fragile Families and Child Wellbeing Study*. Robert Wood Johnson Foundation. https://fragilefamilies.princeton.edu/sites/fragilefamilies/files/rwjf_program_results_report.pdf.

Browne, A., & Bassuk, S. (1997). Intimate violence in the lives of homeless and poor housed women: Prevalence and patterns in an ethnically diverse sample.

American Journal of Orthopsychiatry, 67(2), 261–278. https://doi.org/10.1037/h0080230.

Bruce, J., Lloyd, C., & Leonard, A. (1995). *Families in focus: New perspectives on mothers, fathers and children*. Population Council.

Buckland, J. (2014). Structural barriers, financial exclusion, and the possibilities of situated learning for financial education. *New Directions for Adult & Continuing Education, 141*, 15–24. https://doi.org/10.1002/ace.20081.

Buller, A. M., Peterman, A., Ranganathan, M., Bleile, A., M., H., & Heise, L. (2018). A mixed-method review of cash transfers and intimate partner violence in low-and middle-income countries. *The World Bank Research Observer, 33*(2), 218–258.

Burke, J., Lee, L., & O'Campo, P. (2008). An exploration of maternal intimate partner violence experiences and infant general health and temperament. *Maternal and Child Health Journal, 12*(2), 172–179.

Busch, N. B., & Valentine, D. (2000). Empowerment practice: A focus on battered women. *Affilia, 15*(1), 82–95.

Butler, S. S., & Deprez, L. S. (2002). Something worth fighting for: Higher education for women on welfare. *Affilia, 17*(1), 30–54.

Bybee, D., & Sullivan, C. M. (2005). Predicting re-victimization of battered women 3 years after exiting a shelter program. *American Journal of Community Psychology, 36*(1/2), 85–96.

Byrne, C. A., & Arias, I. (2004). Predicting women's intentions to leave abusive relationships: An application of the Theory of Planned Behavior. *Journal of Applied Social Psychology, 34*(12), 2586–2601.

Cajner, T., Radler, T., Ratner, D., & Vidangos, I. (2017). *Racial gaps in labor market outcomes in the last four decades and over the business cycle* (Finance and Economics Discussion Series 2017-071). Federal Reserve.

Calvès, A. (2009). Empowerment: Généalogie d'un concept clé du discours contemporain sur le développement. *Revue Tiers Monde, 200*(4), 735–479. https://doi.org/10.3917/rtm.200.0735.

Capaldi, D. M., Knoble, N. B., Shortt, J. W., & Kim, H. K. (2012). A systematic review of risk factors for intimate partner violence. *Partner Abuse, 3*(2), 231–280. https://doi.org/10.1891/1946-6560.3.2.231.

Casanueva, C., Martin, S. L., Runyan, D. K., Barth, R. P., & Bradley, R. H. (2008). Quality of maternal parenting among intimate partner violence victims involved with the child welfare system. *Journal of Family Violence, 24*, 413–427.

Casey, A. E., & Ohler, K. (2012). Being a positive bystander: Male antiviolence allies' experiences of "stepping up." *Journal of Interpersonal Violence, 27*(1), 62–83.

Cattaneo, L. B., & Chapman, A. R. (2010). The process of empowerment: A model for use in research and practice. *American Psychologist, 65*(7), 646–659.

Cavanaugh, C. E., Messing, J. T., Del-Colle, M., O'Sullivan, C., & Campbell, J. (2011). Prevalence and correlates of suicidal behavior among female victims of intimate partner violence. *Suicide & Life-Threatening Behavior, 14*(4), 372–383.

Centers for Disease Control and Prevention. (2020). *Behavioral risk factor surveillance system.* https://www.cdc.gov/brfss/index.html.

Centers for Disease Control and Prevention. (2012). *Understanding intimate partner violence: Fact sheet.* http://www.cdc.gov/violenceprevention/pdf/IPV_factsheet-a.pdf.

Centers for Disease Control and Prevention. (2003). *Costs of intimate partner violence against women in the United States.* https://www.cdc.gov/violenceprevention/pdf/IPVbook-a.pdf.

Centers for Disease Control and Prevention. (n.d.). *Intimate partner violence.* https://www.cdc.gov/violenceprevention/intimatepartnerviolence/index.html.

Chowbey, P. (2017). Women's narratives of economic abuse and financial strategies in Britain and South Asia. *Psychology of Violence, 7*, 459–468.

Christy-McMullin, K. (2003). Asset-building policies and safety for women: Stretching social work's conceptual framework. *The Social Policy Journal, 2*(4), 19–37.

Christy-McMullin, K., Shobe, M. A., & Wills, J. (2009). Arkansas IDA programs: Examining asset retention and perceptions of well-being. *Journal of Social Service Research, 35*(1), 65–76. https://doi.org/10.1080/01488370802477485.

Chronister, K. M., & McWhirter, E. H. (2003, Fall). Applying Social Cognitive Career Theory to the empowerment of battered women. *Journal of Counseling & Development, 81*(4), 418–425.

Collins, J. M., & Holden, K. C. (2014). Measuring the impacts of financial literacy: Challenges for community-based financial education. *New Directions for Adult & Continuing Education, 141*, 79–88. https://doi.org/10.1002/ace.20087.

Correia, A. (2000, January). Strategies to expand battered women's economic opportunities. *Building Comprehensive Solutions to Domestic Violence, 9*, 1–36.

Cox, J. W., & Stoltenberg, C. D. (1991). Evaluation of a treatment program for battered wives. *Journal of Family Violence, 6*(4), 395–413.

Crenshaw, K. (1991). Mapping the margins: Intersectionality, identity politics, and violence against women of color. *Stanford Law Review, 43*, 1241–1299.

Crowne, S. S., Juon, H. S., Ensminger, M., Burrell, L., McFarlane, E., & Duggan, A. (2011). Concurrent and long-term impact of intimate partner violence on employment stability. *Journal of Interpersonal Violence, 26*(6), 1282–1304.

Cunradi, C. B., Caetano, R., & Schafer, J. (2002). Socioeconomic predictors of intimate partner violence among White, Black, and Hispanic couples in the United States. *Journal of Family Violence, 17*(4), 377–389. https://doi.org/10.1023/A:1020374617328.

Dalal, K., Dahlstrom, O., & Timpka, T. (2013). Interactions between microfinance programmes and non-economic empowerment of women associated with intimate partner violence in Bangladesh: A cross-sectional study. *BMJ Open, 3*(12). https://doi.org/10.1136/bmjopen-2013-002941.

Danes, S. M., Huddleston-Casas, C., & Boyce, L. (1999). Financial planning curriculum for teens: Impact evaluation. *Financial Counseling and Planning, 10*(1), 25–37.

Davies, J., Lyon, E., & Monti-Catania, D. (1998). *Safety planning with battered women: Complex lives/difficult choices*. Sage.

Deininger, K., & Liu, Y. Y. (2013). Economic and social impacts of an innovative self-help group model in India. *World Development, 43*, 149–163. https://doi.org/10.1016/j.worlddev.2012.09.019.

Dillon, G., Hussain, R., Loxton, D., & Rahman, S. (2013, January 23). Mental and physical health and intimate partner violence against women: A review of the literature. *International Journal of Family Medicine*, 1–15. https://doi.org/10.1155/2013/313909.

Dobash, R. E., & Dobash, R. (1979). *Violence against wives*. Free Press.

Drigotas, S. M., & Rusbult, C. E. (1992). Should I stay or should I go? A dependence model of breakups. *Journal of Personality and Social Psychology, 62*(1), 62–87. https://doi.org/10.1037/0022-3514.62.1.62.

Dunham, K., & Senn, C. Y. (2000). Minimizing negative experiences: Women's disclosure of partner abuse. *Journal of Interpersonal Violence, 15*(3), 251–261.

Edwards, K. M., Gidycz, C. A., & Murphy, M. J. (2015). Leaving an abusive dating relationship: A prospective analysis of the investment model and theory of planned behavior. *Journal of Interpersonal Violence, 30*(16), 2908–2927.

Ellison, C. G., Trinitapoli, J. A., Anderson, K. L., & Johnson, B. R. (2007). Race/ethnicity, religious involvement, and domestic violence. *Violence Against Women, 13*(11), 1094–1112. https://doi.org/10.1177/1077801207308259.

England, P., & Farkas, G. (1986). *Households, employment, and gender: A social, economic, and demographic view*. Aldine.

English, L. M. (2014). Financial literacy: A critical adult education appraisal. *New Directions for Adult & Continuing Education, 141*, 47–55. https://doi.org/10.1002/ace.20084.

Evans, S. E., Davies, C., & DiLillo, D. (2008). Exposure to domestic violence: A meta-analysis of child and adolescent outcomes. *Aggression and Violent Behavior, 13*(2), 131–140.

Farmer, A., & Tiefenthaler, J. (1997, Fall). An economic analysis of domestic violence. *Review of Social Economy, 55*(3), 337–358.

Farmer, A., & Tiefenthaler, J. (2003). Explaining the recent decline in domestic violence. *Contemporary Economic Policy, 21*(2), 158.

Farrell, L., Fry, T. R., & Risse, L. (2016). The significance of financial self-efficacy in explaining women's personal finance behavior. *Journal of Economic Psychology, 54*, 85–99.

Fawole, O. I. (2008, July 1). Economic violence to women and girls: Is it receiving the necessary attention? *Trauma Violence Abuse, 9*(3), 167–177. https://doi.org/10.1177/1524838008319255.

Federal Deposit Insurance Corporation. (2017). *FDIC national survey of unbanked and underbanked households*. https://www.fdic.gov/householdsurvey/.

Fishbein, M., & Ajzen, I. (2010). *Predicting and changing behavior: The reasoned action approach*. Psychology Press.

Fisher, P. (2010). Gender differences in personal saving behaviors. *Journal of Financial Counseling and Planning, 21*(1), 14–24.

Fraser, N. (1989). *Unruly Practices*. University of Minnesota Press.

Garcia, P.R.J. M., Ng, C. S., Capezio, A., Restubog, S.L.D., & Tang, R. L. (2017). Distressed and drained: Consequences of intimate partner aggression and the buffering role of supervisor support. *Journal of Vocational Behavior, 103*, 106–116.

Gardner, C. V. (2013). *Empowerment and interconnectivity: Toward a feminist history of unitarian philosophy*. Pennsylvania State University Press.

Gelles, R. J. (1976). Abuse wives: Why do they stay? *Journal of Marriage and the Family, 38*, 659–668. https://doi.org/10.2307/350685.

Gibbs, A., Dunkle, K., & Jewkes, R. (2018). Emotional and economic intimate partner violence as key drivers of depression and suicidal ideation: A cross-sectional study among young women in informal settlements in South Africa. *PloS One, 13*(4).

Glinski, J. (2022). *Post-Separation Economic Power and Control Wheel* [Unpublished doctoral dissertation]. University of Glasgow, Scotland.

Goodman, L. A., Banyard, V., Woulfe, J., Ash, S., & Mattern, G. (2016). Bringing a network-oriented approach to domestic violence services: A focus group exploration of promising practices. *Violence Against Women, 22*(1), 64–89.

Goodman, L. A., Cattaneo, L. B., Thomas, K., Woulfe, J., Kwan Chong, S., & Fels Smyth, K. (2014, November 10). Advancing domestic violence program evaluation: Development and validation of the Measure of Victim Empowerment Related to Safety (MOVERS). *Psychology of Violence*. https://doi.org/10.1037/a0038318.

Goodman, L. A., Dutton, M. A., Weinfurt, K., & Cook, S. (2003). The intimate partner violence strategies index: Development and application. *Violence Against Women, 9*, 163–186.

Goodman, L. A., Fauci, J. E., Sullivan, C. M., DiGiovanni, C. D., & Wilson, J. M. (2016). Domestic violence survivors' empowerment and mental health: Exploring the role of the alliance with advocates. *American Journal of Orthopsychiatry, 86*(3), 286.

Gordon, J. S. (1996). Community services for abused women: A review of perceived usefulness and efficacy. *Journal of Family Violence, 11*(4), 315–329.

Gottlieb, A., & Mahabir, M. (2019, January 2). The effect of multiple types of intimate partner violence on maternal criminal justice involvement. *Journal of Interpersonal Violence.* https://doi.org/10.1177/0886260518820705.

Gottschalck, A. O. (2008). *Net worth and the assets of households: 2002.* U.S. Census Bureau. http://www.census.gov/prod/2008pubs/p70-115.pdf.

Gowdy, E. A., & Pearlmutter, S. (1993). Economic self-sufficiency: It's not just money. *Affilia, 8*(4), 368–387.

Gowdy, E. A., & Pearlmutter, S. (1994). Economic self-sufficiency is a road I'm on: Results of focus group research with low-income women. In L. Davis (Ed.), *Building on women's strengths: A social work agenda for the 21st century* (pp. 81–113). Haworth.

Graham-Bermann, S. A., & Perkins, S. (2010). Effects of early exposure and lifetime exposure to intimate partner violence (IPV) on child adjustment. *Violence and Victims, 25*(4), 427–439.

Green, E. P., Blattman, C., Jamison, J., & Annan, J. (2015). Women's entrepreneurship and intimate partner violence: A cluster randomized trial of microenterprise assistance and partner participation on post-conflict Uganda. *Social Science & Medicine, 133*, 177–188.

Greenfeld, L. A., & Rand, M. R. (1998). *Violence by intimates: Analysis of data on crimes by current or former spouses, boyfriends, and girlfriends* (NCJ-167237). U.S. Dept. of Justice.

Gregoire, T. K., & Snively, C. A. (2001). The relationship of social support and economic self-sufficiency to substance abuse outcomes in a long-term recovery program for women. *Journal of Drug Education, 31*(3), 221–237.

Gu, D., Martin, S., Sprague, W., & Rowe, L. (2010). *Where the ends don't meet: Measuring poverty and self-sufficiency among Oregon's families.* Institute of Portland Metropolitan Studies, Portland State University.

Guarnieri, E.R.H. (2018). *Female empowerment and male backlash: An analysis of domestic violence and women's employment using Cameroon's colonial past as a lab.* Munich Society for the Promotion of Economic Research. https://www.cesifo.org/DocDL/cesif01_wp7009.pdf.

Gudmunson, C. G., & Danes, S. M. (2011). Family financial socialization: Theory and critical review. *Journal of Family and Economic Issues, 32*, 644–667.

Gupta, J., Falb, K. L., Lehmann, H., Kpebo, D., Xuan, Z., Hossain, M., Zimmerman, C., Watts, C., & Annan, J. (2013). Gender norms and economic empowerment intervention to reduce intimate partner violence against women in rural Côte d'Ivoire: A randomized controlled pilot study. *BMC International Health and Human Rights, 13*(46), 1–12. https://doi.org/10.1186/1472-698X-13-46.

Gutiérrez, L. M., GlenMaye, L., & DeLois, K. (1995, March). The organizational context of empowerment practice: Implications for social work administration. *Social Work, 40*(2), 249–258.

Gutman, L. M., McLoyd, V. C., & Tokoyawa, T. (2005). Financial strain, neighborhood stress, parenting behaviors, and adolescent adjustment in urban African American families. *Journal of Research on Adolescence, 15*(4), 425–449.

Gutter, M., & Copur, Z. (2011). Financial behaviors and financial well-being of college students: Evidence from a national survey. *Journal of Family and Economic Issues, 32*, 699–714.

Hagen, J. L., & Owens-Manley, J. (2002). Issues in implementing TANF in New York: The perspective of front-line workers. *Social Work, 47*(2), 171–182.

Hallerod, B., Diaz, C., & Stocks, J. (2007). Doing gender while doing couple: Concluding remarks. In J. Stocks, C. Diaz, & B. Hallerod (Eds.), *Modern couples sharing money, sharing life* (pp. 143–155). Palgrave Macmillan.

Hamby, S., Finkelhor, D., Turner, H., & Ormrod, R. (2010). The overlap of witnessing partner violence with child maltreatment and other victimizations in a nationally representative survey of youth. *Child Abuse & Neglect, 34*, 734–741.

Hamilton, G. (2002). *Moving people from welfare to work: Lessons from the National Evaluation of Welfare-to-Work Strategies.* U.S. Department of Health and Human Services, Administration for Children and Families, Office of the Assistant Secretary for Planning and Evaluation.

Harrington, C., Smith, W., & Bauer, R. (2016). Influencing business student intent to use a personal budget. *The Accounting Educators' Journal, 26*, 135–153.

Hart, B. (1993). The legal road to freedom. In M. Hansen & M. Harway (Eds.), *Battering and family therapy* (pp. 13–28). Sage.

Hasenfeld, Y. (1987). Power in social work practice. *Social Service Review, 61*, 469–483.

Hensing, G., & Alexanderson, K. (2000). The relation of adult experience of domestic harassment, violence, and sexual abuse to health and sickness absence. *International Journal of Behavioral Medicine, 7*(1), 1–18. https://doi.org/10.1207/S15327558IJBM0701_1.

Hetling, A. (2011). Welfare casework assessments and domestic violence services: Findings from administrative data and case narratives. *Violence Against Women, 17*(8), 1046–1066.

Hetling, A., Hoge, G. L., & Postmus, J. L. (2016). What is economic self-sufficiency? Validating a measurement scale for policy, practice, and research. *Journal of Poverty, 20*(2), 214–235. https://doi.org/10.1080/10875549.2015.1094768.

Hetling, A., Postmus, J. L., & Kaltz, C. (2015). A randomized field-based evaluation of a financial literacy curriculum for survivors of intimate partner violence. *Journal of Family & Economic Issues, 37*(4), 672–685. https://doi.org/10.1007/s10834-015-9479-7.

Hetling, A., Stylianou, A. M., & Postmus, J. L. (2015). Measuring financial strain in the lives of survivors of intimate partner violence. *Journal of Interpersonal Violence, 30*(6), 1046–1064. https://doi.org/10.1177/0886260514539758.

Hidrobo, M., & Fernald, L. (2013). Cash transfers and domestic violence. *Journal of Health Economics, 32*(1), 304–319. https://doi.org/10.1016/j.jhealeco.2012.11.002.

Hidrobo, M., Peterman, A., & Heise, L. (2016). The effect of cash, vouchers, and food transfers on intimate partner violence: Evidence from a randomized experiment in northern Ecuador. *American Economic Journal: Applied Economics, 8*(3), 284–303. https://www.aeaweb.org/articles?id=10.1257/app.20150048.

Hilgert, M. A., Hogarth, J. M., & Beverly, S. G. (2003). Household financial management: The Connection between knowledge and behavior. *Federal Reserve Bulletin, 89*(7), 309–322.

Hobfoll, S. E. (2001). The influence of culture, community, and the nested-self in the stress process: Advancing conservation of resources theory. *Applied Psychology, 50*, 337–370.

Hoge, G. L. (2016). *Understanding and measuring economic self-sufficiency in the context of intimate partner violence and immigration: A mixed-method study.* Rutgers University Graduate School.

Hoge, G. L., & Postmus, J. L. (2014). *Evaluating the impact of the "Moving Ahead through Financial Management" curriculum: Final report—Interviews with immigrant Latina participants.* Center on Violence Against Women and Children, Rutgers School of Social Work. https://socialwork.rutgers.edu/file/657/download?token=ZGob6ivf.

Hoge, G. L., Stylianou, A. M., Hetling, A., & Postmus, J. L. (2020). Developing and validating the Scale of Economic Self-Efficacy. *Journal of Interpersonal Violence, 35*(15/16), 3011–3033. https://doi.org/10.1177/0886260517706761.

Holcomb, S., Johnson, L., Hetling, A., Postmus, J. L., Steiner, J. J., Braasch, L., & Riordan, A. (2017). Implementation of the Family Violence Option twenty years later: A review of state welfare rules for domestic violence survivors. *Journal of Policy Practice, 16*(4), 415–431. https://doi.org/10.1080/15588742.2017.1311820.

Holt, S., Buckley, H., & Whelan, S. (2008). The impact of exposure to domestic violence on children and young people: A review of the literature. *Child Abuse & Neglect, 32*(8), 797–810. http://www.sciencedirect.com/science/article/B6V7N-4T9BXJP-2/2/5e8b84ed9430fd4de80ce008b4ff1d5c.

hooks, b. (1984). *Feminist theory: From margin to center.* South End.

Hopley, V. (2003, Spring). *Financial education: What is it and what makes it so important?* Community Reinvestment Report, Federal Reserve Bank of Cleveland. https://www.clevelandfed.org/newsroom-and-events/publications/discontinued-publications/cr-report/crr-20030605-financial-education--what-is-it-and-what-makes-it-so-important.aspx.

HSBC UK. (2019). *HSBC UK introduces untraceable sort code to protect victims of financial abuse*. https://www.about.hsbc.co.uk/news-and-media/hsbc-uk-introduces-untraceable-sort-code-to-protect-victims-of-financial-abuse.

Huang, C. C., Postmus, J. L., Vikse, J. H., & Wang, L. R. (2013). Economic abuse, physical violence, and union formation. *Children and Youth Services Review, 35*, 780–786. https://doi.org/10.1016/j.childyouth.2013.01.020.

Huang, C. C., Vikse, J. H., Lu, S., & Yi, S. (2015). Children's exposure to intimate partner violence and early delinquency. *Journal of Family Violence, 30*(8), 953–965.

Huang, C. C., Wang, L., & Warrener, C. (2010). Effects of domestic violence on behavior problems of preschool-aged children: Do maternal mental health and parenting mediate the effects? *Children and Youth Services Review, 32*(10), 1317–1323.

Huang, J., Nam, Y., & Sherraden, M. (2013). Financial knowledge and child development account policy: A test of financial capability. *Journal of Consumer Affairs, 47*(1), 1–26.

Hungerford, A., Wait, S. K., Fritz, A. M., & Clements, C. M. (2012). Exposure to intimate partner violence and children's psychological adjustment, cognitive functioning, and social competence: A review. *Aggression and Violent Behavior, 17*, 373–382. https://doi.org/10.1016/j.avb.2012.04.002.

Jackson, S. L., & Hafemeister, T. L. (2011). *Financial abuse of elderly people vs. other forms of elder abuse: Assessing their dynamics, risk factors, and society's response*. U.S. Dept. of Justice. https://www.ncjrs.gov/pdffiles1/nij/grants/233613.pdf.

Jamal, A.A.A., Ramlan, W. K., Karim, M. A., & Osman, Z. (2015). The effects of social influence and financial literacy on savings behavior: A study on students of higher learning institutions in Kota Kinabalu. *International Journal of Business and Social Science, 6*(11), 110–119.

Johansson de Silva, S., Paci, P., & Posadas, J. (2013). *Lessons learned and not yet learned from a multicountry initiative on women's economic empowerment*. World Bank Studies.

Johnson, E., & Sherraden, M. S. (2007). From financial literacy to financial capability among youth. *Journal of Sociology & Social Welfare, 34*(3), 119–146.

Jones, L. P., & Gross, E. (2000). Perceptions and practice with domestic violence among child protective service workers. *Children and Youth Services Review, 22*(5), 355–371. https://doi.org/10.1016/S0190-7409(00)00085-2.

Joo, S. H., & Grable, J. E. (2004). An exploratory framework of the determinants of financial satisfaction. *Journal of Family and Economic Issues, 25*(1), 25–50.

Joseph, M. (2013). Gender, entrepreneurial subjectivity, and pathologies of personal finance. *Social Politics, 20*(2), 242–273.

Jury, A., Thorburn, N., & Weatherall, R. (2017). "What's his is his and what's mine is his": Financial power and economic abuse in Aoetearoa. *Aotearoa New Zealand Social Work, 29*(2), 69–82. https://doi.org/10.11157/anzswj-vol29iss2id312.

Kalmuss, D. S., & Straus, M. A. (1990). Wife's marital dependency and wife abuse. In M. A. Straus & R. J. Gelles (Eds.), *Physical violence in American families: Risk factors and adaptations in 8,145 American families* (pp. 369–382). Transaction Publishers/Routledge.

Katz, M., Lopen, Y. P., & Lavan, H. (2017). Domestic violence spillover into the workplace: An examination of the difference between legal and ethical requirements. *Business and Society Review, 122*(4), 557–587.

Kernsmith, P. (2005). Treating perpetrators of domestic violence: Gender differences in the applicability of the Theory of Planned Behavior. *Sex Roles, 52*, 757–770.

Khandker, S. R. (2005). Microfinance and poverty: Evidence using panel data from Bangladesh. *World Bank Economic Review, 19*(2), 23–286. https://doi.org/10.1093/wber/lhi008.

Kim, J., Ferrari, G., Abramsky, T., Watts, C., Hargreaves, J. R., Morison, L. A., Phetla, G., Porter, J. D., & Pronyk, P. M. (2009). Assessing the incremental effects of combining economic and health interventions: The IMAGE study in South African. *Bulletin of the World Health Organization, 87*(11), 824–832. https://doi.org/10.2471/blt.08.056580.

Kim, J., & Gray, K. A. (2008, October 1). Leave or stay? Battered women's decision after intimate partner violence. *Journal of Interpersonal Violence, 23*(10), 1465–1482. https://doi.org/10.1177/0886260508314307.

Kim, J. C., Watts, C., Hargreaves, J. R., Ndhlovu, L. X., Phetla, G., Morison, L. A., Busza, J., Porter, J. D., & Pronyk, P. (2007). Understanding the impact of a microfinance-based intervention on women's empowerment and the reduction of intimate partner violence in South Africa. *American Journal of Public Health, 97*(10), 1794–1802. https://doi.org/10.2105/AJPH.2006.095521.

King, K., Murray, C. E., Crowe, A. L., Hunnicutt, G., Lundgren, K., & Olson, L. (2017). The costs of recovery: Intimate partner violence survivors' experiences of financial recovery from abuse. *The Family Journal: Counseling and Therapy for Couples and Families, 25*(3), 230–238. https://doi.org/10.1177/1066480717710656.

Kulkarni, S., & Ross, T. C. (2016). Exploring employee intimate partner violence (IPV) disclosures in the workplace. *Journal of Workplace Behavioral Health, 31*(4), 204–221. https://doi.org/10.1080/15555240.2016.1213637.

Kutin, J., Russell, R., & Reid, M. (2017). Economic abuse between intimate partners in Australia: Prevalence, health status, disability and financial stress. *Australian and New Zealand Journal of Public Health, 41*(3), 269–274. https://doi.org/10.1111/1753-6405.12651.

Laffaye, C., Kennedy, C., & Stein, M. B. (2003). Post-traumatic stress disorder and health-related quality of life in female victims of intimate partner violence. *Violence and Victims, 18*(2), 227–238.

Laharnar, N., Perrin, N. A., Hanson, G. C., Anger, W. K., & Glass, N. (2015).

Workplace domestic violence leave laws: Implementation, use, implications. *International Journal of Workplace Health Management, 8*(2), 109–128. https://doi.org/10.1108/IJWHM-03-2014-0006.

Lapp, W. M. (2010). *Behavioral models for prosperity: A statistical assessment of savings and behavioral change.* EARN. http://www.earn.org/static/uploads/files/EARN_Research_Behavioral_Models_Statistical_Assessment_Nov2010.pdf.

LeBlanc, M. M., Barling, J., & Turner, N. (2014). Intimate partner aggression and women's work outcomes. *Journal of Occupational Health Psychology, 19*(4), 399–412.

Lehmann, P., Simmons, C. A., & Pillai, V. K. (2012). The validation of the Checklist of Controlling Behaviors (CCB): Assessing coercive control in abusive relationships. *Violence Against Women, 18*(8), 913–933. https://doi.org/10.1177/1077801212456522.

Lein, L., Jacquet, S. E., Lewis, C. M., Cole, P. R., & Williams, B. B. (2001). With the best of intentions: Family Violence Option and abused women's needs. *Violence Against Women, 7*(2), 193–210.

Levin, R., McKean, L., & Raphael, J. (2004). *Pathways to and from homelessness: Women and children in Chicago shelters.* Center for Impact Research.

Levy-Simon, B. (1994). *The empowerment tradition in American social work: A history.* Columbia University Press.

Lindquist, C. H., McKay, T., Clinton-Sherrod, A. M., Pollack, K. M., Lasater, B. M., & Walters, J.L.H. (2010). The role of employee assistance programs in workplace-based intimate partner violence intervention and prevention activities. *Journal of Workplace Behavioral Health, 25*(1), 46–64. https://doi.org/10.1080/15555240903538980.

Lipsky, M. (1980). *Street-level bureaucracy: Dilemmas of the individual in public services.* Russell Sage Foundation.

Littwin, A. (2012). Coerced debt: The role of consumer credit in domestic violence. *California Law Review, 100*(4), 951–1026. https://www.jstor.org/stable/23249825.

Logan, T. K., Shannon, L., Cole, J., & Swanberg, J. E. (2007). Partner stalking and implications for women's employment. *Journal of Interpersonal Violence, 22*(3), 268–291.

Logan, T. K., & Walker, R. (2018a). Advocate safety planning training, feedback, and personal challenges. *Journal of Family Violence, 33*(3), 213–2225. https://doi.org/10.1007/s10896-017-9949-9.

Logan, T. K., & Walker, R. (2018b). Looking into the day-to-day process of victim safety planning. *Journal of Family Violence, 33*(3), 197–211. https://doi.org/10.1007/s10896-018-9951-x.

Lorde, A. (1982, February). *Learning from the 60s.* Presentation at Malcom X Weekend, Harvard University. https://www.blackpast.org/african-american-history/1982-audre-lorde-learning-60s/.

Luken, P. C., & Vaughan, S. (2005). "Be a genuine homemaker in your own home": Gender and familial relations in state housing practices. *Social Forces, 83*(4), 1603–1626.

Lusardi, A., & Mitchell, O. S. (2007). Financial literacy and retirement preparedness: Evidence and implications for financial education. *Business Economics, 42*(1), 35–44. https://doi.org/10.2145/20070104.

Lusardi, A., Mitchell, O. S., & Curto, V. (2010). Financial literacy among the young. *Journal of Consumer Affairs, 44*(2), 358–380.

Lyon, E. (1998, April 30). *Poverty, welfare and battered women: What does the research tell us?* National Resource Center on Domestic Violence. http://www.vaw.umn.edu/Vawnet/welfare.htm.

Macmillan, R., & Gartner, R. (1999). When she brings home the bacon: Labor-force participation and the risk of spousal violence against women. *Journal of Marriage and the Family, 61*(4), 947–958. https://doi.org/10.2307/354015.

Magen, R. H., Conroy, K., & Tufo, A. D. (2000). Domestic violence in child welfare preventative services: Results from an intake screening questionnaire. *Children and Youth Services Review, 22*(3/4), 251–274.

Malone, K., Stewart, S. D., Wilson, J., & Korsching, P. F. (2009). Perceptions of financial well-being among American women in diverse families. *Journal of Family and Economic Issues, 31*, 63–81.

Mancoske, R. J., Standifer, D., & Cauley, C. (1994). The effectiveness of brief counseling services for battered women. *Research on Social Work Practice, 4*(1), 53–63.

Mann, S. A., & Grimes, M. (2001). Common and contested ground: Marxism and race, gender & class analysis. *Race, Gender & Class, 8*, 3–22.

Matheson, K., Foster, M. D., Bombay, A., McQuaid, R. J., & Anisman, H. (2019). Traumatic experiences, perceived discrimination, and psychological distress among members of various socially marginalized groups. *Frontiers in Psychology, 10*, 416. https://doi.org/10.3389/fpsyg.2019.00416.

Mayoux, L. (1998). Women's empowerment and micro-finance programmes: Strategies for increasing impact. *Development in Practice, 8*(2), 235–241. https://doi.org/10.1080/09614529853873.

McBride, A. M., Lombe, M., & Beverly, S. (2003). The effects of individual development account programs: Perceptions of participants. *Social Development Issues, 25*(1/2), 59–73. https://doi.org/10.7936/K72N51TG.

McDonald, K., & Keys, C. (2008). How the powerful decide: Access to research participation by those at the margins. *American Journal of Community Psychology, 42*(1/2), 79–93.

McDonald, R., Jouriles, E., Ramisetty-Mikler, S., Caetano, R., & Green, C. E. (2006). Estimating the number of American children living in partner-violent families. *Journal of Family Psychology, 20*(1): 137–142.

Meier, S., & Sprenger, C. D. (2013). Discounting financial literacy: Time preferences and participation in financial education programs. *Journal of Economic Behavior & Organization, 95*, 159–174. https://doi.org/10.1016/j.jebo.2012.02.024.

Miller, M. S. (1995). *No visible wounds: Identifying nonphysical abuse of women by their men*. Random House.

Moe, A. M. (2007). Silenced voices and structured survival: Battered women's help seeking. *Violence Against Women, 13*(7), 676–699. https://doi.org/10.1177/1077801207302041.

Moe, A. M., & Bell, M. P. (2004). Abject economics: The effects of battering and violence on women's work and employability. *Violence Against Women, 10*(1), 29–55. https://doi.org/10.1177/1077801203256016.

Molina, O., & Abel, E. M. (2010). Abused Latina women's perceptions of their post-divorce adjustment. *Journal of Divorce & Remarriage, 51*, 124–140.

Mollica, K., & Danehower, C. (2014, October). Domestic violence and the workplace: The employer's legal responsibilities. *Journal of Management and Marketing Research, 17*, 1–11.

Morgen, S. (2001). Negotiating devolution, privatization, and the meaning of self-sufficiency. *American Anthropologist, 103*(3), 747–761.

Murray, C. E., Horton, G. E., Johnson, C. H., Notestine, B. G., Pow, A. M., Flasch, P., & Doom, E. (2015). Domestic violence service providers' perceptions of safety planning: A focus group study. *Journal of Family Violence, 30*, 381–392. https://doi.org/10.1007/s10896-015-9674-1.

Murshid, N. S. (2016). Men's response to their wives' participation in microfinance: Perpetration and justification of intimate partner violence in Bangladesh. *Public Health, 141*, 146–152. https://doi.org/10.1016/j.puhe.2016.09.016.

Nancarrow, H., S. Lockie, & S. Sharma. (2009). *Intimate partner abuse of women in a central Queensland mining region*. Trends and Issues in Crime and Criminal Justice. Criminology Research Council, Australian Institute of Criminology, Australian Government.

National Australia Bank. (2020). Financial abuse and keeping your banking safe. https://www.nab.com.au/about-us/social-impact/customers/domestic-and-family-violence/financial-abuse.

National Endowment for Financial Education. (2006). Closing the gap between knowledge and behavior: Turning education into action. *Financial Counseling and Planning, 17*(1), 73–90.

Nikolova, K., Buttner, C., Cardenas, I., Khetarpal, R., Postmus, J. L., & Simmel, C. (2021). Caseworkers' attitudes about domestic violence (DV): Does personal experience with DV matter? *Human Service Organizations: Management, Leadership, & Governance, 45*(2), 95–108.

Niolon, P. H., Kearns, M., Dills, J., Rambo, K., Irving, S., Armstead, T. L., & Gilbert, L. (2017). *Preventing intimate partner violence across the lifespan: A technical package of programs, policies, and practices*. Division of Violence Prevention, National Center for Injury Prevention and Control, Centers for Disease Control. https://www.cdc.gov/violenceprevention/pdf/ipv-technicalpackages.pdf.

Nussbaum, M. C. (2000). *Women and human development: The capabilities approach*. Cambridge University Press.

Nussbaum, M. C. (2011). *Creating capabilities: The human development approach*. Harvard University Press.

Nyman, C., & Dema, S. (2007). An overview: Research on couples and money. In J. Stocks, C. Diaz, & B. Hallerod (Eds.), *Modern couples sharing money, sharing life* (pp. 7–29). Palgrave Macmillan.

Office of Manhattan Borough President, Sakhi for South Asian Women, & The Worker Institute at Cornell ILR. (2012). *Economic abuse: The untold cost of domestic violence*. https://archive.ilr.cornell.edu/sites/default/files/Economic-Abuse-Untold-Cost-of-DV.pdf

Orton, L., Pennington, A., Nayak, S., Sowden, A., White, M., & Whitehead, M. (2016). Group based microfinance for collective empowerment: A systematic review of health impacts. *Bulletin of the World Health Organization, 94*(9), 694–704A. https://doi.org/10.2471/BLT.15.168252.

Outlaw, M. (2009). No one type of intimate partner abuse: Exploring physical and non-physical abuse among intimate partners. *Journal of Family Violence, 24*, 263–272. https://doi.org/10.1007/s10896-009-9228-5.

Pandey, S., Zhan, M., Barnes-Neely, S., & Menon, N. (2000). The higher education option for poor women with children. *Journal of Sociology and Social Welfare, 27*, 109–170. https://scholarworks.wmich.edu/cgi/viewcontent.cgi?article=2686&context=jssw.

Pecnik, N., & Bezensek-Lalic, O. (2011). Does social workers' personal experience with violence in the family relate to their professional responses and how? *European Journal of Social Work, 14*(4), 525–544.

Pence, E., & Paymar, M. (1985). *Power and control: Tactics of men who batter*. Domestic Abuse Intervention Project.

Perez, S., Johnson, D. M., & Wright, C. V. (2012). The attenuating effect of empowerment on IPV-related PTSD symptoms in battered women living in domestic violence shelters. *Violence Against Women, 18*(1), 102–117.

Perrin, N. A., Yragui, N. L., Hanson, G. C., & Glass, N. (2011). Patterns of workplace supervisor support desired by abused women. *Journal of Interpersonal Violence, 26*(11), 2264–2284. https://doi.org/10.1177/088626-510383025.

Peterman, A., Behrman, J., & Palermo, T. (2015). *Effect of education on women's experience of intimate partner violence: Universal primary education as a natural experiment in Malawi and Uganda* [Paper presentation]. Population Association of American Annual Conference, San Diego, CA. http://paa2015.princeton.edu/abstracts/151336.

Peterson, N. A., & Hughey, J. (2002). Tailoring organizational characteristics for empowerment: Accommodating individual economic resources. *Journal of Community Practice, 10*(3), 41–59.

Pollack, K. M., Austin, W., & Grisso, J. A. (2010). Employee assistance programs: A workplace resource to address intimate partner violence. *Journal of Women's Health, 19*(4), 729–733. https://doi.org/10.1089/jwh.2009.1495.

Postmus, J. L. (2010). *Economic empowerment of domestic violence survivors.* VAWnet.org. https://vawnet.org/sites/default/files/materials/files/2016-09/AR_EcoEmpowerment.pdf.

Postmus, J. L., Hetling, A., & Hoge, G. L. (2013). *Evaluating the impact of the "Moving Ahead through Financial Management" curriculum: A randomized control study.* Center on Violence Against Women and Children, Rutgers School of Social Work. https://socialwork.rutgers.edu/file/660/download?token=NgbOhlCd.

Postmus, J. L., Hetling, A., & Hoge, G. L. (2015). Evaluating a financial education curriculum as an intervention to improve financial behaviors and financial well-being of survivors of domestic violence: Results from a longitudinal randomized controlled study. *Journal of Consumer Affairs, 49*(1), 250–266. https://doi.org/10.1111/joca.12057.

Postmus, J. L., Hoge, G. L., Breckenridge, J., Sharp-Jeffs, N., & Chung, D. (2020). Economic abuse as an invisible form of domestic violence: A multicountry review. *Trauma, Violence, & Abuse, 21*(2), 261–283. https://doi.org/10.1177/1524838018764160.

Postmus, J. L., Huang, C.-C., & Stylianou, A. M. (2012). The impact of physical and economic abuse on maternal mental health and parenting. *Children and Youth Services Review, 34*, 1922–1928.

Postmus, J. L., McMahon, S., Warrener, C., & Macri, L. (2011). Factors that influence attitudes, beliefs, and behaviors of students toward survivors of violence. *Journal of Social Work Education, 47*(2), 303–319.

Postmus, J. L., & Merritt, D. (2010). When child abuse overlaps with domestic violence: The factors that influence child protection workers' beliefs. *Children and Youth Services Review, 32*, 309–317.

Postmus, J. L., & Ortega, D. (2005). Serving two masters: When domestic violence and child abuse overlap. *Families in Society, 86*(4), 483–490.

Postmus, J. L., & Plummer, S. B. (2010). *Validating the Allstate Foundation's national model on helping survivors of violence achieve economic self-sufficiency: Final report.* Center on Violence Against Women and Children, Rutgers School of Social Work.

Postmus, J. L., Plummer, S. B., McMahon, S., Murshid, N., & Kim, M. (2012). Understanding economic abuse in the lives of survivors. *Journal of Interpersonal Violence, 27*, 411–430. https://doi.org/10.1177/0886260511421669.

Postmus, J. L., Plummer, S. B., McMahon, S., & Zurlo, K. (2013). Financial literacy:

Building economic empowerment with survivors of violence. *Journal of Family and Economic Issues, 34*, 275–284. https://doi.org/10.1007/s10834-012-9330-3.

Postmus, J. L., Plummer, S. B., & Stylianou, A. M. (2016). Measuring economic abuse in the lives of survivors: Revising the Scale of Economic Abuse. *Violence Against Women, 22*(6), 692–703. https://doi.org/10.1177/1077801215610012.

Postmus, J. L., Severson, M. E., Berry, M., & Yoo, J. A. (2009). Women's experiences of violence and seeking help. *Violence Against Women, 15*(7), 852–868.

Postmus, J. L., Silva-Martinez, E., Hetling, A., & Danis, F. (2013). *Evaluating the impact of the "Moving Ahead through Financial Management" curriculum: The advocate perspective.* Center on Violence Against Women and Children, Rutgers School of Social Work. https://socialwork.rutgers.edu/file/658/download?token=dg9gn8LB.

Potito, C., Day, A., Carson, E., & O'Leary, P. (2009). Domestic violence and child protection partnerships and collaboration. *Australian Social Work, 62*(3), 356–387. http://doi.org/10.1080/03124070902964657.

Powers, L. E., Renker, P., Robinson-Whelen, S., Oschwald, M., Hughes, R., Swank, P., & Curry, M. A. (2009). Interpersonal violence and women with disabilities: Analysis of safety promoting behaviors. *Violence Against Women, 15*(9), 1040–1069. https://doi.org/10.1177/1077801209340309.

Pronyk, P. M., Hargreaves, J. R., Kim, J. C., Morison, L. A., Phetla, G., Watts, C., Busza, J., & Porter, J. D. (2006). Effect of a structural intervention for the prevention of intimate partner violence and HIV in rural South Africa: A cluster randomised trial. *Lancet, 368*(9551), 1973–1983. https://doi.org/10.1016/S0140-6736(06)69744-4.

Ptacek, J. (1999). *Battered women in the courtroom: The power of judicial responses.* Northeastern University Press.

Pyles, L. (2005). Toward safety for low-income battered women: Promoting economic justice strategies. *Families in Society: The Journal of Contemporary Human Services, 87*, 1–8.

Raj, A., Silverman, J. G., Klugman, J., Saggurti, N., Donta, B., & Shakya, H. B. (2018). Longitudinal analysis of the impact of economic empowerment on risk for intimate partner violence among married women in rural Maharashtra, India. *Social Science & Medicine, 196*, 197–203.

Ramisetty-Mikler, S., Caetano, R., & McGrath, C. (2007). Sexual aggression among White, Black, and Hispanic couples in the US: Alcohol use, physical assault and psychological aggression as its correlates. *American Journal of Drug and Alcohol Abuse, 33*(1), 31–43. https://doi.org/10.1080/00952990601082639.

Ranganathan, M., Knight, L., Abramsky, T., Muvhango, L., Polzer Ngwato, T., Mbobelatsi, M., Ferrari, G., Watts, C., & Stöckl, H. (2019). Associations between women's economic and social empowerment and intimate partner violence: Findings from a microfinance plus program in rural north west province,

South Africa. *Journal of Interpersonal Violence*, 1–29. https://doi.org/10.1177/0886260519836952.

Rappaport, J. (1981). In praise of paradox: A social policy of empowerment over prevention. *American Journal of Community Psychology, 9*(1), 1–25.

Reeves, C., & O'Leary-Kelly, A. M. (2007). The effects and costs of intimate partner violence for work organizations. *Journal of Interpersonal Violence, 22*(3), 327–344. https://doi.org/10.1177/0886260506293582.

Reutebuch, T. G. (2001). An exploration into individual development accounts as an anti-poverty strategy. *Journal of Sociology and Social Welfare, 28*, 95–107.

Richards, K. V., & Thyer, B. (2011). Does individual development account participation help the poor? A review. *Research on Social Work Practice, 21*(3), 348–362. https://doi.org/10.1177/1049731510395609.

Richie, B. (2000). A Black feminist reflection on the antiviolence movement. *Signs, 25*, 1133–1137. https://doi.org/10.1086/495533.

Riger, S., Ahrens, C. E., & Blickenstaff, A. (2000). Measuring interference with employment and education reported by women with abusive partners: Preliminary data. *Violence and Victims, 15*(2), 161–172. https://doi.org/10.1891/0886-6708.15.2.161.

Riger, S., & Staggs, S. L. (2004). Welfare reform, domestic violence, and employment: What do we know and what do we need to know? *Violence Against Women, 10*(9), 961–990.

Roberts, A. L., Gilman, S. E., Fitzmaurice, G., Decker, M. R., & Koenen, K. C. (2010). Witness of intimate partner violence in childhood and perpetration of intimate partner violence in adulthood. *Epidemiology, 2*, 809–818.

Roche, S., & Sadoski, P. (1996). Social action for battered women. In A. Roberts (Ed.), *Helping battered women: New perspectives and remedies* (pp. 13–30). Oxford University Press.

Rose, L. E., & Campbell, J. (2000). The role of social support and family relationships in women's responses to battering. *Health Care for Women International, 21*, 27–39.

Rothman, E. F., Hathaway, J., Stidsen, A., & de Vries, H. F. (2007). How employment helps female victims of intimate partner violence: A qualitative study. *Journal of Occupational Health Psychology, 12*(2), 136–143. https://doi.org/10.1037/1076-8998.12.2.136.

Rothwell, D. W., Khan, M. N., & Cherney, K. (2015). *The mediating role of financial self-efficacy in the financial capability of low-income families*. SSRN. https://ssrn.com/abstract=2646966.

Ruiz, E., Ruvalcaba, Y., Berenstain, N., & Fluegeman, S. (2020). Measuring the economic impact of COVID-19 on survivors of color: Research findings. me too. https://metoomvmt.org/wp-content/uploads/2020/11/MeTooFreeFrom_CovidImpactReport2020.pdf.

Rusbult, C. E., & Martz, J. M. (1995). Remaining in an abusive relationship: An investment model analysis of nonvoluntary dependence. *Personality and social psychology Bulletin, 21*(6), 558–571. https://doi.org/10.1177/0146167295216002.

Sanders, C. K. (2014). Savings for survivors: An individual development account program for survivors of intimate partner violence. *Journal of Social Service Research, 40*(3), 297–312. https://doi.org/10.1080/01488376.2014.893950.

Sanders, C. K. (2015). Economic abuse in the lives of women abused by an intimate partner: A qualitative study. *Violence Against Women, 21*(1), 3–29. https://doi.org/10.1177/1077801214564167.

Sanders, C. K., & Schnabel, M. (2006). Organizing for economic empowerment of battered women: Women's savings accounts. *Journal of Community Practice, 14*(3), 47–68.

Sanders, C. K., Weaver, T. L., & Schnabel, M. (2007, Fall). Economic education for battered women: An evaluation of outcomes. *Affilia, 22*(3), 240–254.

Sauber, E. W., & O'Brien, K. M. (2017). Multiple losses: The psychological and economic well-being of survivors of intimate partner violence. *Journal of Interpersonal Violence, 35*(15/16), 3054–3078. https://doi.org/1177/0886260517706760.

Saunders, D. G., & Anderson, D. (2000). Evaluation of a domestic violence training for child protection workers and supervisors: Initial report. *Children and Youth Services Review, 22*, 375–398.

Schmidt, L., & Sevak, P. (2006). Gender, marriage, and asset accumulation in the United States. *Feminist Economics, 12*(1/2), 139–166.

Schramm, D. G., & Harris, V. W. (2011). Marital quality and income: An examination of the influence of government assistance. *Journal of Family and Economic Issues, 32*, 437–448.

Schuchardt, J., Hanna, S. D., Hira, T. K., Lyons, A. C., Palmer, L., & Xiao, J. J. (2009). Financial literacy and education research priorities. *Journal of Financial Counseling and Planning, 20*(1), 84–95.

Schultz, K., Cattaneo, L. B., Sabina, C., Brunner, L., Jackson, S., & Serrata, J. V. (2016). Key roles of community connectedness in healing from trauma. *Psychology of Violence, 6*(1), 42–48. https://doi.org/10.1037/vio0000025.

Schwarzer, R., & Jerusalem, M. (1995). Generalized Self-Efficacy Scale. In J. Weinman, S. Wright, & M. Johnston (Eds.), *Measures in health psychology: A user's portfolio. Causal and control beliefs* (pp. 35–37). NFER-NELSON.

Scott, E. K., London, A. S., & Gross, G. (2007). "I try not to depend on anyone but me": Welfare-reliant women's perspectives on self-sufficiency, work and marriage. *Sociological Inquiry, 77*(4), 601–625.

Seith, C. (2001, July). Security matters: Domestic violence and public social services. *Violence Against Women, 7*(7), 799–820. https://doi.org/10.1177/10778010122182749.

Sen, A. (1981). *Poverty and families: An essay on entitlement and deprivation.* Clarendon.

Serido, J., Curran, M. J., Wilmarth, M., Ahn, S. Y., Shim, S., & Ballard, J. (2015). The unique role of parents and romantic partners on college students' financial attitudes and behaviors. *Family Relations, 64*(5), 696–710.

Sharp, N. (2008). *"What's yours is mine": The different forms of economic abuse and its impact on women and children experiencing domestic violence.* Refuge.

Sharp-Jeffs, N. (2015a). *Money matters: Research into the extent and nature of financial abuse within intimate relationships in the UK.* The Co-Operative Bank in partnership with Refuge. https://www.refuge.org.uk/files/Money-Matters.pdf.

Sharp-Jeffs, N. (2015b). *A review of research and policy on financial abuse within intimate partner relationships.* Child and Woman Abuse Studies Unit, London Metropolitan University. http://repository.londonmet.ac.uk/1482/1/Review-of-Research-and-Policy-on-Financial-Abuse.pdf.

Shepard, M., & Campbell, J. A. (1992). The Abusive Behavior Inventory: A measure of psychological and physical abuse. *Journal of Interpersonal Violence, 7*(3), 291–305. https://doi.org/10.1177/088626092007003001.

Sherraden, M. (2013). Building blocks of financial capability. In J. Birkenmaier & M. Sherraden (Eds.), *Financial education and capability: Research, education, policy, and practice* (pp. 3–43). Oxford University Press.

Shim, S., Serido, J., Bosch, L., & Tang, C. (2013). Financial identify-processing styles among young adults: A longitudinal study of socialization factors and consequences for financial capabilities. *Journal of Consumer Affairs, 47*(1), 128–152.

Shippee, T. P., Wilkinson, L. R., & Ferraro, K. F. (2012). Accumulated financial strain and women's health over three decades. *Journals of Gerontology Series B: Psychological Sciences and Social Sciences, 67*(5), 585–594.

Shiraz, M. S. (2016). The impact of education and occupation on domestic violence in Saudi Arabia. *International Journal of Social Welfare, 25*, 339–346. https://doi.org/10.1111/ijsw.12214.

Shobe, M. A., & Boyd, A. S. (2003). Increasing the economic self-sufficiency of rural families: Individual development accounts. *The Social Policy Journal, 2*, 63–87.

Shobe, M. A., & Christy-McMullin, K. (2005). Savings experiences past and present: Narratives from low-income African American Women. *Affilia, 20*(2), 222–237. https://doi.org/10.1177/0886109905274566.

Shobe, M. A., & Dienemann, J. (2007). Intimate partner violence in the United States: An ecological approach to prevention and treatment. *Social Polity & Society, 7*, 185–195.

Showalter, K. (2016). Women's employment and domestic violence: A review of the literature. *Aggression and Violent Behavior, 31*, 37–47. https://doi.org/10.1016/j.avb.2016.06.017.

Silva-Martinez, E., Stylianou, A. M., Hoge, G. L., Plummer, S. B., McMahon, S., & Postmus, J. L. (2016). Implementing a financial management curriculum with survivors of IPV: Exploring advocates' experiences. *Affilia, 31*(1), 112–128. https://doi.org/10.1177/0886109915608218.

Slegh, H., Barker, G., Kimonyo, A., Ndolimana, P., & Bannerman, M. (2013). "I can do women's work": Reflections on engaging men as allies in women's economic empowerment in Rwanda. *Gender & Development, 21*(1), 15–30. https://doi.org/10.1080/13552074.2013.767495.

Smallwood, E. (2015). *Stepping stones: Legal barriers to economic equality after family violence.* Women's Legal Service. https://pdfs.semanticscholar.org/7bdb/9a34dc735e39a7f77ce5fcc54274dcec42ba.pdf?_ga=2.159248122.1768423504.1613949546-1820838487.1613949546.

Smith, S. G., Chen, J., Basile, K. C., Gilbert, L. K., Merrick, M. T., Patel, N., Walling, M., & Jain, A. (2017). *The National Intimate Partner and Sexual Violence Survey (NISVS): 2010–2012 state report.* Atlanta: Center for Injury Prevention and Control, Centers for Disease Control and Prevention. https://www.cdc.gov/violenceprevention/pdf/nisvs-statereportbook.pdf.

Sokoloff, N. J., & Dupont, I. (2005). Domestic violence at the intersections of race, class, and gender. *Violence Against Women, 11*(1), 38–64. https://doi.org/10.1177/1077801204271476.

Staggs, S. L., Long, S. M., Mason, G. E., Krishnan, S., & Riger, S. (2007). Intimate partner violence, social support, and employment in the post-welfare reform era. *Journal of Interpersonal Violence, 22*(3), 345–367.

Stark, E. (2007). *Coercive control: How men entrap women in personal life.* Oxford University Press.

Stark, E. (2013). Coercive control. In N. Lombard & L. McMillan (Eds.), *Violence against women: Current theory and practice in domestic abuse, sexual violence and exploitation* (pp. 17–33). Jessica Kingsley.

Stockl, H., & Penhale, B. (2015). Intimate partner violence and its association with physical and mental health symptoms among older women in Germany. *Journal of Interpersonal Violence, 30*(17), 3089–3111.

Straus, M. A. (1979). Measuring intrafamily conflict and violence: The Conflict Tactics (CT) Scales. *Journal of Marriage and the Family, 41*(1), 75–88. https://doi.org/10.2307/351733.

Stylianou, A. M. (2018a). Economic abuse experiences and depressive symptoms among victims of intimate partner violence. *Journal of Family Violence, 33*(6), 381–392. https://doi.org/10.1007/s10896-018-9973-4.

Stylianou, A. M. (2018b). Economic abuse within intimate partner violence: A review of the literature. *Violence and Victims, 33*(1), 3–22. https://doi.org/10.1891/0886-6708.VV-D-16-00112.

Stylianou, A. M., Counselman-Carpenter, E., & Redcay, A. (2018). "My sister is the one that made me stay above water": How social supports are maintained and strained when survivors of intimate partner violence reside in emergency shelter programs. *Journal of Interpersonal Violence*. https://doi.org/10.1177/0886260518816320.

Stylianou, A. M., & Pich, C. (2019). Beyond domestic violence shelter: Factors associated with housing placements for survivors exiting emergency shelters. *Journal of Interpersonal Violence*. https://doi.org/10.1177/0886260519858393.

Stylianou, A. M., Postmus, J. L., & McMahon, S. (2013). Measuring abusive behaviors: Is economic abuse a unique form of abuse? *Journal of Interpersonal Violence, 28*(16), 3186–3204.

Sullivan, C. M., & Bybee, D. I. (1999). Reducing violence using community-based advocacy for women with abusive partners. *Journal of Consulting and Clinical Psychology, 67*(1), 43–53.

Sullivan, C. M., Campbell, R., Angelique, H., Eby, K. K., & Davidson, W. S. (1994). An advocacy intervention program for women with abusive partners: Six-month follow-up. *American Journal of Community Psychology, 22*(1), 101–122.

Sullivan, C. M., Tan, C., Basta, J., Rumptz, M., & Davidson, W. S. (1992). An advocacy intervention program for women with abusive partners: Initial evaluation. *American Journal of Community Psychology, 20*, 309–332.

Surviving Economic Abuse. (2021). *Economic abuse and the Domestic Abuse Act*. https://survivingeconomicabuse.org/i-need-help/economic-abuse-and-the-law/domestic-abuse-bill/.

Suvak, M. K., Taft, C. T., Goodman, L. A., & Dutton, M. A. (2013). Dimensions of functional social support and depressive symptoms: A longitudinal investigation of women seeking help for intimate partner violence. *Journal of Consulting and Clinical Psychology, 81*(3), 455–466. https://doi.org/10.1037/a0031787.

Swain, R. B., Van Sanh, N., & Van Tuan, V. (2008). Microfinance and poverty reduction in the Mekong Delta in Vietnam. *African and Asian Studies, 7*(2–3), 191–215. https://doi.org/10.1163/156921008x318736.

Swanberg, J. E., & Logan, T. K. (2005). Domestic violence and employment: A qualitative study. *Journal of Occupational Health Psychology, 10*(1), 3–17. https://doi.org/10.1037/1076-8998.10.1.3.

Swanberg, J. E., Logan, T. K., & Macke, C. (2005). Intimate partner violence, employment and the workplace. *Trauma, Violence, & Abuse, 6*, 286–312. https://doi.org/10.1177/1524838005280506.

Swanberg, J. E., & Macke, C. (2006). Intimate partner violence and the workplace consequences and disclosure. *Affilia, 21*(4), 391–406. https://doi.org/10.1177%2F0886109906292133.

Swanberg, J. E., Ojha, M. U., & Macke, C. (2012). State employment protection statutes for victims of domestic violence: Public policy's response to domestic violence as an employment matter. *Journal of Interpersonal Violence, 27*(3), 587–619. https://doi.org/10.1177/0886260511421668.

Tamborini, C. R., Iams, H. M., & Reznik, G. L. (2011). Women's earnings before and after marital dissolution: Evidence from longitudinal earnings records matched to survey data. *Journal of Family and Economic Issues, 33*, 69–82. https://doi.org/10.1007/s10834-011-9264-1.

Telford, C. (2020, January 6). Financial abuse. *Mother of All Lists*. https://motherofalllists.com/2020/01/06/financial-abuse/.

Tenkorang, E. Y., & Owusu, A. Y. (2019). Does economic abuse affect the health outcomes of women in Ghana? *Health Education Behavior, 46*(2), 340–348. https://doi.org/10.1177/1090198118806970.

Thomas, D. (1990). Intra-household resource allocation: An inferential approach. *The Journal of Human Resources, 25*, 635–664.

Tjaden, P., & Thoennes, N. (1998). *Prevalence, incidence, and consequences of violence against women: Findings from the national violence against women survey*. National Institute of Justice. https://www.ojp.gov/pdffiles/172837.pdf.

Tolman, R. M., & Raphael, J. (2000). A review of research on welfare and domestic violence. *Journal of Social Issues, 56*(4), 655–682. https://doi.org/10.1111/0022-4537.00190.

Tolman, R. M., & Rosen, D. (2001). Domestic violence in the lives of women receiving welfare: Mental health, substance dependency and economic well-being. *Violence Against Women, 7*(2), 141–158.

Tolman, R. M., & Wang, H. C. (2005). Domestic violence and women's employment: Fixed effects models of three waves of Women's Employment Study data. *American Journal of Community Psychology, 36*(1/2), 147–158. https://doi.org/10.1007/s10464-005-6239-0.

Turner, S. F., & Shapiro, C. H. (1986). Battered women: Mourning the death of a relationship. *Social Work, 31*, 372–376.

Tutty, L. M., Bidgood, B. A., & Rothery, M. A. (1993). Support groups for battered women: Research on their efficacy. *Journal of Family Violence, 8*(4), 325–343.

UK Finance. (2018). *Financial abuse code of practice*. https://www.ukfinance.org.uk/system/files/Financial-Abuse-Code-of-Practice.pdf.

Universal Living Wage. (2018). *Universal living wage formula*. http://www.universallivingwage.org.

U.S. Bureau of Labor Statistics. (2006). *Survey of workplace violence prevention* (USDL 06-1860). http://www.bls.gov/iif/home.htm.

U.S. Bureau of Labor Statistics. (2013). Injuries, illnesses, and fatalities. *Census of fatal occupational injuries charts, 1992–2011*. http://www.bls.gov/iif/oshwc/cfoi/cfch0010.pdf.

U.S. Bureau of Labor Statistics. (2018). *There were 500 workplace homicides in the United States in 2016*. https://www.bls.gov/opub/ted/2018/there-were-500-workplace-homicides-in-the-united-states-in-2016.htm.

U.S. Bureau of Labor Statistics. (2019). *Civilian labor force participation rate (May 2019)*. U.S. Department of Labor. https://www.bls.gov/charts/employment-situation/civilian-labor-force-participation-rate.htm.

U.S. Department of Health and Human Services. (2010). *Report to Congress: Assets for Independence program, status at the conclusion of the tenth year*. http://www.idaresources.org/page?pageid=a0470000000ArRQE.

U.S. Government Accountability Office. (2004). *Highlights of a GAO forum: The federal government's role in improving financial literacy* [Report].

Van Campenhout, G. (2015). Revaluing the role of parents as financial socialization agents in youth financial literacy programs. *Journal of Consumer Affairs, 49*(1), 186–222.

Vitt, L. A., Anderson, C., Kent, J., Lyter, D. M., Siegenthaler, J. K., & Ward, J. (2000). *Personal finance and the rush to competence: Financial literacy education in the U.S.* Institute for Socio-Financial Studies. https://www.isfs.org/documents-pdfs/rep-finliteracy.pdf.

VonDeLinde, K. C. (2002). *How are domestic violence programs meeting the economic needs of battered women in Iowa? An assessment and recommendations* (Building Comprehensive Solutions to Domestic Violence, Publication 16). National Resource Center on Domestic Violence. https://vawnet.org/material/how-are-domestic-violence-programs-meeting-economic-needs-battered-women-iowa-assessment.

VonDeLinde, K. C., & Correia, A. (2005). *Economic education programs for battered women: Lessons learned from two settings* (Building Comprehensive Solutions to Domestic Violence, Publication 18). National Resource Center on Domestic Violence. https://vawnet.org/material/economic-education-programs-battered-women-lessons-learned-two-settings.

Voth Schrag, R. J. (2015). Economic abuse and later material hardship: Is depression a mediator? *Affilia, 30*(3), 341–351.

Voth Schrag, R. J. (2019). Experiences of economic abuse in the community: Listening to survivors voices. *Affilia, 34*(3), 313–324.

Voth Schrag, R. J., & Edmond, T. (2017). School sabotage as a form of intimate partner violence: Provider perspectives. *Affilia, 32*(2), 171–187.

Voth Schrag, R. J., Edmond, T., & Nordberg, A. (2019). Understanding school sabotage among survivors of intimate partner violence from diverse populations. *Violence Against Women, 26*(11), 1286–1304. https://doi.org/10.1177/1077801219862626.

Voth Schrag, R. J., Edmond, T., Tlapek, S. M., & Auslander, W. (2017). Exposure to economically abusive tactics among adolescent girls in the child welfare system. *Child and Adolescent Social Work Journal, 34*(2), 127–136.

Voth Schrag, R. J., Robinson, S. R., & Ravi, K. (2018). Understanding pathways within intimate partner violence: Economic abuse, economic hardship, and mental health. *Journal of Aggression, Maltreatment & Trauma*, 222–242. https://doi.org/10.1080/10926771.2018.1546247.

Vyas, S., & Watts, C. (2009). How does economic empowerment affect women's risk of intimate partner violence in low and middle income countries? A systematic review of published evidence. *Journal of International Development, 21*(5), 577–602. https://doi.org/10.1002/jid.1500.

Walker, L. E. (1979). *The battered woman.* Harper & Row.

Warrener, C., Postmus, J. L., McMahon, S., & Macri, L. (2013). Professional efficacy and working with survivors of domestic violence or sexual assault. *Affilia, 28*(2), 194–206.

Wathen, C. N., MacGregor, J.C.D., & MacQuarrie, B. J. (2015). The impact of domestic violence in the workplace: Results from a pan-Canadian survey. *Journal of Occupational and Environmental Medicine, 57*(7), e65–71. https://doi.org/10.1097/JOM.0000000000000499.

Waugh, F., & Bonner, M. (2002). Domestic violence and child protection: Issues in safety planning. *Child Abuse Review, 11*, 282–295.

Weaver, T. L., Sanders, C. K., Campbell, C. L., & Schnabel, M. (2009). Development and preliminary psychometric evaluation of the Domestic Violence–Related Financial Issues Scale (DV-FI). *Journal of Interpersonal Violence, 24*(4), 569–585. https://doi.org/10.1177/0886260508317176.

Weber, O., & Ahmad, A. (2014). Empowerment through microfinance: The relation between loan cycle and level of empowerment. *World Development, 62*, 75–87. https://doi.org/10.1016/j.worlddev.2014.05.012.

Weisz, A. N. (1999). Legal advocacy for domestic violence survivors: The power of an informative relationship. *Families in Society, 80*(2), 138.

Weisz, A. N., Tolman, R. M., & Bennett, L. (1998). An ecological study of nonresidential services for battered women within a comprehensive community protocol for domestic violence. *Journal of Family Violence, 13*(4), 395–415.

Weitzman, A. (2018). Does increasing women's education reduce their risk of intimate partner violence? Evidence from an education policy reform. *Criminology, 56*(3), 574–607. https://doi.org/10.1111/1745-9125.12181.

Wettersten, K. B., Rudolph, S. E., Faul, K., Gallagher, K., Trangsrud, H. B., Adams, K., Graham, S., & Terrance, C. (2004). Freedom through self-sufficiency: A qualitative examination of the impact of domestic violence on the working lives of women in shelter. *Journal of Counseling Psychology, 51*(4), 447–462. https://doi.org/10.1037/0022-0167.51.4.447.

Woffordt, S., Mihalic, D. E., & Menard, S. (1994). Continuities in marital violence. *Journal of Family Violence, 9*, 195–225. https://doi.org/10.1007/BF01531948.

Wood, R., & Bandura, A. (1989). Impact of conceptions of ability on self-regulatory mechanisms and complex decision making. *Journal of Personality and Social Psychology, 56*, 407–415.

Wright, A. C., & Bertrand, L. D. (2017). Access to legal services in women's shelters. *Journal of Family Violence, 32*(1), 101–114.

Xiao, J. J., Tang, C., Serido, J., & Shim, S. (2011). Antecedents and consequences of risky credit behavior among college students: Application and extension of the Theory of Planned Behavior. *Journal of Public Policy & Marketing, 30*(2), 239–245.

Yoo, M. C. (2012). Credit program participation and decline in violence: Does self-selection matter? *World Development, 40*(8), 1690–1699. https://doi.org/10.1016/j.worlddev.2012.04.003.

Yoshihama, M., & Mills, L. (2003). When is the personal professional in public child welfare practice? The influence of intimate partner and child abuse histories on workers in domestic violence cases. *Child Abuse & Neglect, 27*(3), 319–336.

Zelizer, V. A. (1994). *The social meaning of money*. Basic Books.

Zhan, M., & Schreiner, M. (2005). Savings for post-secondary education in Individual Development Accounts (IDA). *Journal of Sociology and Social Welfare, 32*, 139–163.

Zhan, M., Sherraden, M., & Schreiner, M. (2004). Welfare recipiency and savings outcomes in individual development accounts. *Social Work Research, 28*, 165–181.

Zimmerman, L., Canale, A., Britt, S. L., & Seay, M. (2015). The Theory of Planned Behavior and the Earned Income Tax Credit. *Journal of Financial Therapy, 6*(1), 44–63.

Zimmerman, M. A. (1990). Taking aim on empowerment research: On the distinction between individual and psychological conceptions. *American Journal of Community Psychology, 18*(1), 169–177.

Zimmerman, M. A. (1995, October). Psychological empowerment: Issues and illustrations. *American Journal of Community Psychology, 23*(5), 581–599.

Zimmerman, M. A. (2000). Empowerment theory. In J. Rappaport & E. Seidman (Eds.), *Handbook of Community Psychology* (pp. 43–63). Plenum.

Zlotnick, C., Johnson, D. M., & Kohn, R. (2006). Intimate partner violence and long-term psychosocial functioning in a national sample of American women. *Journal of Interpersonal Violence, 21*(2), 262–275.

Zorza, J. (1991). Woman battering: A major cause of homelessness. *Clearinghouse Review, 25*, 421–429.

Index

Page numbers in italics indicate illustrations.

About the Authors

Judy L. Postmus is dean of the School of Social Work, University of Maryland. She is the editor of *Sexual Violence and Abuse: An Encyclopedia of Prevention, Impacts, and Recovery* (2012) and the series editor of the Violence Against Women and Children series at Rutgers University Press. Her research focuses on physical, sexual, and economic victimization of women, including an examination of strategies to financially empower survivors. Her work is strongly influenced by her twenty years as a practitioner and administrator.

Amanda M. Stylianou is the vice president of population health at Easterseals NJ. Her research focuses on improving services at the intersection of trauma, violence, and mental health. She has over fifteen years of experience working as an advocate, therapist, researcher, and leader in the field of violence against women.